W9-AKE-176

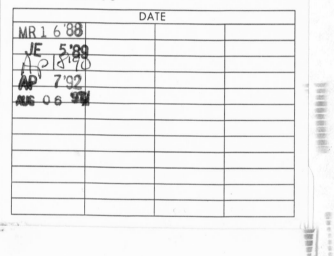

796.6 Van der Plas, Rob
VA
        The bicycle touring
        manual

$9.95

DATE			
MR 1 6 '88			
JE 5 '89			
AP 18 '90			
AP 7 '92			
AUG 06 '94			

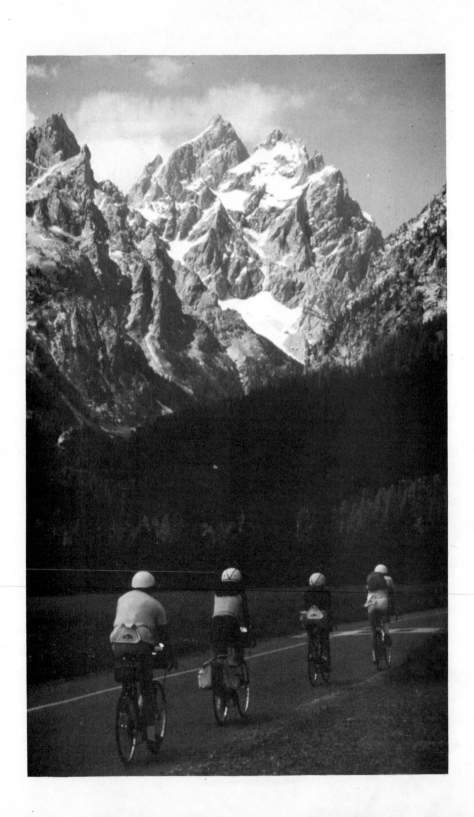

The Bicycle Touring Manual

Using the bicycle for touring and camping

Rob Van der Plas

Bicycle Books – San Francisco

Copyright © Rob Van der Plas, 1987

First printing, 1987

Cover photograph and frontispiece courtesy Backroads Bicycle Touring, San Leandro, California

Published by:
Bicycle Books (Publishing), Inc.
1282a – 7th Avenue
San Francisco, CA 94122

Distributed to the book trade by:
(USA) Kampmann & Co, New York, NY
(Canada) Raincoast, Vancouver, BC
(UK) Fountain Press, Tolworth, Surrey

Library of Congress Cataloging in Publication Data:
Van der Plas, Robert, 1938 –
The Bicycle Touring Manual
Using the bicycle for touring and camping
Bibliography: p. Includes Index
1. Bicycles and bicycling, Manuals and Handbooks, etc.
2. Bicycle touring, Manuals and Handbooks, etc.
3. Camping and Backpacking, Manuals and Handbooks, etc.
I. Title.
Library of Congress Catalog Card Number 86-72641

ISBN 0-933201-15-X

Printed in the United States of America

Table of Contents

About the Author

Rob Van der Plas is a professional engineer and a lifelong cyclist. He has toured by bicycle extensively in Europe and America. As a child, he was taken on camping trips by his parents ever since he was old enough to sit upright in a child's seat on the bike, and continued to do so ever since he could ride a bike of his own. In this book he shares with his readers the experience gained over many years of active bicycle touring and camping.

In addition to the present book, Rob Van der Plas has written extensively on all matters related to bicycles and bicycling. His *Bicycle Repair Book*, *Bicycle Racing Guide*, *Mountain Bike Book* and *Roadside Bicycle Repairs* also appeared in this series, published by Bicycle Books. His technical contributions regularly appear in the form of books and articles with major publishers and in specialized periodicals both sides of the Atlantic.

Part I
Selecting Your Equipment

1
Bicycle Touring, Anyone?

There is probably no greater way to appreciate the delights of riding a bicycle than by using it for touring. Nor is there perhaps a better way to appreciate nature on its grander scale. No offense to hikers and mountaineers, skiers and canoeists – all folks who are similarly self-propelled and closely in touch with nature. Yet all seem to get only a thin slice of God's greatest works, as compared to what is meted out to the touring bicyclist.

The cyclist travels at some speed through the vastness, finding

Taking a break in the Grand Tetons. (Photograph courtesy Backroads)

himself now following a river, now ascending a mountain slope, now skirting a town, getting the full experience of nature's variety. The other muscle-powered tourists are mostly limited to a small region, characterized by either one type of terrain or the other. Whereas the bicyclist can travel quite significant distances, crossing entire continents in a matter of weeks or at most months, the others usually make very slow progress indeed.

Yet bicycle use for touristic purposes is not restricted to continental crossings and other major expeditions. In fact, a lot of bicycle touring may be done much closer to home. You can start biking right outside your own front door. You can ride all the way and return home on the bike, be it for a long trek or a short trip. By bicycle, you may choose to go for months, a week, a weekend, a day, or just a few hours. The bike gives you the freedom to use even the tiniest bit of time and the most unlikely starting points for your trips. The bicycle can make you free.

This book is written to help not only those who have little bicycling experience, but also experienced cyclists who want to get the most out of their hobby. I shall try to help you make optimal use of the bicycle, by sharing with you the experience I and others have gained over many years of active bicycle touring. Together, we shall try to cover all the many facets of bicycling over longer and shorter distances. I'll show you how to choose your equipment, ranging from the bike itself to accessories, such as racks, packs, tents and sleeping bags.

Not only will you learn to choose your equipment, but also to get the best use from your material and how to expand your bicycling skills. You will be shown how to ride your bike safely and efficiently, how to plan your tour and how to choose your route. I'll show how to maintain both the bicycle itself and the rest of your equipment, how to pack the bike and how to find your way at home and abroad. You will learn to be self-sufficient and you'll find out where to get help when you need it.

I also hope to share something else with you, namely the feeling of inspiration and the sense of true freedom that for me and many other touring bicyclists will always turn the activity of cycling into something more than merely using a bike to get around, instead of a car. If all is well,

you will yourself discover with the aid of this book the oneness with nature and the peace with civilization that I have found to make bicycle touring one of the best things man has ever learned to do.

It matters little whether you go on long tours or on short trips. Though different kinds of rides and distances do involve varying levels of preparation and involvement, the quality of these is the same each time. On the long tour, you generally have to carry more luggage than on a shorter trip, you will need more aids to orientation and you may encounter more diverse experiences. Yet anything that helps you on one kind of ride will also help you, more or less, on any other kind of bicycle tour.

Sure, all these things can be learned without a manual. I never read any of this in a book. Instead, I assimilated it from my parents, and I have continued learning from my own experiences and from other cyclists with whom I have kept company ever since. Others have learned mainly from their own mistakes – perhaps the most thorough, though also the most time consuming, frustrating and sometimes dangerous way of gaining proficiency in any skill.

Organized and Individual Cycling
For many years, bicycling has been largely a club activity, especially in Great Britain, but to some extent also in the United States and a number of other countries. No doubt cycling clubs preceded motorization by many years. More recently, bicycling was regarded such an anachronism in a society geared to motorized transportation, that those who participated in it seemed most at ease in the company of others who shared their interests.

Active membership in a bicycle club was, certainly in those days, the most effective form of schooling for beginning bicyclists.

Even today, joining others in a club remains a great way to enjoy the sport. However, with the remarkable revival of interest in biking, and the similarly spectacular influx of new bicyclists since the early 'seventies, two factors have reduced the overall benefit of the potential propagation of skills via the cycling clubs. In the first place, more people for whom club membership is either impractical or unappealing have joined the sport. Secondly, the average level of skill and experience in many clubs has suffered in direct proportion to the increase in membership.

In the mid 'seventies a brand new organization, established by long-time bicycle PR genius Dan Burden,

The British isles offer superb cycling with or without a family. The wide open landscape exposes you to wind and weather, but the wide vistas are a constant reward for your efforts.

mushroomed in America. Called Bikecentennial, this group set out to celebrate the second centennial of the United States and the first centennial of organized cycling with bicycle tours clear across the North American continent. An enormous amount of work, both physical and mental, was rewarded with an unbelievable increase in popularity of bicycle touring in the US, which would never have achieved its present popularity without Bikecentennial. Today this organization is still active and helps its members with their bicycle touring needs.

At about the same time quite a number of local and regional bicycle organizations of a different type were formed. These Coalitions, Associations, Cooperatives and what else they may be called, all have as their major purpose either the propagation of bicycling or the defense of the real or presumed interests of cyclists – objectives that are by no means always identical. Most of these groups are very loosely organized, and members almost invariably do more talking than cycling together. Necessary and useful work is done by several of these groups. Yet only a handful of them really serve to help or educate their newer members in practical matters associated with cycling, whether touring or otherwise.

Another nationwide organization, one that has represented cycling in the United States for over a hundred years now, is the League of American Wheelmen. In the mid 'eighties this national association, with chapters in most states, chose both a new name and a new image. Now calling itself Bicycle USA, the old League ventured away from helping existing cyclists to promoting the image of cycling and trying to attract newcomers to the sport. By whatever name, I hope the League will continue to play a prominent part in the American cycling scene, and it is similarly to be hoped that such nationwide organizations also establish themselves in countries like Canada, New Zealand and Australia.

Another form of organized cycling that should not be ignored is the commercial or voluntary touring agency. In many states, one or more such establishments organize bicycle tours, some only at home, others also abroad. They supply all the necessary route planning, taking care of the accommodation, food and luggage transportation problems for their patrons. Certainly for inexperienced riders, who would like to try out bike touring without wanting to go in at the deep end, this form of touring can be highly recommended. All this assuming we're talking about a serious agency that is well established in the field and can keep its promises. The advice in this book will apply as much to those

who travel alone as to those who prefer to tour under any such form of expert guidance.

Although much of this book is written primarily for an American audience, I hope it will prove equally useful to other readers. Great Britain remains a wonderful place to go touring for natives and foreign bicyclists alike. It is an area that can also be highly recommended as a goal for US touring cyclists. And no account of bicycle organizations active on behalf of bicycle touring can be complete without mentioning the British CTC (Cyclists' Touring Club), which is probably internationally the one with the highest proportion of really competent touring cyclists.

Cycling clubs continue to exist and have indeed experienced an increase in membership throughout the last one or two decades. Many clubs cater to racers, others mainly to casual or recreational bicyclists. They organize local rides over various distances – ranging all the way from afternoon trips to day tours of 100, 200 and even 300 miles, referred to as single, double and triple centuries, respectively. Most of these rides are open to members and outsiders alike. They are well organized, replete with food stops, repair service and a so-called sag wagon to transport stragglers and their equipment. Patches or other mementos are usually offered to those who complete such an event.

But even amongst the many active clubs, only few have enough really experienced people available to help and advise all those who want to take up bicycle touring. Neither can they organize educational programs, nor can they offer adequate help to those who would like to become more effective at pulling off their own tours. In fact, there isn't even very much going on by way of regular club riding in the US, as I know it from England, where new members were quickly and effortlessly coached in a truly social manner.

Although I still heartily recommend joining a bicycle club today, the proportion of adequately competent cyclists in many clubs is at an all time low. So, not as much can be learned there these days as used to be the case. Furthermore, the modern trend of wanting to be self-sufficient, of learning alone, with or without the aid of written instructions, applies as much in cycling as it does elsewhere. Perhaps it is a loss, because the social aspect of community in its many diverse forms is more and more receding from our lifestyle.

Today's bicyclist should be entitled to get the best help that can be offered in the form of written instruction. That's what this book is intended to achieve. Even so, I hope it can be a little more than a kind of cook book manual on bike touring. I would also like it to whet your appetite for bicycle use, and increase your spontaneous awareness of the many wonderful aspects of this unique form of transportation, whether for touring or for more mundane purposes.

Sources of Supply

Throughout this book, I shall describe and discuss various kinds of equipment, ranging from clothing to bike parts and camping gear. In general, the best places to buy either the finished products or the materials used in their construction will be in specialized shops. I recommend you shy away from non-specialized sources, such as department stores and general mail order establishments, as much as

possible. Go to a bike shop to get bikes and bike parts, to an outdoor equipment shop for camping gear, to a book shop for books or maps.

Just the same, there is a place for the mail order business. I myself keep several catalogs of specialized mail order suppliers handy, even if only as a source of reference. They inform me every six months of what is available, and there is hardly a better place to get general information about many useful items of equipment. You will find such mail order establishments advertised in the cycling, backpacking and camping press, which itself is also an excellent additional source of information.

Especially amongst bike shops, you will find great differences. There are some that stock only the basics, others that offer an adequate choice only for a particular type of bike and matching accessories. Some stores specialize more than others in touring equipment. Chances are that somewhere near your home there is such a store with an excellent collection of the kind of materials you need. Otherwise, you may have to venture further out. As you patronize various shops, you will find that many are run by people who will gladly go out of their way to oblige you by offering useful advice and assistance, while others are interested only in a quick sale.

It will be worth your while to choose your suppliers as carefully as you select your equipment. Look around to find the best sources, both for bike parts and other items. I suggest you try several stores and ask other people who are active in bike touring. On your search for good suppliers, it will be best to start closest to your home. Only in very rare cases, perhaps when you live many miles away from a major town, or for items that are just not available locally, should you fall back on the several major specialized mail order companies. Once you have found a good source, continue to patronize it and give the operator some feedback with your experience.

If you are not sure the whole thing is for you, you may consider renting all or at least some of the equipment. Certainly if you entertain the thought of bicycle camping, but have never tried camping before, you would be well advised to obtain some of the rather expensive parts of the necessary equipment through a rental outlet. Once you have established whether it really turns you on, you can always decide to buy your own gear. In some instances, such as when travelling abroad or when mountain bike touring in certain areas, bikes and some accessories may also be rented locally. For addresses of reputable rental outfits, check the advertising pages of the major national cycling and camping periodicals.

A Personal Note

Perhaps you wonder what gives me the crazy notion of wanting to write a book about bicycle touring, and what gives me the qualifications to speak with authority on the subject. Sometimes I wonder myself. Though a keen and experienced cyclist, I lack some of the talents that make bike touring a natural to some. I am not the world's greatest adventurer. While I have toured extensively in Europe and North America, I have never had the ambition to venture into the unknown. In fact, I have the awful habit of getting lost in my own town, and I have at times been caught improperly prepared for what I was doing myself.

Just the same, the combination of many years of personal experience, together with the advice from other, more organized cyclists and the forced inventiveness that I had to develop to get by despite my own shortcomings, has probably prepared me well for the task at hand. Even so, when I first came to America in 1967, I never thought I would finish up eking out a living by writing bicycle books. At that time hardly a soul seemed to ride a bike, and those who did seemed to know a lot about the subject.

I myself had been touring by bike in Holland and later in England since I was a kid, accompanying my cycling parents on summer tours all over Europe. As a youth, I started touring with friends or alone, learning more from my own and my companions' mistakes than any other way. Over the years I became a truly competent touring cyclist, one who can solve all of the many problems he ever encounters. But above all, experience had made me inventive enough to solve problems that I had not faced before.

During my first years in the US, I seemed to have forgotten all about cycling, living the life that was typical for the urban young in San Francisco, as it was probably elsewhere too. I mostly drove a car, and bicycling seemed just a happy memory of a quickly receding earlier age. Until bicycles started cropping up everywhere around me. Within a short time, bike shops seemed to open up everywhere. Soon enough I decided myself to replace the bike I had left in Europe upon the recommendation of Americans, who had convinced me that one just could not ride a bike in the New World, something I had blindly believed, though never really accepted.

By the middle of the 'seventies, lots of people were riding bikes, and I found what I had learned over the years could benefit many others who were newer to the sport. The bits of knowledge, skills and experiences that I had taken for granted, even though their accumulation had taken many years of conscious and unconscious learning, appeared to be treasured morsels of wisdom to the less initiated. Soon I found myself giving advice, and it was a short step to writing articles for the then emerging bicycle periodicals.

Eventually, it became obvious that the most important facts about bicycling could be wrapped up systematically in the form of a book. That is how my first English book, *The Penguin Bicycle Handbook*, evolved. But oddly enough, this book, covering perhaps 90% of the things most cyclists wanted or needed to know, left as many questions unanswered as it addressed. What about obscure details of bike maintenance, what about mountain bikes, what of training practices, commuting, racing, touring? My efforts to answer those additional and more detailed questions resulted in a number of books, each addressing quite specific fields of interest.

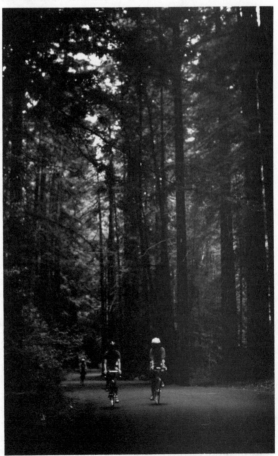

Bike touring in the Redwoods National Park region near the Russian River, about 80 miles North of San Francisco. Cycling through the woods is particularly enjoyable since you are protected from the wind. (Photograph courtesy Backroads)

Whereas the initial reaction to my proposal to write a bicycle book had been that one couldn't possibly fill a whole book about such a trivial subject, the attitude soon changed. As cyclists became more knowledgeable, they also became aware of their need to know even more. So this book is just one in an extended series of books, each of which tries to adequately address one aspect of bicycling. Other books published so far by Bicycle Books in this series are *The Mountain Bike Book, The Bicycle Repair Book, The Bicycle Racing Guide* and *Roadside Bicycle Repairs*. The latter book may be of particular interest to the reader, being a companion volume to the present book: compact enough to be carried on the bike.

About This Book

Like the other books in this series, the present volume makes no claim to being the complete manual on everything worth knowing about bicycling. Instead, it tries to give the absolute maximum of really relevant information on the subject at hand, being bicycle touring in the present instance. Consequently, you will not find much on some of the wide and confusing array of irrelevant subjects often treated in books like this. Instead, I have chosen to use the available space to the maximum for the purpose of helping you with touring by bike. If you really want to know about training or history, about diet or wheel building, there are excellent guides on those subjects available, and this would be the wrong place to look for that kind of information.

Some of the points raised here could perhaps also be found in other manuals on bicycles or bicycling. But I have tried to concentrate the information to maximize its useful-ness with regard to the subject. Consequently, I have selected the topics very carefully, excluding only what is trivial or irrelevant to the touring bicyclist. Instead, I have included all the related material that will be useful both to people with a minimum of previous exposure to cycling, and to those who have used bikes for other purposes but not for touring. Though I have done my utmost to strike a good balance, I welcome any comments from readers, both regarding the choice of subjects and their treatment.

The book is divided up into three distinct parts and an appendix. Each of the main parts covers as fully as I consider practicable one of the three major stages of involvement in bicycle touring. In the first part, you will find all the help I can offer you on the subject of equipment selection. Here you will be shown how to choose items ranging from the bike itself to major components and auxiliaries, including racks, packs, clothing and camping gear.

The second part of the book is devoted to the basics of bicycle riding and touring. Though many people will think immediately of heavily loaded touring with camping gear and survival methods, I shall first make you familiar with all the techniques you have to master in order to enjoy any kind of touristic cycling, be that for a continental crossing or for short evening or day trips, whether heavily loaded or carrying nothing but a credit card. You will be shown how to ride safely and effectively, how to adapt to the weather and how to go about planning your trip.

In the third part, I shall concentrate on some of the less everyday aspects of bicycling and touring. Here are covered those problems that are peculiar to bike touring in general and to quite specific forms of this pursuit. This applies to the various problems that are perhaps useful or important on one trip but not necessarily on the other, let alone on every tour. Included will be advice on orientation, feeding yourself, and bicycle camping. Also covered will be special forms of bicycle touring, such as off-road and tandem touring, cycling with children and touring abroad.

The appendix, finally, contains some of the information that would make dull reading, though it is essential to have easy access to such facts. Here you will find tables and summaries, ranging from frame sizing and gearing tables to packing lists. Also included are a list of addresses, a bibliography and an extensive alphabetical index.

Buffalo encounter in Yellowstone National Park (Photograph courtesy Backroads)

Choice of Words

Let me conclude this introductory chapter with some remarks about the language that will be used in this book. Since the book is purposely written for both the American and other English speaking readership, it would be nice to offer a different version to each market. However, the hard facts of publishing dictate that the same version has to be offered both sides of the Atlantic. Consequently, I must ask my British readers to put up with the peculiar version of the English language as it has become modified in the New World, since I will be using American spelling conventions throughout.

Thus, you will find words like *center, fiber, tire* and *aluminum*, where the British reader expects to read *centre, fibre, tyre* and *aluminium*. On the other hand, my proofreaders and I have done everything possible to avoid the use of words and expressions that make sense only one side of the Atlantic. Some things are known by different names in the two countries. Wherever several distinct names are in common use for the same concept, only one word will be used in most places, after the different terms are explained the first time the concept is mentioned.

Finally, there is the subject of gender. Bicycle touring, like most other activities, is equally accessible to people of either sex. Though I am probably as open to equality of the sexes as any male can be expected to be (which is perhaps still not quite enough), I also feel expressions such as *he/she, him/her* and composites with *-person* are monstrous constructions that stifle any language. That's not the way any sane person speaks, so why should anyone want to write that way? In short, I ask you to accept that the use of the masculine form typically covers both sexes, while the feminine form is generally used only when a statement applies specifically to women.

2
The Bicycle's
Frame, Steering and Saddle

In the present chapter and the two that follow, you will be shown what to look for when choosing and buying a touring bike. Here we will deal only with the bicycle's backbone: its frame with the steering system and saddle. In the next chapter we'll consider the many components installed on every bike, such as wheels, drive system, gears and brakes. In the fourth chapter, finally, we'll consider the accessories that make a touring bicycle particularly suited to its specific purpose.

Of necessity, all this will involve some rather basic explanations and definitions of terminology, in addition to specific advice about touring bicycles and their components. Especially the former is required reading for those who are not fully familiar with the details of the bicycle. Readers who are quite familiar with the bicycle for other uses may

Touring bike with aluminum frame from Cannondale. Note the oversize frame tubes, needed to make up for aluminum's low inherent rigidity. It is equipped with a sturdy rear rack, designed to prevent bag sway, and a low rider front rack.

be tempted to skip these chapters, assuming they contain nothing new.

Yet even these readers would do well to take this material to heart, since it contains quite a bit of information that will help them select bike and components specifically for the intended purpose. Furthermore, it will be helpful to at least check the illustrations and their labels, so you become familiar with the terms I shall be using to identify parts of the bike throughout the book. Often some of these things are called by different names in different parts of the world and indeed by different people in the same area. Thus, confusion can only be avoided if we agree on the terminology that will be used elsewhere in this book.

Parts of the Bike

The illustration Fig. 2.1 gives the names of just about all the major parts on a bicycle. The model illustrated is a fully equipped derailleur bike as might be used for touring. This illustration is chosen because it shows so many different parts, even though not all the components shown will be installed on every bike. In a subsequent part of this chapter and the next, we shall more specifically examine the criteria each of these parts should satisfy to qualify the bicycle for touring.

Before we get into such details, however, here is a summary of the way any bike is built up, and what the various parts are called. The easiest way to do this, at the same time explaining roughly how the bike works, is by grouping the many different parts together in functional assemblies. Thus, one can distinguish the following major component groups:

☐ The frame, which is the bicycle's tubular 'backbone', to which all the other components are attached.
☐ The steering system, required for balance and control.
☐ The drivetrain, comprising all the parts that transmit power to the rear wheel.
☐ The gearing system, allowing the rider to adapt the transmission ratio to the terrain conditions.
☐ The wheels.
☐ The brakes, together with their controls.
☐ The saddle with its seat post that attaches it to the frame.
☐ The various accessories, which play a vital role if we want to distinguish a touring machine from any run-of-the-mill bike.

Frame, steering system and saddle will be treated here. The accessories will be dealt with in Chapter 4. All other functional groups of components will be examined in Chapter 3.

Most bicycles sold these days are made by major bike manufacturers. Although there still is a domestic bicycle industry in the US, the vast majority of quality bikes sold through the specialized bicycle trade are imported these days. Most domestically made bikes are the low end mass products sold through non-specialized outlets. Even those major US companies that do sell through the bike trade import most of their products from places like Taiwan, South Korea and Japan. However, several of these, such as Trek and Schwinn, still make several top line models in their own US factories. With the falling Dollar during the years since 1984, chances are that some manufacturers will increase their domestic production.

In addition to these American firms and a number of East Asian manufacturers, the Europeans are

Fig. 2.1 Parts of the touring bike

not quite dead, although even some of the bikes with European names may well be made elsewhere. Thus, you will find presumably Italian Bianchis or French Peugeots with a sticker proclaiming, 'made in Taiwan', not to mention the name Raleigh, which in the US is in no way associated with the British manufacturer of that same name. Many of these bikes, wherever they may be manufactured, are perfectly good quality machines. What matters more than the country of origin, is the care that went into making them. I will try to show you in the present chapter what to look for to recognize products of satisfactory quality.

Besides factory bikes, there are custom-built machines, based on frames made either to the rider's specifications or at least built by a specialist frame builder. Though this is a very personal way to go, and assures you will get a distinct looking machine that generally costs a lot of money, there is no absolute certainty this will necessarily give you a better bike than you could have bought off the peg for less money. In recent years so many manufacturers have introduced and perfected special touring machines, that it should be no problem to find one to suit your needs at an affordable price.

It is not even realistic to think of most custom-built bikes as being made to measure. Most frame builders also use standard sizing tables with fixed proportions, even though theirs may be a little different from those used by others. However, when you order a custom built frame, you can usually specify just which components should be used and what kind of attachments for the installation of accessories you want to have installed. That may be interesting for a very experienced rider, who has tried all the standard solutions and knows exactly what he wants. For most of us, it will be smarter to choose one of the standard touring bikes now offered by most manufacturers.

Fig. 2.2 The frame

Now for an overview of the bike, it consists of a frame to which a whole lot of otherwise standard parts are installed. Virtually all frames for the same type of bike are made with similar materials, and all the other components come from the series production lines of a limited number of specialized component manufacturers. On bikes from many different manufacturers, even custom-built machines, you will find the same frame tubes, brakes, gears, tires, handlebars and a hundred other parts that all come from one of a limited number of manufacturers who specialize in those particular items.

Even so, not all parts made by the same firm are of the same quality. A maker of brakes, for instance, may have half a dozen or more different models, ranging in price, type, size and quality from one end of the scale to the other. Typically, it will be impossible to give you very detailed information indicating which make and model of any part will be better than other ones, if only because manufacturers change their product specifications and designations from time to time. Instead, I shall explain which general types are suitable and what to look for to make sure you are getting a satisfactory product.

The thing to check is the ultimate functionality on the finished bike. To give but one example, the Campagnolo Record brake is a superb mechanism – on a racing bike. Mount the same model on a touring machine, and you'll find it won't even clear the tires, let alone provide good braking. When buying a complete bike, you should try out all the various components as they work on that bike. When replacing any component, make sure to take the bicycle on which it must be mounted, or at a minimum the matching parts, to the bike store. This way the sales person or mechanic may help you select an item that is really satisfactory for your specific application.

The Frame

The bicycle's frame, shown in Fig. 2.2, is its biggest single component. It consists of the main frame, built up of relatively large diameter tubes, and the rear triangle, consisting of double sets of tubes with smaller diameters. The main frame is made up of top tube, bottom tube, seat tube and head tube. The pairs of tubes that form the rear triangle are called seat stays and chain stays, respectively.

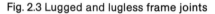

Fig. 2.3 Lugged and lugless frame joints

Fig. 2.4 Plain gauge and butted tubes

On most bikes, the large diameter tubes of the main frame are joined by means of parts referred to as lugs, though these tubes may be joined directly on some bikes. The seat lug, which connects seat tube and top tube, is slotted in the back, allowing it to clamp around the saddle there. The lug that connects down tube and seat tube is called bottom bracket or chain hanger and accommodates the bearings for the crankset. The two forward lugs, connecting the head tube to down tube and top tube, respectively, accept the headset bearings. These are called head lugs and hold the bike's steering system. Fig. 2.3 shows the difference between typical lugged and lugless frame joints.

The rear triangle's pairs of seat and chain stays each come together in flat plates, referred to as dropouts or (rear) fork-ends, in which the rear wheel is installed. At the top, the seat stays are attached to the seat lug, while the chain stays run to the bottom bracket. The pairs of these stays are each stiffened by means of short transverse tubular bridge pieces.

Materials, Strength and Rigidity

Although some manufacturers now offer very attractive bikes with frames made of aluminum tubing, welded or bonded together with or without lugs, the majority of touring bikes continue to be made with more traditional materials: various qualities of steel. On cheap bikes, the frame is made of simple carbon steel tubes that must have significant wall thicknesses (about 1.4 mm) to give adequate strength for a touring bike. This results in a rather heavy and 'dead' bike.

For more expensive machines, strong steel alloys are used. These alloys contain small percentages of other materials, such as chrome, molybdenum and manganese. Generally, their strength is further increased through the tube forming operation. Due to these materials' greater inherent strength, the resulting frame is strong enough even when the tube wall thickness is much smaller. On the highest quality frames, these materials are used in tubes that have a greater wall thickness towards the ends (for adequate strength and resistance to the heat when joining the tubes) than elsewhere along the length of the tube, as shown in Fig. 2.4. The use of such tubes, referred to as butted tubes, results in a lighter, more responsive and comfortable bike.

Given adequate strength and rigidity, the lighter bike is distinctly more enjoyable to ride, even if the difference seems minor relative to the total weight of bike, luggage and rider. This is due to the fact that, unlike the rider's own body weight, most of the weight of bicycle and luggage should be considered 'dead' weight or mass. Essentially, it is unsprung mass, which is not cushioned, as the equivalent weight of a car or motorcycle. Nor can it be transferred or shifted, as is the case for the rider's weight, which can be raised off the saddle in response to anticipated road shocks. This argument not only applies to the weight of the frame, but to virtually all parts of the bike and the luggage carried on it when touring.

Another desirable feature, besides high strength and low weight, is adequate lateral and torsional rigidity of the bike. Rigidity means absence of flexibility. On a rigid bike, there is little deformation in response to a force applied to it at one point. Inadequate rigidity leads to the propagation of vibrations, oscillations and swaying, particularly while riding fast on poor road surfaces or when changing direction abruptly. For a real touring bike, used to carry luggage in difficult terrain, rigidity is of particular importance.

Unfortunately, rigidity is largely affected by some of the same factors as weight: for a given material and tube diameter, the rigidity decreases with decreasing wall thickness. Thus it is harder to get an adequately rigid bike with strong, light and expensive tubes, due to their smaller wall thickness. In consequence, good touring bike frames should be made of tubing materials that are as strong as those used on racing bikes, yet built with thicker walls to be adequately rigid.

Particularly sensitive to undesirable flexing is the down tube, which should therefore have a considerable wall thickness for a good touring bike, even if that makes the frame a little heavier.

There is an even more effective way to achieve greater rigidity: increase the diameter of the tubes. Whereas a 20% increase in wall thickness only leads to a proportional 20% increase in rigidity, the effect of a 20% greater outside diameter, even with an unchanged wall thickness, is on the order of 70%. Both methods lead to the same 20% weight increase. This is the reason why the frame's down tube, which is most heavily subjected to torsional forces, is always made with a greater diameter than the other main tubes.

A third factor to keep in mind with regard to rigidity, is the material used for the tubes. On the one hand, all types of steel, from the cheapest and weakest to the strongest and most exotic, have the same inherent rigidity. Given the same diameter and wall thickness, the tubes are equally rigid, whatever kind of steel is used. On the other hand, aluminum with all its alloys is considerably less rigid. Consequently, an aluminum frame should have tubes that have a greater wall thickness (required to compensate for this material's lower strength anyway) as well as a greater outside diameter, if it is to be satisfactory for touring use.

In addition to the tube diameter, the wall thickness and the tubing material, also the bicycle's frame geometry affects its rigidity. The longer the individual tubes, the more flexible they become. And the frame for a touring bike must be made to more generous dimensions than that for a racing machine, to accommodate fatter tires and allow the installation of certain accessories. A real rigidity nightmare is of course the tandem frame, which is incomparably longer than that of a regular touring bike, not to mention a nimble racing frame. The problems of tandem frames will be addressed separately in Chapter 21, *Tandem Touring*.

Within certain limitations, the bicycle manufacturer is at liberty to select greater wall thicknesses and diameters for certain tubes, to achieve the desired combination of strength, weight and rigidity required for a good touring bike. Especially for heavily loaded touring on a bike that should itself be kept as light as possible, it should be obvious that only the diamond shaped frame gives the required rigidity. That applies to bikes for men

and for women alike, and all special women's models without a horizontal top tube are potentially dangerous at higher speeds when loaded. Oddly enough, that applies particularly if they are made with high strength tubing, since it will have thinner walls.

Many women have particular difficulties getting a bike to fit them properly. That is due to the manufacturer's desire to standardize. They provide off-the-peg frames to fit the averagely proportioned male. However, the typical woman has different proportions that don't fit this standard scheme. Their legs tend to be shorter in relation to their trunks and arms. Their arms are weaker and their hip area heavier. In addition, women tend to be shorter, though short men have at least as much trouble finding a properly proportioned bike. At least one female American frame designer now offers a special series of bikes that are

Bikes are available in all sizes. Here two extremes: the one with 24 inch wheels and an 16 inch frame, the other with 700 mm wheels and a 27 inch frame.

right for the averagely proportioned woman. Very fine machines that are available in many of the more sophisticated bike shops around the country.

For quality bikes, virtually all major bicycle manufacturers and individual frame builders use butted alloy steel tubing. These materials are made by specialized manufacturers, such as Reynolds, Columbus, Tange and Ishiwata. Since each of them offers a wide range of different tubing sets of various strength levels and different wall thicknesses, it is important to find out whether the variety intended for touring bikes has been used for the frame in question. The lighter thin-walled tubes intended for racing frames would not be rigid enough, even if their strength may be adequate.

If you should get a custom frame built, ask the frame builder to give you details on the various tube sets available, so you can select one that is beefy enough. This is especially critical for the down tube and the chain stays, which must be pretty hefty. Whether the frame is custom built or not, I would say for a normal touring bike with conventional tubing diameters (i.e. 1⅛ in seat tube and down tube, 1 in top tube and 1¼ in head tube), the down tube should nowhere have a wall thickness less than 1 mm, while the seat stays should have a diameter of at least 15 mm.

Special frame designs and materials should be considered carefully. Mountain bikes, quite suitable for many touring uses, tend to have tubes of greater diameters, usually welded together without lugs. This makes them quite satisfactory, despite their generous dimensions. Aluminum frames must also have tubes of greater diameters, as well as a greater wall thickness. Since

Fig. 2.5 Frame dimensions

aluminum is so much lighter than steel, the overall weight will still be quite low.

Frame Dimensions

A bicycle's nominal size is determined by the frame size, which is defined as the length of the seat tube. Unfortunately, different manufacturers measure this dimension differently, as shown in Fig. 2.5. In the English speaking world, the distance between the center of the bottom bracket and the top of the seat lug used to be quoted. Today, it is becoming more customary to follow the French custom of measuring between the center of the bottom bracket and the center of the top tube. The same frame will be quoted as being 15 mm or about ½ inch smaller in the latter case than in the former.

To select a frame of the right size, you can either use the advice contained in Table 1 in the Appendix, or you can try out some frames for fit. With wheels of the correct size installed, the top tube should be at such a height that you can straddle it with both feet flat on the ground, wearing thin-soled shoes with minimal heels. Most people seem to buy a bike that is too big. Though less critical for a touring

Fig. 2.6 Touring frame versus racing frame geometry

Fig. 2.7 Parts of the steering system

bike than for a racing machine, I would suggest you deviate on the smaller, rather than on the larger side. See Chapters 20, 21 and 22 for the size selection of special children's bikes, tandems and mountain bikes, respectively.

A good touring bike's frame distinguishes itself from that designed for a racing machine in the following details:

□ The touring bike frame comprises relatively thick walled tubing of the same high quality butted alloy steels and a greater seat stay diameter.

□ The touring bike frame should have slightly more generous dimensions and clearances, including shallower angles between the horizontal and the seat tube and steering axis (fork and head tube), respectively, as shown in Fig. 2.6.

□ Corresponding to many touring cyclists' choice to sit more upright, the touring frame may perhaps be selected about an inch bigger than the optimal racing bike size, which should be kept rather small to allow a really low handlebar position. Table 1 in the Appendix suggests a range of frame sizes as a function of the rider's leg length, measured as shown there. Whatever else applies, you should be able to straddle the frame with both feet flat on the ground.

□ The touring bike frame should be equipped with a number of threaded bosses and lugs for the installation of accessories such as racks and fenders (in Britain called carriers and mudguards, respectively) and on the frame for water bottles, lighting equipment, racks and sometimes for special brakes.

The Steering System
This is the assembly of parts that keeps the bike on track and balanced, by allowing the rotational plane of the front wheel to pivot relative to the rest of the bike. As shown in Fig. 2.7, it comprises the fork, headset bearings, handlebar stem or extension, and the handlebars.

The Fork
The front fork, shown in Fig. 2.8, consists of two blades, terminating in fork-ends or front drop-outs, a fork crown and a steerer tube or fork shaft, which is threaded at one end to accept the adjustable parts of the headset. The fork should be of similar materials to those used for a good steel frame: strong alloy

Fig. 2.8 The front fork

Fig. 2.9 Steering geometry

tubing, brazed onto the fork crown and with relatively thick fork-ends. The latter should have threaded eyelets for the installation of a rack and a mudguard. There should be additional threaded bosses on the fork blades to accept a rack, and pivot bosses may be provided for special brakes. Even on bikes with aluminum frames, the forks must be of steel tubing to stand up to touring abuse.

Due to the shallower angle of the steering system axis relative to the horizontal, the touring bike's fork should have a greater off-set or rake than what is customary on a racing bike. This is necessary to achieve the same steering characteristics, as shown in Fig 2.9. Typical values for a touring bike are a steerer tube angle of 71–72 degrees and a rake of 50–55 mm.

This combination of greater rake and shallower angle results in more clearance between the pedals and the wheel. This allows for the installation of mudguards without interference with the rider's toes when steering around a steep curve at low speed. It also gives better shock absorption, which is essentially a

Fig. 2.10 Typical fork damage

function of front fork design and construction. On the other hand, the touring bike's fork should be made of thicker wall tubing for adequate strength, which tends to detract from its shock absorption qualities.

In a collision, the fork will generally be the first thing to get damaged, being bent back as illustrated in Fig. 2.10. Although such a bent fork can sometimes be straightened again, it will be smart to check with a qualified bike mechanic, rather than experimenting around yourself. When in doubt, have a new fork installed.

The length of the fork's steerer tube is a function of the frame size. It is determined by adding the head tube length to the headset bearing's stacking height, deducting 2 mm

Fig. 2.11 Steerer tube length determination

— locknut

— lockring (lock washer)

— adjustable cup (race)

— fixed cup (race)

Fig. 2.12 The headset

(about $^1/_{16}$ inch), as illustrated in Fig. 2.11. There are two distinct threading standards in use: French and English. The latter standard is used on most bikes. Nowadays, even some frames made for export by French manufacturers are originally supplied with English threading. It will be a good idea to take the old fork and a matching threaded part of the headset along when replacing a bent fork. If the bike has cantilever brakes (as explained under *The Brakes* in Chapter 3), pivot bosses for their installation must be present, in addition to the threaded eyelets and bosses required for the installation of rack and fender.

ALIGN SLOT
CONE   WEDGE

Fig. 2.13 Handlebar expander devices

The Headset

The headset, shown in Fig. 2.12, consists of a double set of ball bearings. These are installed at the upper and lower ends of the head tube, with the matching parts fixed on the fork crown and screwed onto the threaded part of the steerer tube, respectively. The headset should be adjusted if the steering is either too loose or too tight. Proceed as follows:

1. Loosen the big locknut on the upper headset bearing by about 3–4 turns.
2. Lift the lock washer far enough to allow turning the bearing race immediately below.
3. Tighten or loosen the adjustable race as required, by turning it clockwise or counterclockwise, respectively.
4. Put the lock washer in place and tighten the locknut, while holding the adjustable race.
5. If problems persist, see a bike shop for lubrication or part replacement, or learn to do it yourself with the aid of a bicycle repair book.

Handlebars and Stem

The handlebars are attached to the fork's steerer tube by means of an L-shaped piece called handlebar stem or gooseneck. The lower end of this device fits inside the steerer tube. As shown in Fig. 2.13, a wedge or cone-shaped part can be pulled into the stem to clamp the two parts

Fig. 2.14 Stem size

Fig. 2.15 Bar-end plugs

Fig. 2.16 Mountain bike handlebars

together by tightening the expander bolt. The latter is reached from the top and is generally operated by means of a hexagonal bar tool, referred to as Allen key. If you are using a relatively high handlebar position, as many touring cyclists do, the extension should be quite long, since at least 65 mm (2.5 in) must remain contained inside the steerer tube for safety reasons.

The handlebar proper, also referred to as handlebar bend, is held in a split or otherwise clamped portion at the forward end of the stem. Here it is clamped by tightening a second bolt, referred to as binder bolt. Stems are generally made of aluminum alloy and are available in various extension lengths, measured horizontally as shown in Fig. 2.14. A different size may be necessary to adapt the distance between saddle and handlebars to the rider for maximum comfort, as will be described in Chapter 8, *Bike Fit and Riding Style*.

Handlebar bends are generally made of aluminum tubing. They are available in several distinct shapes, ranging from the wide flat things installed on mountain bikes to the nar-row and deep models used on pure racing machines. For touring, most riders prefer bars similar to those used on racing bikes, though with less depth and greater width. One popular model is referred to as Randonneur, on which the curved sections are raised relative to the straight center.

The middle part of the handlebars must be reinforced by an interior or exterior reinforcing sleeve (resulting in a section of greater diameter) over a length of at least 5 cm (2 in) to eliminate the chance of breaking the bar at the point where it projects from the stem. Handlebar bend and stem must be matched, since handlebar diameters vary from one make and model to the other.

The drop bar is finished off by wrapping cloth or plastic handlebar tape around it. Alternately, you may choose installing flexible foam plastic sleeves. The latter solution appears to be most comfortable for touristic cycling on less than perfect road surfaces. The open ends of the

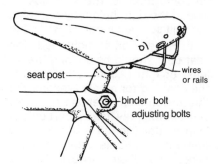

Fig. 2.18 Leather saddle and seat post

Fig. 2.17 Women's and men's saddle widths

Fig. 2.19 Nylon based padded saddle

handlebar bend are closed off by inserting plastic plugs, of which there are several kinds, as shown in Fig. 2.15. If you use a mountain bike with flat wide bars, shown in Fig. 2.16, I suggest cutting the bars down to a width not exceeding about 55 cm (22 in) if the bike is mainly used on the open road. Use firm foam grips at the end of the mountain bike handlebars.

Saddle and Seat Post

On a touring bike, the saddle or seat had better be comfortable. Most touring cyclists prefer to sit more upright than is customary for bicycle racing. This riding style results in more weight resting on the saddle and more difficulty lifting the weight to relieve pain. Consequently, a different saddle design may be required. In general, a good touring saddle should be somewhat wider in the back, though still as long and narrow in the front as the racing saddle. In particular women, who usually have a considerably wider pelvis then most men, may need an extra-wide and more generously padded model, as shown in Fig. 2.17.

Although I and many other experienced touring bicyclists prefer leather saddles, the trend is towards nylon-based seats with some padding in the main pressure areas, covered by thin leather. The two types are shown in Fig 2.18 and Fig. 2.19, respectively. The former illustration also shows the way the saddle is attached to the frame at the seat lug by means of a seat post, referred to as seat pin or seat pillar in Britain. The attachment bolts that hold the saddle to the seat post may be either on top, underneath or by the side of the seat clip that holds the saddle wires to the seat post.

The seat post should be of a model that allows fine adjustment of the position and the angle relative to the horizontal plane. Select one of the micro-adjustable models, as shown in Fig. 2.20. The seat post diameter should match the inside diameter of the seat tube, being 27.2 mm on most quality frames built with butted tubing, though this value may differ on some models. The seat post is held at the right height by clamping the split seat lug around it when the seat binder bolt is tightened. The seat post should be so long that at least 65 mm (2.5 in) is held inside the seat lug for safety reasons. For this reason, a tall rider on a relatively short frame may need a particularly long model, though a better fitting frame is preferable. See Chapter 8, *Bike Fit and Riding Style*, for a step-by-step description of the saddle adjustment procedure.

Fig. 2.20 Micro-adjusting seat posts

3
The Bicycle's Other Components

Having considered the overall configuration of the bicycle and its main structural parts in the preceding chapter, we shall now look at the remaining regular components. These will be grouped into several major categories: drivetrain, wheels, gearing system and brakes. The accessories – those items that adapt a touring bike to its particular purpose – will be treated separately in Chapter 4. In addition, the gearing system, which is handled here

summarily, will be covered more fully in Chapter 9, *Selecting and Using the Gears*.

Some elementary repair and maintenance instructions are included here for the components discussed. This is only done in those cases where it seems relevant in the context of a touring book. When you get into trouble *en route* because you have a flat (referred to as a puncture in Britain) or the chain comes off, you'll want to know what to do about it. On the other hand, there are numerous other possible maintenance or repair jobs that are not relevant to the average touring cyclist. Those who want to do these

Fixing a flat on San Juan Island in Puget Sound, Washington. (Photograph courtesy Backroads)

Fig. 3.1 Adjustable bottom bracket bearings

jobs themselves get full information from a complete repair book, while the less ambitious may choose to take their machine to a bike store to alleviate the problems.

The Drivetrain

The bicycle's drivetrain comprises all the parts that transmit the power from the rider's legs to the rear wheel. The gearing system, which allows adjusting the transmission ratio, can be considered part of the drivetrain as well. I have chosen to treat it separately, not only in the present chapter, but also in conjunction with a discussion of its theoretical and practical implications in Chapter 9, *Selecting and Using the Gears*.

The heart of the drivetrain is the crankset, referred to as chainset in Britain, which is installed in the frame's bottom bracket. It turns around a spindle or axle that is supported in ball bearings. The two types of bottom bracket bearing systems used on quality bicycles are the adjustable cup-and-cone type and the non-adjustable cartridge type, usually referred to as sealed bearing unit. These two varieties are depicted in Fig. 3.1 and Fig. 3.2, respectively.

On virtually all quality bikes built nowadays, the spindle has tapered square ends, matching correspondingly shaped recesses in the cranks. The cranks are held on the spindle by means of a bolt, covered by a dust

Fig. 3.2 Cartridge type bottom bracket bearings

cap in the crank. This method of attachment is referred to as cotterless and is shown in Fig. 3.3. Spindle lengths, bottom bracket widths, screw threading and taper shape all may differ, even if (different) models of the same make are installed. Consequently, all parts of the bottom bracket can only be replaced when the original and the matching parts are taken along to the shop, to make sure they fit as a system.

On a new bike, the cranks tend to come loose after some use, as they may at more infrequent intervals later on. For this reason, and for other maintenance or replacement work, I suggest you obtain a matching crank tool for the particular make and model of the crankset installed on your bike. Check and tighten the crank every 50 km (30 miles) during the first 250 km, and perhaps once a month afterwards. On models with a one-key release, which were popular for a while, only a matching Allen key is required, which is simply used to tighten the crank insert bolt like any other bolt. For all other models, proceed as described below:

Fig. 3.3 Cotterless crank attachment

Fig. 3.4 Tightening crank

Tighten Cotterless Crank

1. Remove the dust cap with any fitting tool (on most models a coin may be used).
2. Using the wrench part of the special crank tool, tighten the recessed bolt firmly, countering at the crank (see Fig. 3.4).
3. Reinstall the dust cap.

The cranks are generally made of aluminum and are available in several different lengths. Unless you have particularly long or short legs, the standard size of 17 cm (about 7 in) will be quite satisfactory. The RH crank has an attachment spider for installation of the chainrings, also called chainwheels. On special touring bikes you will generally find three chainrings installed. In many types of terrain the 10 or 12-speed gearing system, with only two chainrings, will be adequate. It tends to cause fewer problems and uses more readily available replacement parts. Check the attachment bolts of the chainrings from time to time, and tighten them evenly if necessary.

Fig. 3.5 Chainring attachment

Whatever the number of chainrings, make sure the spider is of such a type that quite small chainrings, down to perhaps 26 teeth or so, may be installed – more under *The Gearing System* below and in Chapter 9. The other point to watch out for is that the RH crank and the attachment spider must be formed in one integral part, rather than two parts swaged together, as often used on cheaper bikes. Swaged attachments usually do not stand up to heavy use in hilly terrain. Fig. 3.5 shows how the chainrings are attached to the RH crank and what basic attachment spider forms are commonly in use. Note that many manufacturers use differently dimensioned attachment spiders, making it mandatory to be cautious, ascertaining you get perfectly matching parts when replacing anything.

The pedals are installed at the ends of the cranks. They come in

CONE   LOCKNUT

LOCK WASHER   DUST CAP

adjusting detail

quill pedal

platform pedal

Fig. 3.6 Pedal types

buckle or clasp

rough side in

twist strap
once

Fig. 3.7 Toeclips with strap

Fig. 3.8 Short toeclips

several basically different models, as shown in Fig. 3.6. The platform model is probably most suitable for touring bikes, although many riders are quite satisfied with quill pedals or even one of the threatening looking devices installed on mountain bikes. In recent years fiber reinforced plastic pedals have come on the market, as have models that can only be used in combination with a matching special shoe. I feel neither are very suitable for touring use.

The pedals may have to be removed from the bike when it is transported, particularly if it has to be placed in a box, as is demanded by many airlines. First check whether your pedals have only flat wrench faces or also a (more convenient) hexagonal recess reached from the back of the crank. In the latter case, use a matching Allen key to unscrew and install them. Otherwise, you will need a

thin open ended wrench of the appropriate size (usually 15 mm). Remember that the LH pedal has LH thread, so it is loosened by turning to the right, fastened by turning to the left. Putting some lubricant on the thread protects the screw thread and makes it easier to loosen the pedals next time.

Whether or not you use special bicycle shoes with shoe plates or cletes, which hold the shoes accurately in place on the pedals, the installation of toeclips seems a must for comfortable cycling over longer distances. I prefer the regular type which has a strap to wrap around the shoe, and which is installed as shown in Fig. 3.7. If you don't like the idea of being semi-permanently wired up to your bike by the feet, install the short open type of toeclips, illustrated in Fig. 3.8, which at least stop the shoes from slipping forward off the pedals.

ROLLER
BUSHING
PIN

CONVENTIONAL   SEDISPORT

Fig. 3.10 Using chain tool

Fig. 3.9 The chain

The Chain

The chain connects the crankset with the rear wheel, where a freewheel block with several different size sprockets is installed. The chain must be routed as explained below under *The Gearing System*. It must have the right size, which means it should neither hang loose nor tightens up excessively when using either of the extreme gearing combinations (big chainwheel with a big sprocket or small chainwheel with small sprocket, respectively).

Fig. 3.9 shows how the chain is constructed. On derailleur bikes an endless chain is used, which may be parted by removing one of the pins connecting two links. The same method is used to add or remove links to adjust the chain's length. It may be necessary to remove the chain for cleaning and lubrication, which will be frequently required under dusty or wet conditions. To do that, you will need a chain tool, which is used as illustrated in Fig. 3.10 and described below:

Chain Maintenance

1. Put the chain on a combination of a small chainwheel with a small sprocket, to release its tension.

JOCKEY WHEEL

SPRING TENSION

TENSION WHEEL

Fig. 3.11 Chain routing at rear derailleur

2. Place the tool on one of the pins connecting two links, and turn it in by 6 turns.
3. Turn the handle of the tool back out and remove the tool from the chain.
4. Wriggle the chain apart.
5. Reinstall the chain, routing it around the derailleur per Fig. 3.11.

Note: This description applies to the removal of the chain for cleaning or replacement. To remove or add an even number of links, one pin must be pushed out completely, turning the tool in as far as needed.

The Freewheel

Depending on the make and type of rear wheel hub, the freewheel is either a separate unit screwed on, or it is integrated in the (special) hub. Amongst the earlier variety, the solu-

Fig. 3.13 The derailleur system

Fig. 3.12 Freewheel with sprockets

Fig. 3.14 Front derailleur

tion with a special easily detachable screw thread, such as the Maillard Helico-matic, is particularly suitable for touring, since it can be easily removed en route. This may become necessary to replace a broken spoke, and is hard to do with other screw-on types. The sprockets are closely associated with the gearing system, which will be covered separately. Fig. 3.12 shows a common screwed-on freewheel with its sprockets.

The Gearing System

In this section we'll discuss only the hardware, while the niceties of the system, including selection and handling, are described in some detail in Chapter 9, *Selecting and Using the Gears*. Whereas hub gearing systems may be suitable for many touristic purposes, they have been essentially eliminated from the American market for that use. Consequently, I shall confine my remarks to derailleur gearing.

A typical derailleur system is shown in Fig. 3.13. It consists of a front changer and a rear derailleur, which are operated by means of shift levers. The shifters may be installed either on the down tube or, in the case of a bike with flat handlebars, on top of the bars. Other shift lever positions, such as in the handlebar ends or at the stem, though seen on some bikes, are inherently unsuitable for touring use, since they are not easily accessible under touring conditions. The shift levers are connected to the changers by

Fig. 3.15 Rear derailleur

Fig. 3.16 Parts of the wheel

means of flexible cables that run over guides and, in the case of handlebar-mounted shifters, partly inside flexible outer cables.

The front changer, shown in Fig. 3.14, is installed on the seat tube, either by means of a clip around the tube or by means of brazed-on lug. The latter solution restricts you to the use of derailleurs of the same make as that lug if you ever have to replace it. The rear derailleur, depicted in Fig. 3.15, is installed on the RH drop-out, which should have a threaded eye for this purpose, though adaptor plates are provided with most derailleurs, to allow installing them on a bike without it. The chain is routed around the rear derailleur as shown in Fig. 3.11, while it is guided through the changer's cage in the front.

The derailleurs are used to shift the chain over sideways to engage a smaller or bigger chainwheel or sprocket, while you continue to pedal forward with reduced pedal force. A combination with a large chainwheel and a small sprocket provides a high gear, suitable for easy terrain conditions. Engaging a small chainwheel and a large sprocket provides a low gear, required to go up an incline, starting off or riding against a head wind. A thorough explanation will be found in Chapter 9.

For serious touring work, especially in hilly terrain, carrying luggage, both front and rear derailleurs should be models suitable for use with wide range gearing. This may be defined as gears ranging from very low to very high, characterized by big differences between the numbers of teeth (and hence the sizes) of individual sprockets and chainwheels. You can recognize these wide range models by the greater size of their cages through which the chain is guided.

The Wheels

A typical bicycle wheel is shown in Fig. 3.16. It is a spoked wheel with regular wired-on tire, which consists of a separate inner tube and a cover that is held tight in a deep bedded metal rim by means of metal wires in the side of the tire cover. The other components of the wheel are hub and spokes. Wheel problems are perhaps the most common category of incidents while touring, and their repair will be covered in some detail below.

The hub, shown in Fig. 3.17, may be either a high flange or a low flange model (referred to as big and small flange, respectively, in Britain). Like

locknut

axle   cone   lock washer
bearing cup

Adjusting detail

LOW (SMALL) FLANGE

HIGH (LARGE) FLANGE

Fig. 3.17 Hub types

Axle nuts

CLOSE

OPEN

Quick-release

Fig. 3.18 Hub attachments

the rim, it must be designed for a minimum of 36 spokes per wheel. An exception is formed for smaller sizes, as used for children's bikes.

On most touring bikes the hubs have quick-release levers, allowing easy wheel removal (see Fig. 3.18). Especially for mountain bikes and tandems, but even for heavily loaded normal touring machines, quick-releases are not such a good idea, since these have hollow axles. The hole weakens the axle somewhat, which is an important drawback, especially for the rear wheel.

The spokes, shown in Fig. 3.19, should be of stainless steel. Each spoke is held to the rim by means of a screwed-on nipple, which should be kept tightened to maintain the spoke under tension, which actually prevents a lot of spoke breakages. The spokes run from the hub to the rim in one of several distinct patterns. Fig. 3.20 shows three-cross and four-cross spoking patterns. The latter appears to be most suitable for the rear wheel, as it has been demonstrated to result in fewer spoke breakages.

A problem on the rear wheel is the fact that the rim with the tire must be centered over the ends of the bearing locknuts. This normally creates a significant off-set relative to the hub flanges, on account of the presence of the freewheel on the RH side. Fig. 3.21 shows several ways the wheel may be centered. The usual off-set in the rear wheel results in much higher forces in the spokes leading to the RH flange than in those on the other side of the wheel.

The length of the spoke is measured as shown in the illustration Fig 3.19. It depends on the wheel size, the type of hub and the spoking pattern. Make sure you know which sizes are needed for your wheels (they may be different for front and rear, and in the rear even for both sides). The strength is a function of the thickness – at least 2.0 mm or 14 gauge is required for a touring bike. Butted spokes have a thinner section in the middle. They are as strong as regular spokes that are as

Fig. 3.19 Spoke details

Fig. 3.20 Spoking patterns

Fig. 3.21 Symmetrical and asymmetric wheels

thick as their thickest section (the lower gauge number in their size designation). If a spoke should brake, carry out a repair according to the following description:

Replace Broken Spoke

1. Remove the freewheel, if the hole in the hub that corresponds to the broken spoke lies inaccessibly under the freewheel.

Fig. 3.22 Rim cross section

2. Remove the old spoke. If possible, unscrew the remaining section from the nipple, holding the latter with a wrench. If not possible, the tire must be deflated and locally lifted first, after which the nipple may be replaced by a new one.
3. Locate a spoke that runs the same way as the broken one: every fourth spoke along the circumference of the rim runs similarly. Check how it crosses the various other spokes that run the other way, using it as an example.
4. Thread the spoke into the nipple until it has the same tension as the other spokes of the wheel.
5. If the spokes do not seem to be under tension, tighten all of them half a turn at a time, until they all seem equally taut and the wheel is reasonably true – if necessary, follow the instructions for *Wheel Truing* below to correct the situation.

The Rims
For a touring bike of any quality, the rims must be of aluminum, which is reasonably light and strong. In addition, aluminum provides much better braking characteristics than heavier chrome plated steel rims.

Correcting radial distortion

Fig. 3.23 Wheel truing

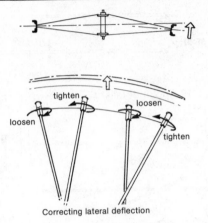

Correcting lateral deflection

Fig. 3.22 illustrates the rim. The rim should match the tire, which will be discussed below. For touring, a relatively strong model should be selected. Stronger models tend to be those that are a little heavier.

If weight is to be saved – and lighter wheels definitely run better than heavier ones – keep the weight down by selecting a relatively narrow model, within the limitation that it must accept the tire selected. The spoke holes should be reinforced by means of ferrules, which on a 'box section' rim design should connect the inner and outer bottom, as shown in the illustration. To protect the tube, a piece of tape should cover the part of the rim bed where the spoke nipples would otherwise touch the inner tube.

Wheel Truing

If the wheel is bent, which may or may not be the result of a broken spoke, proceed as follows to straighten it by retensioning certain spokes, as shown in Fig. 3.23:

1. Check just where it is offset to the left, where to the right, by turning it slowly while watching at a fixed reference point, such as the brake shoes. Mark the relevant sections.

2. Tighten LH spokes in the area where the rim is off-set to the RH side, while loosening the ones on the RH ones – and vice versa.
3. Repeat steps 1 and 2 several times, until the wheel is true enough not to rub on the brakes. This will get you by but, unless you are quite good at it, I suggest you get the job done properly by a bike mechanic as soon as possible.

Tires and Tubes

The size of the tire defines the nominal size of the wheel. Adult touring bikes usually have either 27 in or 700 mm tires of various tire widths. Such nominal sizes are a far cry from their actual dimensions. To give an example: the supposed 700 mm tires normally measure anywhere from 666 mm to 686 mm, depending on the tire width. Though these things are also known as 28 in tires, they are actually smaller than those of nominal size 27 in. The inner tube should be of a size to match the tire. For any given size, it seems the lighter and thinner tube and tire give a better ride. Only in terrain with thorns and other frequent puncture causes, should the very thick thorn-proof tubes be used.

Fig. 3.24 Tire sizing

Fig. 3.25 Valve types

Tire and rim must match. The critical dimension determining tire interchangeability, especially important if you ever run into trouble on a trip abroad, is the rim bed or rim shoulder dimension. For 27 in and 700 mm tires this diameter should be 630 mm and 622 mm, respectively. Mountain bikes that roll on 26 in tires have rims of 559 mm rim bed diameter. Certainly the European tire and rim manufacturers now quote the critical dimensions in mm on both tires and rims in the form of the so-called ETRTO designation, illustrated in Fig. 3.24. On tires this is e.g 25–622 for a 25 mm wide tire for use on a 622 mm rim. On a rim the ETRTO code may e.g. read 622 x 19 for a 622 mm diameter rim with a width of 19 mm.

As for the recommended tire width, I feel it depends on the terrain encountered. The minimum width suitable for touring is probably 25 mm, while 28 or even 32 mm are good choices for heavily loaded bikes on mixed road surfaces. If you want to tour off-road or in regions where roads are maintained less scrupulously than they are in the US or Western Europe, mountain bike wheels with tire widths anywhere from 35 mm to 54 mm are an excellent choice, as they are for tandem use. Whenever long life and resistance to abuse are required, select a tire with plenty of rubber in the tread area. Even in that case, look for a model with flexible sidewalls, which I have found to roll significantly lighter, especially on rough surfaces.

The tube is inflated by means of a valve, several types of which are illustrated in Fig. 3.25. By far the most suitable is the Presta valve, which requires much less force to inflate properly, though it can't be done by means of a gas station air hose, unless you can find an adaptor nipple. Unscrew the round nut at the tip before inflating, and tighten it again afterwards. Inflation pressure is the key to low rolling resistance and immunity to puncturing. Maintain at least the pressure quoted on the tire side wall, and don't hesitate to inflate at least the rear wheel by about 20 percent more than that minimum value. On the road, use a hand pump and regularly check the pressure with the aid of a tire pressure gauge, both described in Chapter 4.

Sooner or later, every cyclist gets a flat. When you are touring, you must be able to handle this repair yourself. Carry a puncture kit, three tire irons (called tyre levers in Britain), a pump and perhaps a spare tube. The adhesive quality of the patches in your kit deteriorates over time, so I suggest replacing them once a year. Proceed as follows to mend a puncture:

Fixing a Flat

1. Remove the wheel from the bike. On a rear wheel, first select the gear with the small chainwheel and sprocket, then hold the chain with the derailleur back as shown in Fig. 3.26.
2. Check whether the cause is visible from the outside. In that case, remove it and mark its location, so you know where to work.
3. Remove the valve cap and locknut, unscrew the round nut (if you have a Presta valve).
4. Push the valve body in and work one side of the tire into the deeper center of the rim, as shown in Fig. 3.27.
5. Put a tire iron under the bead on that side, at some distance from the valve, then use it to lift the bead over the rim edge and hook it on a spoke, as shown in Fig. 3.28.
6. Do the same with the second tire iron two spokes to the left and with the third one two spokes over to the right. Now the first one will come loose, so you may use it in a fourth location, if necessary.
7. When enough of the tire sidewall is lifted over the rim, you can lift the rest over by hand.
8. Remove the tube, saving the valve until last, when it must be pushed back through the valve hole in the rim.
9. Try inflating the tire and check where air escapes. If the hole is very small, so it can't be easily detected, pass the tube slowly

Fig. 3.26 Hold back derailleur

Fig. 3.27 Shift tire sidewall

past your eye, which is quite sensitive. If still no luck, dip the tube under water, a section at a time: the hole is wherever bubbles escape. Mark its location and dry the tire if appropriate. There may be more than just one hole.
10. Make sure the area around the patch is dry and clean, then roughen it with the sand paper or the scraper from the puncture kit and remove the resulting dust. Treat an area slightly larger than the patch you want to use.
11. Quickly and evenly, spread a thin film of rubber solution on the treated area. Let dry about 3 minutes.
12. Remove the foil backing from the patch, without touching the adhesive side. Place it with the adhesive side down on the treat-

Fig. 3.28 Use of tire levers

ed area, centered on the hole. Apply pressure over the entire patch to improve adhesion.

13. Sprinkle talcum powder from the patch kit over the treated area.

14. Inflate the tube and wait long enough to make sure the repair is carried out properly.

15. Meanwhile, check the inside of the tire and remove any sharp objects that may have caused the puncture. Also make sure no spoke ends are projecting from the rim bed – file flush if necessary and cover with rim tape.

16. Let enough air out of the tube to make it limp but not completely empty. Then reinsert it under the tire, starting at the valve.

17. With your bare hands, pull the tire back over the edge of the rim, starting opposite the valve, which must be done last of all. If it seems too tight, work the part already installed deeper into the center of the rim bed, working around towards the valve from both sides.

18. Make sure the tube is not pinched between rim and tire bead anywhere, working and kneading the tire until it is free.

19. Install the valve locknut and inflate the tire to about a third its final pressure.

20. Center the tire relative to the rim, making sure it lies evenly all around on both sides.

21. Inflate to its final pressure, then install the wheel. If the tire is wider than the rim, you may have to release the brake (just make sure you tighten it again afterwards). On the rear wheel, refer to point 1 above.

Note: If the valve leaks, or if the tube is seriously damaged, the entire tube must be replaced, which is done following the relevant steps of these same instructions. Replacement of the tire cover is done similarly. Always make sure the rim tape that covers the spoke ends is intact.

The Brakes

Basically, there are four different types of rim brakes suitable for touring bicycles. In some countries hub brakes are also used, but only rim brakes are commonly applied for serious cycling of any kind in the English speaking world. Fig. 3.29 shows the various types, which may be referred to as centerpull, sidepull, cantilever, and cam-operated brakes, respectively.

On the sidepull brake, the brake arms pivot around the attachment bolt, while they pivot around separate bosses installed on a common yoke on the centerpull brake and on the regular cam-operated brake. On the cantilever brake and the frame-mounted variety of the cam-operated model, the pivots are installed on bosses that are attached directly to the fork or seat stays, which must be welded on in those locations.

With any rim brake, the force applied by pulling the lever is transmitted to the brake unit by means of flexible cables. These cables are partly contained in flexible outer cables and restrained at anchor points on the frame. The force is

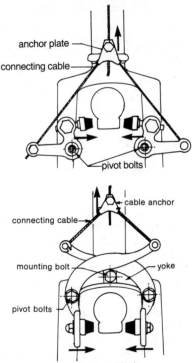

Fig. 3.29 Brake types

transmitted to the parts of the brake unit to which the cable is attached. A pivoting action then pulls the ends of the brake arms with the brake blocks against the sides of the rim to create the drag that slows down the bike.

Touring cyclists are fortunate compared to racing cyclists, because the best brakes for their application are relatively reasonably priced. The paramount criterion for a good touring brake is that it must be rigid, while still opening up far enough to clear the rather fat tire and leaving enough space for fenders. Of the models shown, the cantilever brake seems to be best suited, since it can easily be designed that way. My second choice would be the centerpull brake.

The brake handle, several models of which are shown in Fig. 3.30, should be designed very rigidly. It must match the handlebar type used and it should be easy to reach, while allowing full application of the brake. The type of levers designed for mountain bikes are quite suitable for any bike with flat handlebars, providing the attachment clamp matches the bar diameter. If you like to hold drop handlebars in the top straight portion, you will be best served with guidonnet models. Models with extension levers are not satisfactory, since they are insufficiently rigid and often shorten the regular handle's range of travel.

All brakes have an adjustment mechanism to shorten the cable, which allows you to apply more force. It

MULTIPLE ADJUSTING

SIMPLE ADJUSTING

Fig. 3.31 Brake shoe types

EXTENSION LEVER

adequate force. Relatively thick inner cables with non-compressing outer cables, such as those by Campagnolo, are best for use with any make or model of brake. Brake cables should be routed as short as

guidonnet

This is the way to adjust the rear brake once the range of the adjusting barrel is exceeded: pull the cable taut with the pliers, then retighten the eye bolt.

ADJUSTER

Fig. 3.30 Brake handles

may be installed at the handle, at the brake unit or at one of the cable anchor points. The adjustment is described below. Most brakes have a quick-release mechanism to allow easy wheel removal and installation, without affecting adjustment of the brake. Brake cables should not be elastic or 'spungy', to allow applying possible, providing they are not forced in excessively tight bends in any position of handlebars or brake.

The brake blocks should be of a composition material that provides adequate braking even in the rain, which is just not the case with any kind of plain rubber brake blocks. Contrary to popular belief, longer brake blocks are not better but poorer than shorter ones, given the same material. Depending on the type of brake used, the brake blocks may be installed in one of the two basic types of brake shoes illustrated in Fig. 3.31, which are adjustable in one and two planes, respectively.

To make sure the brakes work properly, it is enough to test them at low speed. Try them out separately at walking speed, which is perfectly safe and still gives a representative test of the deceleration reached with each brake. Used alone while riding the bike, the rear brake must be strong enough to skid the wheel when applied firmly. The front brake should decelerate the bike so much that the rider notices the rear wheel lifting off when it is fully applied. If their performance is inadequate, carry out the adjustment described below.

Adjust Brake

We will assume the brake must be adjusted because its performance is insufficient. In this case, the cable tension must be increased by decreasing its length. Should the brake touch the rim even when not engaged, the opposite must be done to lengthen the cable slightly. The adjuster mechanism is shown in Fig. 3.32.

Before starting, check to make sure the brake blocks lie on the rim properly over their entire width and length when the brake is applied, as shown in Fig. 3.33. Ideally, the front

Fig. 3.32 Brake adjuster

Fig. 3.33 Brake block adjustment

Fig. 3.34 Brake quick release

of the brake block should touch the rim just a little earlier than the back. If necessary, adjust by loosening the brake block bolt, moving the block as appropriate. Retighten it while holding the brake block in the right position. If necessary, the brake block may be replaced, after which the adjustment steps that follow must be carried out as well.

Fig. 3.35 Brake cable nipple

1. Release brake quick-release, as shown in Fig. 3.34.
2. Loosen locknut on the adjusting mechanism for the brake cable, which may be installed on the brake, on the handle or at a cable anchor point.

Moderately priced touring bike from Raleigh USA. Equipped with fifteen-speed gearing, sturdy racks and large cross-section tires.

3. While holding the locknut, screw the barrel adjuster out by several turns; then tighten the quick-release again.
4. Check the brake tension: the brake must grab the rim firmly when a minimum of 2 cm (¾ in) clearance remains between the brake handle and the handlebars.
5. If necessary, repeat steps 1–4 until the brake works properly.
6. Tighten the locknut again, while holding the adjusting barrel to stop it from turning.

Replace Brake Cable

To avoid the unsettling experience of breaking your brake cable just when it is most needed, I suggest you replace it as soon as individual strands show signs of damage at the end nipple. Since a cable may have to be replaced while you are touring, it will be smart to carry a spare. Make sure the spare cable has a nipple that matches the particular brake handle used on your bike. Proceed as follows:

1. Loosen the brake quick-release.
2. Loosen the eye bolt that holds the cable at the brake, until you can pull the old cable out.
3. Push the old cable out, working towards the handle, where you can dislodge the nipple as shown in Fig. 3.35. Then pull the entire inner cable out, catching the outer cable section or sections, as well as any other parts, memorizing their installation locations.
4. Lubricate the new cable. Back off on the locknut, then screw the adjusting barrel in all the way.
5. Starting at the handle, push the new cable through, securing the nipple by pulling it taut. Thread the cable through the various anchor points, outer cable sections and other parts, through the adjuster. Finally push it through the eye bolt at the brake, where it must be clamped in. Secure the nipple into the handle by pulling the cable taut from the brake end.
6. Tighten the eye bolt while continuing to keep the cable taut.
7. Adjust the cable tension, following the preceding instruction.
8. Test the brake in operation, followed by a final adjustment if necessary.
9. Finally, cut off the free end of cable until about 3 cm (1¼ in) projects, using sharp cutters.

4
Useful Touring Accessories

Having examined the bicycle itself with its essential components in the two preceding chapters, we shall now look at its accessories: the additional equipment that can be installed to advantage on the touring bike. In some cases, any more or less regular derailleur bicycle, whether a model with drop handlebars or a mountain bike, can be turned into an acceptable touring machine by merely installing addi-

Room enough on even the smallest frame to mount the essentials: water bottle, pump and lock. (Photograph Bill de Simone / Kryptonite)

tional equipment, such as luggage racks, fenders, lights etc. In recent years quite a few manufacturers have introduced purpose-built touring bikes, more or less completely equipped with such accessories.

Either way, the following descriptions deal with all those accessories that are particularly suitable for a touring bicycle. They may be readily installed on the bike when purchased, or installed at a later date. They may be mounted on a machine specifically designed for touring, or on a relatively common derailleur bike with the aid of special adaptors and clamping devices.

Braze-ons, Lugs and Eyelets

It is not impossible to attach many items on the bike by means of more or less improvised clamps, as will be shown in various places throughout this chapter for different accessories. Ideally, however, the touring bicycle should be equipped with a number of attachment points for the installation of accessories. In most cases that is not only the most convenient solution, it is also the safest way: reliable and secure. Even if sold without these touring accessories, the bike should preferably have the following attachment provisions:

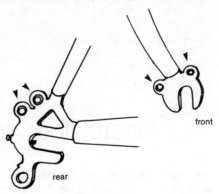

front

rear

Fig. 4.1 Double eyelets

☐ Double threaded eyelets on front and rear drop-outs, to attach the stays for front and rear luggage racks and mudguards simultaneously, as shown in Fig. 4.1.

Fig. 4.2 Threaded bosses for racks

☐ Threaded bosses, as shown in Fig. 4.2, on the fork blades and on the seat stays, to attach the upper supports for front and rear luggage racks.

☐ If the bike will be equipped with cantilever brakes or other models designed for frame-mounted pivots, as described in Chapter 3, pivot bosses for these on the fork blades and the seat stays, as shown in Fig. 4.3. If a cam-operated brake with fixed pivots will be used, as is frequently the case on high quality mountain bikes, those for the rear wheel may be installed at the bottom of the chain stays, instead.

Fig. 4.3 Pivot bosses for brake

☐ Stops, tunnels and guides for the brake cables on the frame, as shown in Fig. 4.4. Included should be guides or tunnels and stops for the outer cables on the top tube of the frame. Those for the rear brake may be on the down tube if a cam-operated rear brake with brazed-on pivots is used.

Fig. 4.4 Tunnels and guides for cables

☐ Anchors or stops for the outer brake cables, as shown in Fig. 4.5. One should be in the form of a bridge between the seat stays to act as a stop for the cable to the rear centerpull or cantilever

Fig. 4.5 Anchors for brake cable

dynamo on seat stay   head light on fork
                            (only if not obstructed)

Fig. 4.6 Attachments for lighting equipment

Fig. 4.7 Chain hanger boss

brake, and a similar device either on the handlebar stem or integrated in the upper headset bearing for the front brake. If a cam-operated brake is used on the rear wheel, the rear brake anchor will probably be installed on the down tube near the bottom bracket.

☐ Threaded bosses on the frame's down tube and seat tube for the installation of two or more water bottles.

☐ Threaded bosses or lugs for the installation of front and rear lights and a dynamo on the front fork and the seat stay, as shown in Fig. 4.6.

☐ A boss or chain hanger on the inside of the RH seat stay, to accept the chain when the wheel is not installed, as shown in Fig. 4.7.

If the pertinent accessories are not installed initially, screws should preferably be installed in the threaded parts to protect the internal screw threads. These bolts should be greased slightly and kept tightened too. Some frame builders use nylon screws here, which is quite acceptable, since they have to be replaced by (steel) bolts of a different length when the accessory is installed anyway.

Clamps and Clips

To install accessories on a bicycle without such special provisions, you will have to rely on provisional clamps and the like. As illustrated in Fig. 4.8, it will be advisable to attach any such clamps only after installing a rubber patch from the bicycle tire patch kit around the bike's tubing locally. This not only protects paintwork or metal finish, it also prevents the clamp from slipping or twisting. Do not use self-adhesive tape for this purpose, since it will slip over time, whereas a tire patch, applied just like you would do to fix a flat tire, will stay in place firmly.

By way of maintenance of most accessories, you merely have to make sure the things are not broken or loose. Tighten the various attachment bolts from time to time, preferably on a regular basis – even daily on a longer tour. To make sure bolts do not come loose, I suggest you use washers and locknuts wherever possible. Thus, racks and fenders attached to eyelets on the drop-outs can be secured more reliably when the installation according to Fig. 4.9 is used, countering the locknut against the metal of the eyelet, while the washer under the bolt head allows you to tighten the screw fully.

Fig. 4.8 Installing patch around frame tube

Luggage Racks

It may be possible to go on shorter trips (up to weekend rides, if you stay in hotels) with no more luggage than can be carried in bags directly attached to the bike or carried on the back. However, you will need luggage racks or carriers for any serious touring over longer distances. The dilemma of carrying luggage, together with the details of bags and racks, will be covered in much more detail in Chapters 5 and 13. Here we'll merely introduce the basic types of racks available.

Fig. 4.9 Bolt attachment at drop-out

Luggage racks are available for the front and the rear. Generally, the rear rack allows carrying relatively large bags by the side and on top, while the one in the front is smaller, being attached to the fork. Their details of construction and the preferred way to combine the various types of racks and bags shall all be covered in the next chapter. Fig. 4.10 shows two typical racks for front and rear, respectively.

Whatever their type, make sure the racks can be attached very firmly to the bike. Preferably, brazed-on attachment lugs or bosses should be installed on the bike, exactly matching the dimensions of the particular rack used. That may become a bit ·of a problem when replacing the rack on a used bike or when installing a rack on a bike for the first time. However, a certain degree of standardization has taken place. Most manufacturers of tour-

Fig. 4.10 Typical racks

ing bikes and racks nowadays design their equipment in line with the attachment details of the racks produced by Jim Blackburn – including his many cut-price competitors.

Do not skimp on the quality of your luggage racks, since they are essential load-bearing parts. As in so many things related to the bike, the price difference comes either out of the weight or the quality. Conse-

Fig. 4.11 Fenders

Fig. 4.12 Fender attachment detail

quently, you should expect to pay a lot for a good aluminum rack, or save quite a bit on a well built, though much heavier steel rack. Just don't look for a rack that is both light and cheap: it probably won't be much good. See the next chapter for more details on recognizing quality and suitability.

Fenders

Although many cyclists in America abhor the idea of installing fenders or mudguards on their bicycle, I suggest no touring bike is complete without them, unless you do all your cycling in one of those areas where it simply doesn't ever rain for a period of several months. Even then, you would be well advised to get fenders, though you may hold off on installing them until the rainy season

starts. Cycling in the rain or on wet roads after it has rained is not as bad as some people think, and it will certainly be less miserable when you are equipped for it.

Yes, you can ride in the rain, or on a wet road after the rain, on a bike without fenders. But you'll be dead miserable. A spray of muddy water will stain your back and your luggage; another jet of water will be shooting at your feet, and there's no way to get comfortable that way. Though you may still need rain gear to keep the rain off the top, you'll find fenders at least keep you reasonably dry and clean from below.

Fig. 4.11 shows typical fenders. At the top, they are attached to the brake bolt behind the front fork and

Light welded aluminum luggage rack from Eclipse. The forward mounting detail allows alignment of the rack, while the rear braces run towards the center to provide adequate rigidity.

in front of the bridge connecting the seat stays, for front and rear fenders, respectively. In the rear, a second point of attachment is by means of a clip over the bridge just behind the bottom bracket. Finally, they are held by means of rather thin rods, called stays, to the front fork-ends and rear drop-outs, respectively. Some attachment details are shown in Fig. 4.12.

Install plain washers between bolts or nuts and the various clips or stays. The fender should be mounted in such a way that about 2 cm (¾ in) radial and at least 1 cm (⅜ in) lateral clearance remains between the tires on the one hand and the fender with its stays on the other. If the fender is either crooked, too close, or too far from the wheel, do not adjust it by bending the stays. Instead, undo the clamping point and move the stays in or out to suit, after which the bolt is tightened again. Any excessive protrusions should be cut off. On the CPSC approved fenders installed as original equipment on bikes sold in the US, the stays are attached on the inside, which means the stays must be cut to size before they are installed.

If you choose to install fenders only occasionally, removable attachments are easy enough to make, as shown in Fig. 4.13. To attach the stays at the fork-ends and drop-outs, make your own wing bolts by soldering a sizable washer in the slot of a normal screw. If the bike has caliper brakes, attached by means of single bolts in fork crown and rear brake bridge, replace their attachment nuts by two thinner nuts, between which the fender clip is clamped. Install and tighten both nuts, even when the fender is not installed, since a single thin nut is not adequate to restrain the brake.

Fig. 4.13 Removable fender installation

On bikes with brakes that are not mounted with a central brake bolt, attach the fenders by means of a similar home-made wing bolt. Use a bolt with a saw cut in the head that is threaded to match the thread of a regular 6 mm or ¼ in wing nut. This is usually a coarser thread than what is used on brake mounting bolts, for which it would not be suitable, though it is adequate for fender installation.

Fenders may be either of plastic or of metal. The lightest satisfactory fenders available are the plastic models that used to be made by Bluemels of England. Since this company's production facilities were taken over by SKS, a major German competitor, the future of these fenders is not assured, but they'll probably be around for a while. The problem is that SKS is used to doing business in a market where a rear light is commonly installed on the rear fender, and even the strongest plastic fenders invariably break after extended use when they are loaded by anything like that in the back. This kind of failure mode is known as fatigue, which will be explained in the next

Fig. 4.14 Mud flap

many less sensible CPSC regulations.

To really keep the water that is splashed up from the road at the front wheel from your feet, you will need a mud flap installed at the bottom of the front fender. Very few models available have one of these things attached, but you can make your own, using a 15–20 cm (6–8 in) square piece of flexible, but relatively thick plastic sheet, installed as shown in Fig. 4.14.

chapter, as it also applies to structural members of luggage racks.

Much more expensive fiber-reinforced fenders, such as those made by ESGE, oddly enough do not last any longer than the lightest and cheapest ones. Much stronger are most metal models, and it is generally agreed that the relatively wide aluminum versions, particularly those made by the French Lefol company, are the ideal touring fenders. On the latter models, the wire stays and other mounting hardware are solidly attached to the metal of the fenders, while such items are only clamped or loosely riveted on most plastic fenders. If you choose aluminum or other metal fenders, make sure the edges are rolled to eliminate potentially dangerous protrusions.

Fenders with unguarded edges are not legal as original equipment in the US. To protect children, the American CPSC (Consumer Product Safety Commission) has the authority to regulate the sale of toys. Curiously defining all bicycles as toys, this agency has instituted some far-out criteria for bicycle equipment, of which this is one of the very few sensible examples. You will, for instance, find out that the mounting hardware for fenders as sold in the US is often highly impractical – simply to satisfy one of the

Lights

Next to fenders, bicycle lights are perhaps the most maligned bicycle accessories. Like fenders, lights are not very common on bicycles sold and ridden in the US. In many other countries they are a prescribed accessory, and I know of at least one cyclist who got into serious trouble on a foreign trip because he thought lights were a waste of time. Of course, they are not. If you have ever seen an unlit cyclist appear out of nowhere in your car headlights or when riding your bike during darkness or at dusk, you will perhaps appreciate just how dangerous it can be to go without. The fact that you didn't run into the turkey does not prove that it is safe to go without lights: the risk is infinitely greater without than it is with lights.

Many cyclists argue they never ride in the dark anyway. However, from experience I can report that just about every one who told me that was not only lying, he was also playing with his life. Sooner or later during any tour, you will want to leave the place you are staying without being able to return before dark. Or your day's trip will take you longer than expected. In short, though you may not plan on using lights, you should have them available in case you do need them.

Bicycle lights may be either battery operated or powered by means of a generator, referred to as a dynamo in Britain. Generator operated models are almost invariably installed permanently, while most battery models may be simply removed from the bike. One advantage of the latter is that they will double for use off the bike as a flash light, called torch in Britain. The removability may be good or bad: bad if it's stolen when you do leave it on, good if you can avoid somebody messing around with it by taking it off yourself.

Fig. 4.15 Generator lights

Though generator lights are not so easily stolen, they can also be tampered with, and unfortunately often are. It may happen if you have to leave your bike for some time in a place that makes it clear you won't be back very soon, such as a public swimming pool. Even if the lights are not stolen or vandalized, they may get damaged, so it will be wise to check their operation regularly and to tighten all mechanical and electric connections.

Fig. 4.16 Roller generator

A typical generator lighting set is depicted in Fig. 4.15. The generator is activated by means of a lever-operated spring-loaded mechanism that pushes a friction roller, connected with the dynamo's rotor, against the side or the tread of a tire, depending on the type used. I find the models shown in Fig. 4.16, referred to as roller dynamo, generally more satisfactory than the ones that rub off the side of the tire. Several of these provide less physical resistance and all of them cause less tire wear, though some models slip even more than many conventional generators. Of the various roller generators available, I have found the one by Union to be the most reliable. The adhesion of a roller dynamo to the tire may be

Fig. 4.17 Block generator light

improved by means of an elastic cord, pulling the roller towards the rear drop-out.

On any kind of generator system, the electric current is carried from the (single) generator contact to the contacts of front and rear lights and returns over the metal-to-metal contacts of the installation hardware and the bicycle frame. If the system malfunctions, it may be either a burnt out-bulb, a bulb that is not fully screwed into its fitting, a loose contact, a broken wire or simply the dynamo's roller slipping off the tire, which is most common in rainy weather. Keep the dynamo aligned, attach all the hardware and the wires properly, and check the whole system at least once a month.

It is possible to use an easily removable form of dynamo lighting. In that case, you will have to make do without a rear light, which is perhaps justified if you use a really big reflector in the rear and make sure it is never obstructed. Removable units are installed to the front fork and consist of a dynamo with light attached. Most of the commercially available models, referred to as block generators, are not very satisfactory. That's why I would suggest making your own, following the proposal by John Forester, illustrated in Fig. 4.17.

Personally, I prefer lights and reflectors that are always there over temporarily installed models, because they are available when I need them unexpectedly. Thus, I could ride without fear through dark tunnels along the Oregon coastline, while other cyclists, who either didn't have them or didn't stop to install their handy clip-on lights and reflectors, felt like members of a suicide squad. In cases like that, you should at least take the trouble to install the temporary goodies whenever there is a need for them.

The many possible trouble sources of most generator lighting systems and the physical resistance caused by their mechanical inefficiency are the reasons why many cyclists prefer battery lights. Not that these are always troublefree, but that will be covered below. The batteries and the bulbs must match the light unit: some use a single flat 4.5 volt battery, other models two D-cells, still others two C-cells. Special lights, powered by a large rechargeable battery, are also available. In general, the larger the battery, the more powerful and longer lasting the light is likely to be. Make sure to get correctly rated bulbs for the batteries used, both in terms of voltage and wattage or amperage.

Don't assume that battery lights are free from problems, but there are indeed fewer potential causes of failures. Whether generator or dynamo powered, take the appropriate spare bulbs along. Furthermore, for a battery light you will need at least one set of spare batteries. I suggest using the krypton or halogen gas filled bulbs, the latter are brighter when new, while both types stay equally bright throughout their useful lifespan, whereas regular bulbs dim to less than half their original and rated light output.

Normal carbon-zinc batteries produce a gradually decreasing electric output over the battery's life. Replace such batteries when the light begins to dim – don't wait until the thing is virtually dead. Rechargeable NiCad (nickel-cadmium) batteries stay equally bright much longer, to go out quite suddenly when the charge is depleted. So make sure the battery is charged regularly, or that you have a charged spare with you, since there is no warning when the light will go off. If you have to leave the bike out in the rain, you'd better remove the batteries and store them in a dry place. This stops them from swelling up, becoming useless themselves and damaging the light unit to boot.

Fig. 4.19 Tire pump

In addition to lights, some reflectors are quite useful. But they can not completely replace lights, and some reflectors are of no protective benefit whatsoever. The CPSC requirement that all bicycles sold in the US must be equipped with a whole plethora of reflectors is a big step in the wrong direction, promptly followed by equally inept agencies in other countries. It gives people the false conviction to be adequately protected with the wrong equipment. Add to that the particular models prescribed show up brightly under certain obvious but irrelevant conditions, and you've been fooled. Useful is only a big rear reflector, even as a substitute for a rear light. It must be mounted where it can not be obstructed by luggage, for example at the back of the rear luggage rack, as shown in Fig. 4.18.

Fig. 4.18 Reflector on rack

Fig. 4.20 Tire pressure gauge

Fig. 4.21 Mushroom clamp

Pump and Tire Gauge

While travelling, you will need to keep your tires inflated properly. Don't count on having gas stations handily available to inflate your tires, and don't just guess at the pressure. For loaded touring, the tire pressure is important, both since it allows efficient performance and because it protects the tire against damage. If you are experienced enough to have developed a calibrated thumb, you may do without a tire gauge for checking the pressure, but nobody should go without a pump. Figures 4.19 and 4.20 show typical examples of these two items.

Fig. 4.22 Water bottle and cage

The pump should be a model suitable for developing an adequately high pressure. Depending on the tire design, that may be anywhere from 4–6 bar (60–90 psi) gauge pressure. That is defined as the pressure relative to that of the atmosphere. Since the atmospheric pressure is about 1 bar, the absolute values corresponding to these pressures are actually 5–7 bar, but all gauges seem to be calibrated so that they read 0 bar when the absolute pressure really is 1 bar.

Be guided by the pressure quoted on the tire sidewalls as an absolute minimum for unloaded cycling on smooth roads. On rough roads you will need 15% more in the back, 5% more in the front. Loaded with luggage, you will need another 10% more on the loaded wheel. Tires on which it says, 'inflate to 60 psi' should at least be inflated to 75 psi in the rear and 65–70 psi in the front. As a basic rule, narrower tires will require and withstand higher inflation pressure than wider models of the same materials.

In the preceding chapter, I recommended getting tires with Presta valves (also referred to as French valves). Make sure both the pump and the gauge have a connection that corresponds to the type of valve used. Don't use a pump with a flexible hose connector, since the air trapped in the hose makes it impossible to reach an adequate pressure with a normal hand pump. For quick tire inflation at home you may keep a big stand pump, which has enough volume to work fine with a flexible hose connector.

Nowadays, pumps are mostly designed to clamp directly between the bike's top tube and bottom bracket along the seat tube. These are referred to as frame-fit pumps, and are available in several sizes to match a range of frame sizes each. That works fine on a diamond frame bike with only one water bottle installed. If you carry two bottles, or if you have a different kind of frame, such as a special reinforce model or a mixte (which I don't recommend), use a short pump, and clamp it between two mushroom clips installed along the bottom of the top tube, as shown in Fig. 4.21. If the pump should not work properly, tighten the screwed nozzle and if necessary replace the underlying rubber washer that seals around the valve, taking care to install it the right way round, so it doesn't leak even more afterwards.

Water Bottle and Cage

Here's another useful touring accessory, especially in hot weather. Of course, you can also stuff a properly closed bottle in your luggage, which has the advantage that it won't get as hot as it would exposed to the sun; but the frame-mounted water bottle is a lot more convenient. Fig. 4.22 shows both a bottle and the cage to which it is mounted. In case your bike lacks the bosses, most bottle cages are sold complete with a pair of rather crude clips to put around a frame tube. If you need to mount the thing that way, first stick a tire patch around the frame tube, as explained elsewhere in this chapter.

Bike water bottles are available in cheap and fancy versions. The more expensive bottles should have the kind of spout illustrated, which is operated by pulling the central part out and closed off by pushing it back in. Don't drink by sucking at the spout: instead, hold the bottle inclined with the spout down at one or two inches from the open mouth and squirt the water in by squeezing on the bottle.

There are some interesting bottle variants on the market these days. One of these actually squirts when held upright, due to an internal tube that runs from the spout to the bottom of the bottle. Then there are thermos bottles, insulated with a foam material, and extra large bottles. One way to keep a cold drink of water cool is by wrapping a cloth (such as a sock) around it. Moisten this cloth occasionally by squirting some water out, so that evaporation will draw enough heat out of the bottle to keep the contents cool. Of course, that is only practical with water. You may also want a bottle with a more nourishing liquid, such as fruit juice. In winter, I use the insulated thermos bottle and keep a hot liquid in it.

Locks

Unfortunately, a good lock is an essential accessory for any kind of cycling. The very best lock is barely good enough to hold on to your bike in many parts of the world nowadays. The best locks are the large U-locks, such as the one shown in the photograph. They may be installed on the bike by means of a bracket. Since that takes away bottle mounting options, I prefer to keep the lock at the top of one of my bike bags.

Don't just lock the bike onto itself, but secure it to some immovable object. Though the U-locks fit nicely around many street furnishings, you may also want to use a strong cable or chain with end loops or shackles big enough to fit the lock. This allows you to tie the bike up to something bigger. Make sure to select an object from which the lock can not be lifted off: a chain around a parking meter is of little use if the cable can be slipped over the top. To help you stop the front wheel from rolling away, the Flick Stand, which clamps between down tube and front wheel, is useful. Unfortunately, this gadget can not be used on a bike with fenders.

Holding on to your bike is a difficult art. The large U-shaped locks, such as the one by Citadel shown here, are the best insurance you can get. But vigilance is still needed.

Even with the best lock, you may not be able to completely protect your bike, equipment, accessories and luggage against vandalism and theft of individual items. The smartest thing to do is to be totally paranoid and suspect thieves and thugs everywhere and anytime. Never go anywhere without securing your gear. If at all possible, don't leave your equipment out of sight. When touring in a group, you may decide to take turns keeping an eye on things. At least keep the most valuable items in a bag that you always take with you on your body. Despite the horror stories told about other countries, the risk of theft and vandalism is probably greater in the USA than it is in any other country I have ever visited.

Warning Devices

When travelling on a narrow, winding mountain road, you may want to alert others to your presence for your own protection. In most European countries a hand operated bell is prescribed, which is totally ineffective. Instead, or in addition, use a compressed gas powered sound horn that can be carried in your back pocket. If you cycle on paths frequented by pedestrians, joggers, roller skaters, dog walkers and casual cyclists, you may prefer to use a bell as well, since it is less offensive, yet adequately audible under the circumstances.

Tools and Spares

Depending on a number of factors, you should carry some tools and spare parts. How many you need depends on several factors, including the distance and the difficulty of the terrain, as well as the population and bike density of the region. In an area with plenty of gas stations and a bike shop every twenty miles, you do not need as many items as you should carry when crossing the desert. Here's a list of the essentials that should probably always be taken along on any longer trip away from home:

☐ A set of three tire irons (tyre levers in Britain).
☐ A tire patch kit, containing patches, rubber solution, chalk, sand paper, talcum powder and a piece of canvas to mend a damaged tire casing.
☐ A small screw driver with a 4 mm (³⁄₁₆ in) wide blade.
☐ Crescent wrench (adjustable spanner), 6 or 8 inches long.
☐ Allen keys in whatever sizes correspond to the recessed hexagon bolts used on your bike.
☐ Crank extractor tool, especially the wrench part, which will be needed to tighten a loose crank.
☐ Spoke wrench (nipple spanner) to straighten a bent wheel.
☐ Chain rivet tool to take the chain apart or to join it up again.
☐ A pair of small pliers, such as needle nose pliers with sharp cutters.
☐ Spare spokes of correct length, brake cable, spare tube, spare chain links and lighting parts. If you also take a spare tire, turn it into three loops, as shown in Fig. 4.23.
☐ Waterless hand cleaning paste.
☐ Cleaning rags to wipe your hands as well as protect or clean any messy parts before working on them.

As this is really only a very basic set, you may want to add quite a number of other items on longer trips. Examples are a small spray can of oil, to keep things like the chain and other moving parts lubricated and to prevent rust, and an assortment of various tools to take apart the

1. fold into three loops   2. fold outer loops in to center   3. tie three loops together to form 9-in ring

Fig. 4.23 Rolling up wired-on tire

Fig. 4.24 Tool pouch

components that may have to be overhauled on your bike. Establish by very conscientiously checking which tools in which sizes and how many of each are needed. Conversely, on a short trip in known terrain, you may feel adequately prepared with nothing more than a pump, a small screw driver and the equipment needed to repair a puncture.

Whenever you are buying tools, consider that under the primitive roadside repair conditions, you should have the best tools available. Get quality tools. That means generally expensive tools, exactly fitting the parts in question. Don't let terms like 'economy tools' fool you: in the long run the best tools are much more economic than any cheap tool will ever be, since the former lasts forever, while the latter quickly wears out and may actually damage the bike's components.

Covers and Pouches

Don't just dump the tools in a side pocket of your bike bag, since they may get lost or they could damage other items that way. I suggest you carry them in a pouch that holds all the tools you ever plan to carry and a few spare slots. If you can't buy one ready-made, it will be easy enough to sew your own. Be guided by Fig. 4.24, using a strong material such as denim from an old pair of blue jeans. Allow enough space between the various items to enable you to roll it all together when it is full. On shorter trips, when you do not need to take everything along, you may leave certain slots blank.

5
Luggage Carrying Equipment

To most people, bicycle touring means riding a heavily loaded machine. Though it will be possible to go on short trips with no more luggage than what fits in a small bag attached to the bike or carried on the back, most serious touring requires more luggage. This chapter is devoted to the equipment for carrying all kinds of luggage. In addition to the information found here, you may refer to the preceding

Top pack for the rear rack. This model from Eclipse has several separate compartments and can be easily removed to be carried off the bike.

chapter, which informed you of the attachments required on the bike to install racks. Finally, it will be smart to consider just what to take along and which items you may be able to do without. For this subject, you are referred to Chapter 13, *What to Take and how to Pack it.*

For heavily loaded cycling at speed, the best is barely good enough when it comes to luggage carrying equipment. That means you will need bags and racks that are strong and rigid enough not to sag, get damaged or come loose. It also means they should not sway during

shake sideways

Fig. 5.1 Torquing test

a fast descent, even on a rough road or in sharp curves. An additional important factor is the location detail of the racks, since that determines how the weight of the luggage will affect the bike's handling and steering.

This is one more instance where mail order companies may be a useful source of information. Their catalogs often list many more different items in this field than your local bike shop can stock. Furthermore, the descriptive information given in these catalogs can be very useful, even if you would finish up buying the equipment at a regular bike shop, as I would do myself whenever I have the choice.

Dividing the Load

The correct distribution of weight for carrying luggage on a bike has been established in computer analyses and confirmed by means of practical tests. The following is a summary of the main conclusions of these tests:

☐ Ideally, the weight should be concentrated close to the bike's mass center (also referred to as center of gravity).
☐ Preferably, loads should be stable relative to the bike's frame, rather than to the steering system.

☐ Anything mounted on the rear should be as far forward as possible, while it need not be particularly low.
☐ Anything mounted on the front and attached to the steering system, should be close to the center of the front wheel and the steering axle, which is most easily achieved by mounting racks and bags as low as possible.
☐ Everything – whether rack or bag – should be attached so that it does not shift or sway as the bike is leaned over or when turning, accelerating, slowing down, climbing, descending or bouncing.

Now for a practical check to verify whether the bike, its racks and the luggage attached are properly constructed and mounted, respectively. To do that, hold the loaded machine by the center of the handlebars, as shown in Fig. 5.1, and shake it. If the bike is well constructed, the racks are well built and mounted properly, and the bags are loaded and tied down correctly, there will be a minimum of noticeable sway propagated over the entire bike. Since the swaying effect is transmitted back to the point of the movement's origin, you will easily feel whether things are constructed, attached and loaded correctly.

Fig. 5.2 Bag attachment

Fig. 5.3 Frame-mounted front rack

The rules listed above can be translated into a number of practical recommendations as follows:

☐ Any bag or rack must be attached as rigidly to the bicycle's frame as possible, tying in general not only the top at two points, but also at least one point at the bottom, as shown in Fig. 5.2.
☐ When carrying little luggage, take it in a bag that is attached as close as possible to the mass center, which is most easily satis-

fied by attaching it directly to the saddle.
☐ Racks must be very rigidly constructed and attached, requiring specifically a form of stiffener or bracing to avoid lateral deflection.
☐ When loading a bike with bags and racks in the back, the load should be carried as far forward as possible. That means that the top of the rack may well be used and that there is no sense installing the bags particularly low, since that would force a rearward installation to prevent interference with the heels while pedalling.
☐ To carry luggage in the front, it would be preferable to have a rack that attaches to the frame, rather than one attached to the steering system. The small-wheeled sprung Moulton bikes from Britain are unique in offering this solution, shown in Fig. 5.3.
☐ If front bags are attached to the steering system, as is usually the case, they should be installed as low and as close to the wheel axle as possible.

Fig. 5.4 Load distribution options

The various possible ways of distri-
buting the luggage over front and
rear racks, with their corresponding
effects on steering and balancing
characteristics, have been investi-
gated by Jim Blackburn, one
competent manufacturer of bicycle
racks and other accessories. It was
found that of the solutions shown in
Fig. 5.4, the one in the middle detail
(low in the front, high and forward in
the rear) provided the best solution.
Consequently, that is the loading
technique I advise you to follow.

Fig. 5.5 Laterally rigid rack stays

Luggage Racks
Heavy luggage and high speeds
over longer distances form a tough
test for any kind of equipment.

Fig. 5.6 Stay configuration for light rack

Speed and the unevenness of the
road surface, combined with the
rider's alternating driving forces,
translate into a combination of different cyclical loading changes that
are likely to propagate along the
bike, presenting serious steering
and handling problems. Furthermore, this kind of thing may lead to a
phenomenon known as fatigue.

Unlike the more familiar form of
fatigue from which you or I may
suffer at times, structural materials
do not recover from the fatigue
caused by frequently repeated high
load changes. After a certain
number of such loading cycles the
part will brake, unless it is designed
with enough safety margin to
consider this kind of thing. Specifically, it can be observed that the
higher loading values are more likely

Fig. 5.7 Lateral bracing

to be avoided when the vibrations
are dampened by a rigid construction.

Consequently, there are a number
of details to look for to make sure
you are getting the best in racks.
These criteria are easy enough to
appreciate once you know and
understand the preceding comments. But the rack is not an independent structure: don't judge a
rack by itself, but insist on inspecting

the rack mounted on a bicycle – preferably your own machine. Holding the bike, check how it responds to vertical and lateral forces applied by hand. This will give you a good idea of what will happen out on the road.

Any rack should be attached firmly in at least four points, preferably by means of sizable bolts with flat washers under the heads. The purpose of these washers is to reduce turning friction when tightening the bolts. Spring washers, which actually increase friction and resist turning, are not satisfactory. The attachments must be to points on the bike that are themselves firm and solid, and the stays of the racks should preferably be stiffened by means of bracing pieces.

The materials most suitable for racks are aluminum rod, steel rod and steel tubing. If aluminum is used for the rack, as it usually is nowadays, it should be at least 8 mm thick, while steel rod should be at least 6 mm, even if that seems like a heavy solution, which is the reason aluminum is so widely used these days. Tubular steel is a light, strong and expensive solution, and requires diameters of 9 mm or more. For moderate loads, tubular aluminum material with a minimum diameter of 12 mm may be suitable.

The method of construction is as important as the materials used. Racks made of solid steel or aluminum should be welded, while tubular materials must be brazed. The difference between the two operations is that in welding the material of the rack itself is heated to such a high temperature that it melts and bonds together. Brazing, on the other hand, is done at a lower temperature by melting a filler material of lower melting point to bond the parts. The thin walls of tubular

members would be weakened excessively if welding were used. Light folding racks have pivot points where the stays attach to the platform. Check to make sure these are of a solid metal construction. Plastic joints are a no-no, whether rigid or pivoted.

Vertical load bearing capacity and rigidity of a larger rack in the back can be assured only if twin stays in an inverse V-pattern are used at both ends, as shown in Fig. 5.5. Even so, the greatest strength can only be expected if each set of stays is

The very sophisticated Moulton bike with small wheels and front and rear suspension is astonishingly suitable for carrying luggage. The front rack is rigidly connected to the frame, rather than to the steering system.

connected by means of a horizontal stiffener, which may be designed quite long, so it also helps to avoid sway of the bag once it is mounted. If only one pair of stays is used on a smaller rack for lighter luggage, they should be attached just beyond the midpoint of the platform along the rack's length, as illustrated in Fig. 5.6.

Lateral rigidity can be best provided when the stays are triangulated laterally as shown in Fig. 5.7. This is a remarkably important criterion, since I have several times observed that otherwise lightly constructed racks with such lateral bracing held up much better than much heavier racks that lacked this kind of lateral stiffener. On one of my bikes, I use a set of very light aluminum racks with tubular stays by the Dutch Steco company and have excellent experience with them, while earlier racks weighing three times as much have failed under similar conditions.

As we've seen, the rear rack should allow placing the load far forward, rather than bringing it as low as possible. Thus, the so-called low-rider racks are of no benefit in the rear. What is important, though, is that the rack should not only provide adequate support at the top, but also a vertical plane for the back of the bags to rest against lower down, to prevent swaying of the bags. A good rear rack is illustrated in Fig. 5.8.

The primary criteria for the front rack are a low and centered mounting position, close to the steering and wheel axes, maximum rigidity and top and bottom support surfaces. The combination of adequate rigidity with a low-rider style is a bit tricky: weird looking constructions with big loops extending around over the top of the front wheel turn out to be necessary in

Fig. 5.8 Rear rack

Fig. 5.9 Low rider front rack

Fig. 5.10 Top platform stop

many cases. Fig. 5.9 shows a typical good low-rider front rack.

To carry (some) luggage on top of the rack, a relatively wide and long flat top frame or platform is useful. In the front you should only put very light things on the top platform, if

Fig. 5.11 Belt pack

waist strap

Fig. 5.12 Large backpack

any at all. In the rear you will actually find this a fine plaoe to carry such luggage as a small rigid suitcase which may contain quite heavy items. To prevent shifting of the load, which might interfere with the operation of the brakes, a stop should protrude from the top of the rack. Fig. 5.10 shows such a provision.

Types of Bags

Depending on your needs, specifically on the amount of luggage to be taken along, several different kinds of bicycle bags may be appropriate. Three basic types can be distinguished: bags that attach to the

rider, models that attach directly to the bike and those that attach to luggage racks on the bike. The various kinds of bags will be described in some detail here, while you will be shown what to look for in materials and construction, whatever the type of bag selected, in the next section. In addition, the general remarks about the distribution of weight given under the heading *Dividing the Load* should be borne in mind.

Bags that are worn directly on the body are of three basic types: light backpacks (referred to as rucksacks in Britain), large backpacks with a separate or integral carrying frame, and belt packs, referred to as fanny packs in the US, where that word does not have quite the vulgar connotation it has across the Atlantic. None of these are the answer to your main luggage carrying problem. However, they can come in handy for short trips and for things that must be taken along when you leave the bike, or for temporary use, such as the shopping purchased shortly before a meal or before setting up camp.

The belt pack, shown in Fig. 5.11, should have a really wide belt part and a stiff but flexible area that rests against the back, also supporting the bottom of the pack. It is at best suitable for carrying small items such as would be carried in a woman's handbag: money, documents, sunglasses, perhaps a camera and a bite to eat. Try it out in the store before buying, to make sure it is comfortable and will not slip around the waist when cycling.

Large backpacks with or without frame, as shown in Fig. 5.12, are to my mind not really very suitable for bike touring. However, they do have the advantage of requiring no racks on the bike. A bike without racks is easier to transport in a car or on public transportation. I know people who occasionally used trains where bikes were not accepted as accompanied luggage. They found a bike without racks and fenders could be dismantled and carried on the train hidden in a light bag, while all the regular luggage could be carried in such a backpack. If you choose a bag of this kind, make sure it has really wide padded straps and an additional waist strap to restrain its movement while cycling. Also this kind of bag should be tried out for comfort before it is purchased.

A small and light backpack, shown in Fig. 5.13, comes in very handy for provisional carrying tasks. I have one that weighs only half a pound and fits in the small side pocket of another bag. I use it to take things along when I leave the bike, or when I have groceries or other shopping that doesn't fit in the regular bike bags. It will only be comfortable to carry if you stiffen the back by means of a light, rigid board. Cut it to the size of the back of your pack. When not in use, it easily slides inside another bag. Since the same board can be used as a writing support or as a tray when preparing food, it need by no means be regarded as ballast.

Bags carried directly on the bike are of three kinds: saddle bags, handlebar bags and frame bags. The saddle bag, shown in Fig. 5.14, is so universally used in Britain that one wonders why it has not found its way to the US in a comparable quality and variety. It is attached to the back of the saddle. That is no problem on a leather model with carrying eyelets, while other saddle types may require the installation of a special clamp as shown in Fig. 5.15. It is also possible to install a handlebar bag, which is more widely available in the US, behind the seat post

Fig. 5.13 Light backpack

Fig. 5.14 Saddle bag

Fig. 5.15 Saddle bag support

by means of a clamping bracket sold under the name Seat Post Thing.

Saddle bags exist in various sizes, ranging all the way from 10 liters, which is barely enough for the absolute essentials, to 30 liters (that's more than a cubic foot). The latter is big enough for a weekend trip if you don't go camping. A large saddle bag, especially if it is used on a bike with a relatively low saddle, should be supported by means of some kind of a rack or bracket to keep it

Fig. 5.16 Handlebar bag

Fig. 5.17 Frame bag

Fig. 5.18 Pannier bags

off the rear wheel and the rear brake. It should have side pockets for small items and straps on the top to carry your rain gear. Before buying such a bag, look at it very critically and ascertain that it is properly support-

ed and will neither interfere with your movements nor drag on the rear wheel or the brake.

Handlebar bags are unreasonably popular in the US and France, though I would put them at the bottom of my list of suitable bags. Alright for carrying small items to which you want frequent access along the way, especially if it is of such a design that it can be easily removed from the bike. The only satisfactory models are those that are supported at the top by a bracket that fits on the handlebars, while the bottom of the bag is held down with elastic shock cords, preferably to the front fork-ends. A few external pockets and a transparent map compartment are helpful. Preferably it should open towards the rider. When buying this kind of bag, make sure it does not interfere with steering, braking or lighting. Fig. 5.16 shows an example of such a bag. A special versions of the handlebar bag is available to carry a camera and photographic accessories.

The frame bag, shown in Fig. 5.17, is a rare birds indeed. World travellers, who have to carry as much as possible, may find a use for a bag like that, in addition to every other bag that can be mounted on the bike. Trapezoidally shaped and tied between the frame tubes, it must be packed compactly to avoid its swelling up to a thickness that interferes with the movement of your legs.

Pannier bags are the kind hung either side of a luggage rack. Available in a whole plethora of shapes and sizes, they are the mainstay of bicycle touring. So many manufacturers offer different bags of this kind, that it will be hard to find the best ones– though there are plenty to choose from, of course. Fig. 5.18 illustrates satisfactory pannier bags for the front and the rear.

Different sizes are intended for front and rear use, though you may find the small front bags quite suitable for the rear as well. It will be just as important to try the bags out on your bike and your racks as it will be to watch all the details of construction and design, described in the next section. Each pannier bag should be attached by means of convenient hooks at two points close to the top and a shock cord clipped to e.g. the drop-out or fork-end. A sizable outside pocket may be installed in the rear, while only a relatively flat pouch (or better still: two even smaller ones, side by side) would be suitable on the side of the bag that faces sideways when installed. Make sure the shape of the bag is such that adequate heel clearance remains on rear bags even when they are stuffed.

Combination bags are single pieces of luggage, comprising three compartments: two panniers and a top compartment. They are hung over the luggage rack, and seem more practical than they are. Hard to pack and even harder to install or to remove from the bike, their rather modest price is the only redeeming feature. Fig. 5.19 shows a combination bag for installation on a rear rack. There are also combination bags without the top compartment, which I find to be generally a lot more convenient, though still less so than separate panniers. One interesting model of the combination bag can be carried off the bike as a large backpack.

Bags to fit on top of a luggage rack are recommended for use only in the rear. They may either be of the stuffsack variety or rectangular cases. My preference is for a small rigid suitcase, mounted sideways. In fact, what I use consists of two relatively rigid halves that can be extended in height almost infinitely in order to accept more or less. This is where I keep my food and cooking gear on a camping trip. It is tied to the top of the luggage rack by means of long webbing straps with buckles.

In general, either webbing straps or leather belts are more suitable to tie things on to the bike than the more popular elastic shock cords or bungees. The disadvantage of the latter is the fact that they stretch when the load shifts or gets unbalanced, which often leads to items shifting or even falling off the bike. Bungees also have hooks at their ends, which tend to get caught in the spokes.

Fig. 5.19 Combination bag

Bag Details

In the present section we shall have a look at the details of construction of all bags described above. We will be looking at materials of the bags and their attachments and at the tricky points such as design, supports, closures and reinforcements.

Whenever there is a chance of rain, the bags should either be water resistant themselves, or everything inside them must be wrapped in plastic. The best material against rain, oddly enough, is not some modern coated synthetic fabric, but old fashioned canvas or ducking, sewn with cotton yarn. In the rain, the cotton fibers expand and seal up both the pores in the fabric and the stitch holes. I have spent whole days in the rain with luggage carried in old fashioned canvas bags without problems, whereas a really rainproof synthetic bag is a very rare thing indeed.

Excellent compact and well cut pannier bags from Eclipse. These bags do not have any external compartments; instead the manufacturer has concentrated his efforts on more important constructive and mounting details.

Today, virtually all bags are made of coated synthetics, and there are ways to keep your gear at least reasonably dry in them. Look for bags made of a relatively heavy cloth: at least 500 g/m^2 or 16 oz/sq yd gives you a reliable material. Bags of this cloth really aren't that much heavier than models of lighter materials, and are much more durable as well. To make bags of such materials reasonably water resistant, all the seams must be sealed with a special sealing compound bought at a backpacking supply store. This applies even to those models that are claimed to be sealed when sold. Don't forget the seams with which zippers are sewn in and the attachment stitchings of the straps.

On any synthetic bag, it may be a good idea to sear the exposed edges where the cloth was cut at the seams (inside) to prevent them from fraying. This is no unnecessary luxury, since the material easily frays and comes undone at the seams if it is not prevented this way. Simply turn the bag inside out and melt the cut edge of the cloth by holding it over a candle flame, as shown in Fig. 5.20. Move along as soon as the fibers begin to melt together and before they generate a nasty black smoke.

As for the design and construction details, look for bags with really big access openings, with zippers or draw cord closures that don't restrict the size of the bag at the entrance. The closure should run all around the top, and any zippers or other openings must be covered with a generously overlapping flap. Preferably, they should be sewn with double seams. Reinforcements should be sewn in or on the bag at exposed points, such as the attachment points of straps, the ends of zippers, points of contact with the bike or the rack and all exposed corners.

The bags should have strong and simply operated means of attachment and closure. The closure flap should be held down by means of wide webbing straps with buckles. These allow the contents to be compressed, keeping the entire bag compact and preventing shifting or rattling, even if it is only half full. These straps should be separate from the devices with which the bag is mounted on the bike, so access to the contents does not affect the attachment to the bike, and conversely the bag's mounting system does not interfere with access. Additionally, most bags require some kind of stiffener board in the back, to assure they retain their shape well enough not to interfere with the bicycle's moving parts. If not built in, you may install one yourself, using any lightweight water resistant fiber board, cut to fit the back of the bag.

The top of any bag that hangs down by the side of a rack, from the saddle or another point of the bike, should be held in two points. For rack-mounted bags, the preferable solution is by means of simple plastic-coated metal hooks at points close to the front and rear ends of the bag. Check to make sure these hooks do not hang loose on the rack and that the rack has the right length to accommodate them. At the bottom, the bag must be held to a fixed point on the bike or the rack at a third point by means of a strap or a tightly stretched elastic cord, securely attached to the bag. The attachment point of this strap must be higher on the bag than it is on the bike, so it tends to put tension on the bag, as shown in Fig. 5.2 near the beginning of this chapter. This strap should be secured so that it does not shift or come undone. At the

Fig. 5.20 Searing edges of nylon bag

same time, it must be easily accessible and simple to attach or loosen.

Check the effectiveness of the mounting system by assuring the bags don't shift perceptibly when the bike is held in several positions. To do that, you have to statically simulate the effect of dynamic conditions that influence the bike and its luggage when riding, steer-

Perhaps loaded more than you can pull when touring. All the same, items like this Equinox Tourlite trailer can be an excellent solution for taking children along.

ing, climbing, descending, bouncing, braking and accelerating. That is done by holding the bike with heavily loaded bags in various orientations as follows:

☐ upside down;
☐ vertically up with front wheel off the ground;
☐ vertically up with rear wheel off the ground;
☐ horizontally to the left;
☐ horizontally to the right;
☐ from the handlebars, shaking the bike loaded with luggage as described previously and as illustrated in Fig. 5.1.

Bicycle Trailers
An alternative to the conventional way of carrying luggage in bags mounted on the bike is the use of a trailer behind the bike. Several models are available, mostly with two wheels and usually attached to the saddle pin by means of a flexible

coupling. There are also single-wheel models attached more rigidly; even side cars have been available. In general, the trailer should have a rigid but light frame and big wheels rolling on ball bearings and pneumatic tires. It will perform best if it has some kind of suspension built in. Their disadvantage is the difficulty they present if they have to be transported or stored, much more than any negative effect on bike handling.

Many years ago I had one disheartening experience with a device like that. The trailer began to lead a life of its own, eventually forcing me to dismount on a long descent. Since then, I have learned that many modern trailers are actually quite satisfactory, certainly when used only on well paved roads. I've heard of experienced cyclists and responsible parents who have crossed the entire North American continent towing their child in a bike trailer, so they obviously must be perfectly safe. Don't buy a trailer unless you have had a chance to try it out in combination with your bike first. Anything carried in the trailer must of course be enclosed in a sturdy bag or fully covered and securely strapped to the trailer's framing structure.

6
Clothing On and Off the Bike

In the present chapter we shall first look at conventional bicycle dress, followed by sections devoted to clothing for cycling under unfavorable weather conditions and things to take on a bike tour to wear when not cycling. Bicycle clothing is probably the most functional gear ever designed for any sport, and though there'll be no need to ride around looking to all the world like Greg LeMond or Rebecca Twigg, it makes sense to aim at the same comfort that has been developed to accommodate racers.

This stuff has been designed the way it is to provide the freedom of movement, the control of temperature and humidity and the protection against chafing that allows a racer to continue non-stop for seven hours, covering 150 miles or more. That, I'm sure, will also be comfortable when touring half the distance at half the speed on a loaded machine.

Gore-Tex bicycle clothing. Keeps rain and wind out, while allowing perspiration to evaporate through the fabric.

Fig. 6.1 Bicycle clothing

In the first section of this chapter, I shall highlight the points that make the various items of bicycle clothing so suitable for their purpose. These will also be the things to watch out for when buying clothing that is not specifically designed for the purpose, to determine whether it will serve you anyway. You may refer to Fig. 6.1 for an idea of what a typical racing outfit looks like. What you don't see there is the colors and the materials. Whereas traditional racing garb used to comprise rather drab looking woollen garments, today's cycling fashion is bright and gary, relying heavily on synthetic fibers.

Shoes and Socks

The shoes are perhaps the single most important item that can make the difference between effective cycling and plodding along. Special bicycling shoes consist of light leather uppers with a thin but very stiff sole, generally with a metal plate built in to achieve that sole stiffness. This helps distribute the pedalling force over a large area of the foot and prevents deformation where the toeclips hold the shoe to the pedal. Consequently, the pressure at any one point of the foot is within the

Fig. 6.2 Shoe cleat

comfortable range, and a more efficient transfer of energy from the legs to the bicycle drivetrain results.

Bicycle racing shoes have metal or plastic cleats, as shown in Fig. 6.2, to hold the feet in place on the pedals. This optimizes the effectiveness of pedalling. Some modern types actually are designed as a system of matching shoe and pedal with something akin to a ski binding. There is little doubt that either system allows more secure pedalling, especially on long trips where there is rarely a need to get off the bike. However, these things make it nearly impossible to walk, and tricky enough to get on and off the bike.

When touring, you will probably want to be able to walk in reasonable comfort as well. That not only rules out all those modern binding systems, but also makes old fashioned cleats highly inconvenient. Either you do without cleats or you should have a spare pair of shoes easily accessible for getting around when off the bike. Depending on how much luggage you are prepared to carry, either solution is satisfactory for long cycling trips with few interruptions. If, on the other hand, you are touring around Europe, stopping frequently to inspect interesting sights, you will be much better off wearing shoes without cleats even when cycling.

In addition to the real things, compromise solutions in the form of walking/cycling shoes exist these days. They have stiff, slightly profiled plastic soles and well ventilated uppers. This kind of shoe is probably the best solution for most touring purposes that involve getting off the bike frequently. The cloth uppers unfortunately cause your feet to get saturated almost instantaneously in the rain – more about that under *Rain Gear* below. Similarly, cycling in cold weather also poses special problems, which will also be covered separately.

Whatever kind of shoes you wear, they must have the right length and width not to hurt. Pull the shoe laces relatively tight in the lower part of the closure, so that the toes do not slip forward, getting pushed against the front of the shoe. Inside the shoes, choose cotton or wool socks that absorb perspiration. To be comfortable, they should be relatively thick, especially in the sole, and they should not have a knotty seam in the toe area. Tennis socks are generally very suitable. I suggest getting socks that are long and elastic enough to fit over your trouser legs when you wear regular street clothing, which keeps these loose rags out of the chain.

Shorts and Pants

Specific bicycle shorts are tight but stretchable knitted garments with rather long tight fitting legs and a high waist. They generally stretch so elastically that they stay up without the need for a belt, though suspenders (called braces in Britain) may be required, depending on your body build. Sewn in the crotch area is a soft and smooth piece of chamois leather, which protects the skin against chafing and absorbs perspiration. Correctly worn directly over the bare skin, they must be washed out daily. Consequently, you need at least two pairs and have to wash one pair out every night.

This laundry problem is reduced by selecting the modern acrylic or polypropylene materials. However, old fashioned woollen pants have the advantage that they regulate your body temperature better and get less smelly when they absorb perspiration. On the other hand, synthetics take up less moisture, dry a lot faster, and are much easier to wash. Being conservative, I still prefer woollen shorts.

One other way of minimizing the laundry problems is by wearing very light, stretchy seamless underpants underneath the cycling shorts. These items are available as regular women's underwear or may be obtained in men's versions from some bicycle outfits. They are much easier to wash out, quicker to dry and perfectly comfortable to wear. If no other source can be found, most men may well succeed in getting something fitting amongst underwear intended for women.

In addition to ordinary bicycle shorts and long legged cold weather versions of these same things, there are special bicycle touring shorts and slacks. These are based on the same materials and construction methods, but are tailored more to look like regular shorts or slacks. They have convenient pockets and look a lot more civil, as shown in Fig. 6.3. Alternately, you may wear any other pair of shorts or pants, providing you establish whether they are comfortable when pedalling.

They can only be comfortable if they are smooth and soft. Stretchable materials are best and they should have no bulky seams. Slacks must be tight enough around the lower leg not to get caught in the chain. If they are not quite tight enough there, tuck the legs inside your socks or keep them together by means of elastic straps with a Velcro closure. Of course, you can also cycle in real racing shorts and put on some light slacks over the top when it is appropriate to dress up a little.

Fig. 6.3 Touring shorts and long pants

Shirts and Tops
The bicycling shirt or jersey is a tight fitting knitted garment with short sleeves, a very long bodice and pockets sewn on in the back. It works well to absorb perspiration, covers the parts of the torso that should be covered even when bending over, and doesn't flap in the wind. Similar things with long sleeves are designed for colder weather. Both long and short sleeved cycling shirts are available in wool and various synthetics. The former material is really most comfortable, even in hot weather, and does not smell as offensively when it has absorbed perspiration. Synthetics, on the other hand, are a lot easier to wash and dry.

Though modern materials and designs make some of these cycling garments remarkably fashionable, they're as unsuitable for visits to medieval churches, theaters and

LEATHER HELMET

SAFETY HELMET

Fig. 6.4 Helmet types

restaurants as are conventional cycling shorts or swim suits. So you may wish to tuck the jersey inside your pants and slip into a kind of dress shirt or jacket to wear over the top when you have to look a bit more respectable. You may consider this unreasonably old fashioned, but you will probably learn, as I did, that you enjoy the trip more if people do not take offense at your appearance.

When it gets cooler, you may either wear a regular long sleeved cycling jersey or a thin, tightly fitting sweater over the top. Except in really cold weather, get a model that can be opened at the neck by means of a zipper. You may also wear a light windproof jacket over the top of your cycling shirt, providing it is made of a densely woven material that allows air and perspiration through. Special cold and wet weather gear will be discussed separately below.

Gloves

Even in warm weather, special cycling gloves are highly recommended, since they make the ride a lot more comfortable. This applies especially to riders who select a low riding style, which places a rather high percentage of the rider's weight on the handlebars. These gloves have leather insides and open knit top panels and have fingers cut off to a length of about an inch. The palm area should be padded. If you do not like to wear gloves, at least use foam handlebar sleeves instead of (or underneath) regular handlebar tape, since this also provides the kind of cushioning effect needed to prevent nerve damage in the area of the palms. For colder weather, special winter cycling gloves are available, as described below.

Head Protection

Back in the 'sixties and early 'seventies, head protection might at best have meant something to keep the rain off your head. Today, at least American and Australian cyclists seem to have ample choice of real accident protection for their heads. In other countries the hard shell helmet, as it is generally called, is taking a long time to get established. I suggest you wear one – even if you go touring abroad, where in many cases there is more chance of being ridiculed than of the thing saving your life. You may never need a helmet, but it will make all the difference if you ever should fall off the bike. See Chapter 11 for more details on the safety aspect of head protection. Fig. 6.4 illustrates some models.

It should be a helmet specifically designed for bicycle use, that is comfortable to wear, well ventilated, and attached so that it will not move out of place upon impact. Most of these important criteria are satisfied if the helmet meets the American standard ANSI Z-90.4. I prefer a model without vent holes but with an open ventilation space between the carrying frame and the shell, such as the Bailen. So many makes and models are now available that nobody has to go without, whatever his preference in style and design. Many helmets can be combined with a shield or visor to keep the sun out of your eyes or the rain off your glasses.

There is one situation where a helmet becomes too uncomfortable to wear for most people. That happens on a steep climb in hot weather. This situation is characterized by a combination of profuse perspiration, due to the heat generated as the result of performing work close to your maximum output, with the slow speed that virtually precludes natural ventilation induced by air movement. I simply take off the helmet in a case like that. Just don't forget to put it back on as soon as the descent begins.

Rain Gear

Yes, it is entirely possible to ride a bike in the rain – in my native Holland you'd never get very far if you'd stop for every shower. Yet more people ride bikes there than anywhere else in the western world. Besides equipping the bike to keep the rain and spray off your body, the bike and the luggage, as explained in Chapter 4, you can make sure to have clothing that will see you through most rain storms in reasonable comfort. Both this kind of clothing and the material described for cold weather cycling in the next section justify the investment in a couple of bicycle mail order catalogs. Most of these companies have a summer and a winter catalog, the latter one often containing lots of useful items in this field, complete with worthwhile information on the properties of various materials and designs.

Fig. 6.5 Rain clothing

Fig. 6.5 illustrates some typical rain garments. The big problem is that perfectly waterproof materials don't only keep rain out, but also perspiration in. Even if you are not usually aware of it, the cyclist is continuously perspiring as a result of performing the work necessary to propel his machine. Normally, this perspiration evaporates immediately as it is absorbed by the air passing along the body. When an impermeable barrier in the form of rubber- or plastic-coated fabric prevents this natural process, the moisture condenses on the inside of the barrier and very soon it penetrates every fiber between your body and the rain gear, until you are as dismally soaked as you would have been without rain wear.

Fig. 6.6 Spats

Sou'wester

Fig. 6.7 Sou'wester

The only satisfactory solution to this dilemma is the use of a special material that is just porous enough to pass water vapor, without allowing the passage of liquid water. One material that satisfies this criterion is Goretex, a trade name for a cloth consisting of woven fabric with a barrier layer of stretched PTFE. Another solution is provided by a material called Tenson, where the fibers are treated so that they

Fig. 6.8 Pedal covers

expand enough to achieve the same effect when a certain humidity is exceeded. There are a few other materials and coatings that do the same after a fashion, varying widely in price, weight and appearance.

Though most garments made with these materials are awfully expensive and often garishly styled, I consider the investment absolutely essential in most climates at any time, and at least for off-season cycling in more blessed regions. Available are jackets, capes, coats, pants and suits, designed either specifically for cycling or for general use. Try a number of different models out in a cycling or backpacking store, to make sure you get a model that is not so generously cut as to be unsuitable for safe cycling.

Personally, I find the rain cape is still the best solution, provided it is combined with spats. The latter are a kind of leggings that are open in the back, as shown in Fig. 6.6. They may be either home-made or purchased from the only known source of these things in the US, Custom Cycling Fitments. The cape should preferably be a model without a built-in hood, since the hood restricts your peripheral vision, which is especially important when checking behind before turning off. The best thing to keep your head dry is a helmet without holes, or – for those who choose not to wear one – a Sou'wester, as shown in Fig. 6.7.

Finally, with regard to rain gear, the feet are a real problem. Cycling shoes are little use when it comes to keeping your feet dry, especially if a constant jet is being thrown up from the front wheel, as will happen when you have not installed fenders with a mud flap on the one for the front wheel. To ward off the rain from above, you may find good spats, with long beak-shaped extensions that

Full rain suit from the Dutch AGU-Sport company, with double overlapping zippers, covered pockets and sealed seams. Due to condensation, perfectly waterproof garment like these are only comfortable for short periods.

long wool pants

long wool socks

lined shoes with thick soles

wool cap

wool sweater

jacket with water-proof front and shoulders

lined gloves

water-proof front

shoe covers

Fig. 6.9 Cold weather cycling

reach over the tops of the shoes, quite effective. Another solution is to simply wear plastic bags around the socks, inside the shoes: not very elegant, but remarkably effective.

Cold Weather Wear

To be comfortable on the bike in cold weather, you will not need quite so much in the way of clothing as you would standing around watching a soccer game or waiting for your wife or husband. In the first place, the cycling activity generates enough heat to keep at least your trunk reasonably warm. In the second place, all that gear would hinder your movements. The heat is mainly generated in the trunk and the upper legs, so these parts will keep warm more easily, while the extremities of ears, hands and feet may need much thicker clothing.

Since the relatively high speed at which the cyclist proceeds causes high resultant air velocities, excessive wind chill may ensue in many cases. That is especially critical during descents, when the speed is high and your energy output low. Besides, even in summer it may get

quite cold at high elevations. Consequently, bicycle touring in the mountains will cause additional problems, since you will be experiencing all the extremes. You'll be exposed to warm weather in the valleys and cold weather on the peaks, hard heat-producing cycling without significant wind cooling when climbing, and cold fast air-cooled descents.

To arm yourself for cases like that, dress in layers that are easily put on and taken off. In addition, the wind must be kept out, for which a wind-proof outer layer is needed. That means a rather closely fitting, long jacket, made of very densely woven cloth that is permeable to water vapor, preferably in two-layer construction. This same kind of outer shell also protects you best in winter, when winds seem to cut right through the warmest woollen wear.

Underneath this outer layer, wear several relatively thin layers of other warm materials. Quite close fitting knitted or other very stretchable materials are ideal. For long underwear, polypropylene is a good solution, since it is very light and not as hard on the skin as many other synthetics and wool. As for design, all these garments must be long, close fitting and easy to put on or take off. Zippers and other closures should be installed in such a way that there is a large enough overlap to keep the cold out, especially in the front.

Hands and feet cause greater problems, since the body's thermostat turns off the supply of heat-carrying blood to these extremities whenever the temperature of head and trunk is in danger of falling below the vital organs' required minimum operating temperature. Thick woollen socks inside special thick-soled and lined winter cycling shoes keep the feet comfortable. Add plastic bags, as described above for rain wear, if the combination of cold with rain or sleet occurs. In addition, you may find pedal covers, as shown in Fig. 6.8, keep the feet comfortable under such conditions. Nylon backed woollen gloves or relatively light lined leather models, such as cross-country skiing gloves, may suffice for the hands. Thick lined mittens may be needed when it gets even colder.

For the head, finally, a helmet without air scoops will be most comfortable, although helmet covers are available, which also serve well in the rain. Makes you wonder why they put those silly holes in most helmets in the first place, because there are better methods of providing ventilation. In very cold weather, you may have to wear a thin cap underneath the helmet to cover the ears and other exposed portions of your head. And if you elect not to wear a helmet, you can get a knitted wool cap of the type worn by the gentleman shown in Fig. 6.9.

Though hard to find, there are specific winter riding garments of the kind that is readily available in traditional cycling countries like France and England. If you should ever get there on your travels, don't forget to stock up on such useful things while you get the chance. These garments are integrated items that combine the warm materials in a design specifically intended for cycling, with wind breaking panels in the front of jacket and pants. Fig. 6.9 shows a cyclist wearing such gear. In addition, there are special add-ons to normal cycling garments that can be put on or taken off easily, although they look awful. These are particularly convenient at times and in areas where significant temperature differences are encountered in the course of a day's ride.

The ultimate in winter touring is a bike equipped with padded hand warmers. These things keep rain, wind and cold off the hands better than any gloves. Though they can't be used with drop handlebars, it is a fine solution for a bicycle equipped with flat bars, such as a mountain bike.

Civil Dress

However effective bicycle clothing is, you probably want to look less conspicuous at certain times when touring for longer periods. That may be appropriate when looking for accommodation or when going for a meal, when sightseeing or whenever you are off the bike. The easiest way to handle that is by wearing normal cycling gear, and carrying light wash-and-wear clothing that is wide enough to be worn over the top.

Especially when travelling outside the US, it will help if you wear things that are relatively unobtrusive: no excessively bright colors or far-out designs. There should always be enough room in your bicycle bags to add a pair of slacks, a shirt, a pair of light dress shoes and perhaps a nylon raincoat. Select easily washable materials that don't suffer too much from storage in full panniers. Alternately, you may consider wearing less obtrusive cycling garments that are suitable off the bike as well.

Campsite Wear

When camping, you'll want to move about in reasonable comfort. I have found that a combination of cycling clothing with some of the more respectable items of dress de- scribed above serves my purposes adequately. An exception should be made for the feet, which need extra protection in wet or merely humid climates. Especially when first getting up in the morning, the ground will be wet, certainly if you are camping in a grassy area. Once your shoes and socks are wet, there is no way of being comfortable for a long time. A pair of light but high plastic overshoes will serve you well under those conditions. If it is not too cold, the smartest solution is perhaps to go barefoot until the grass is dry, keeping a towel handy near the entrance to the tent.

If you like to add more to your packing list for campsite wear – 'apres pitch', so to speak – you may consider a track suit. It is very easy to put on or take off, as the tempera- ture dictates, and can be worn over the top of other clothes. It even doubles as pajamas and allows you to get up at night quickly and with- out embarrassment – whether to visit the bathroom or to check up when it sounds as though some- body is snooping around, ready to take off with your bike. Just how much more you take is up to you. Keep in mind that everything taken has to be carried the entire duration of the trip, even if you only use it once or twice.

7
Selecting Camping Gear

This chapter may seem to be of interest only to those who plan to spend their nights out in nature while bicycle touring. Yet much of the information contained here will also prove useful to many others. Though you may not plan on camping out all the time, you may have to spend at least some nights under the open sky, and it will be infinitely more comfortable when you are adequately prepared to do that. Here you are introduced to the various kinds of camping equipment, while remarks on the practice of camping will be found in Chapter 18.

This can not possibly be an elementary and complete manual on the selection of camping equipment. Instead, I shall only cover those points that are essential to the bike camper, highlighting the different considerations that will be of importance when selecting materials and equipment. The most basic equipment needed to spend the night outside consists of nothing more than a sleeping bag and a ground sheet. Depending on the intensity of the camping experience desired, you may expand this list with tent and cooking gear.

In addition to the information imparted here, you may find quite a lot of useful information relevant to this subject in the catalogs of some specialized camping and backpacking mail order companies. You may find that some of this information and some of the equipment recommended in the present chapter is not the same as you have seen recommended in authoritative backpacking and camping manuals. This is justified, since the touring bicyclist has different problems and potentials than the mountaineer and hiker, not to mention the camper who carries his gear in the back of a car or pick-up.

To give an example, the bicyclist can usually descend from great heights to milder, lower lying regions in a matter of an hour or so, while the backpacker might spend much more time at higher elevations. Similarly, the bicyclist can more frequently obtain fresh stores of food than the backpacker. Compared to the car camper, on the other hand, he has to economize with respect to luggage volume and weight. He must plan ahead more, since he won't be able to go far out of his way to get food or other supplies before pitching the tent.

Sleeping Bags

Sleeping bags are available in many different designs, materials and quality levels. The sleeping bag selected for bicycle camping generally need not be quite as superb as what would be selected for backpacking. On the one hand, you will probably not camp at such high elevations as to need the ultimate in warmth. On the other hand, the risk of getting the bag wet are greater – not so much when camping as when carrying the gear.

Of the available filling materials, natural down is still the lightest and – even more important on the bike – the most compact. A down bag weighs about two thirds as much and packs in about half the space as a qualitatively comparable bag with synthetic filling. On the other hand, the down bag is invariably more expensive, more delicate and more sensitive to moisture than its synthetic counterparts. If you do select down, which remains my preference, you will have to take extreme precautions to keep the thing dry, for instance by keeping it in a fully closed plastic bag, in addition to its own pouch.

Both down and synthetic fillings come in a number of different qualities. In general, you get what you pay for. I suggest, rather than selecting one make in preference over another, you simply buy the most expensive bag of the chosen kind of material that meets your basic criteria, which will be outlined below. With down, you'll find that the more expensive bag has a softer quality down, which quickly recovers from the compacted to the lofted state once released from its pouch.

Loft refers to the thickness achieved by the non-compacted bag. When you put the bag flat down loosely, it will attain a certain thickness: that thickness is defined as the bag's loft. Since the bag's ability to keep you warm is primarily a function of the thickness of insulation, this loft is a simple guide to the warmth the bag offers. Use the lofting figures only as a basis for comparison, between individual bags of the same material. Don't assume the thickest loft must necessarily give you the best bag for your purpose, since you will probably not be exposed to the extremes in low temperatures for which the high loft bag is designed.

Fig. 7.1 Square cut and mummy bag designs

Nowadays, bags are often rated by their comfort range. Take the temperatures quoted by the manufacturers with a pinch of salt, though. A bag advertised with a comfort range from 60 to 15°F probably does not give you the cosy comfort you may expect if the temperatures drop below freezing. In fact, my experience is that a comfort range to a minimum of 20 or 25°F is about right to handle most situations, even if it never freezes. When the temperature does stay high at night, you can always open the bag or lie on top of it. Don't choose too fancy a bag either: get one that is comfortable in summer, and sew a cover out of flannel cloth that can be used around the bag to upgrade it if you ever camp out during the colder time of the year.

The materials used for the outside are either polyamide, cotton or a combination of the two. Polyamide, usually simply referred to as nylon, which is just a trade name, is invariably lighter, whereas cotton feels more comfortable, especially if you tend to develop allergies. When you first get into a bag, the polyamide probably feels a little colder; however, after a very short time the polyamide warms up. It also stays warmer throughout the night.

Furthermore, cotton takes up the moisture that is given off by the body, whereas it passes straight through the polyamide. Consequently, the cotton often feels clammy in the mornings, whereas the polyamide bag remains dry more easily. I like a bag that has cotton on one side and polyamide on the other. I can use it whichever way round seems most comfortable for a particular situation: the polyamide inside when it is cold or humid, the cotton inside when it is hot and dry.

The two basic sleeping bag designs are the square cut (or blanket) and mummy styles, both shown in Fig. 7.1. The former is somewhat less space and material effective, and a little less warm than the latter. However, the square cut offers more room to spread out, can be opened up to serve as a blanket and is cheaper to make. On the whole, I think the square cut is an excellent design for bicycle use. Amongst the mummy designs, the preferred configuration should be one with a full length zipper, so the bag may be opened when it gets too warm. Two matching bags with full length zippers can usually be combined to form a bag for two. Either way, the zipper should be covered by a generous padded flap to keep the cold out when needed.

The cross section of the bag may be any one of the designs shown in Fig. 7.2. Sewn through is the simplest way to make a sleeping bag. For a down bag, that may be good enough for temperatures down to about 40°F (5°C), if the bag is otherwise well constructed, and that is adequate for almost all summer and a good deal of spring and autumn use. If the bag has enough loft, the thin sections where the inner and outer layers are sewn together do not significantly detract from the warmth offered by the filling in the thicker sections.

A little more sophisticated is the straight box section design. These things are divided up into tubes, separated by walls, referred to as baffles. This allows a more even distribution of the filling material, leading to a slightly warmer bag with a given filling weight – at a correspondingly higher price, due to its more complex construction. The tubes may run either lengthwise or circumferentially. The former method generally allows a more consistent distribution of the filling, thus offering more durable comfort. The next step up is the slant baffle design, which theoretically results in an even warmer bag given the same amount of down. Finally, there is the overlapping baffle design, which is perhaps the ultimate (and most expensive) way of getting the most out of a given weight of filling.

Apart from the stitching or baffling method used, mummy bags may be either cut evenly or differentially. The different basic designs are represented in Fig. 7.3. Some manufacturers claim that a given amount of filling results in a warmer bag when the inside is cut smaller than the outside, while others claim that their bag is warmer because the inside is cut just as big as the outside. Then there are those who cut the bag differentially, yet recommend using it inside-out. I prefer a bag that is not differentially cut, but you are free to differ.

The closure and the hood of the bag are important details. To be warm enough, it should be possible to tighten the bag around the top at some point above the shoulders. A hood may not seem necessary at all times, but I've often found one loses so much heat through the head, that

Fig. 7.2 Sleeping bag partitioning

Fig. 7.3 Even and differential cut

it had to be tucked in. In those situations, a sleeping bag with a close fitting hood is a fine solution. Essentially all mummy bags have some kind of hood, but not all are equally comfortable. Square cut bags generally have a very simple hood that can only be kept in place by means of a draw cord.

Take good care of your sleeping bag. After the night, hang it out to air before packing it away. It dries quickest in wind and sunlight. Just don't keep polyamide bags out in the sun more than necessary, since the ultraviolet rays eventually ruin the material. Especially cotton bags and down fillings should be dried and aired very thoroughly. To put the bag in its pouch, do not roll it up tightly, but literally stuff it into its pouch, starting at the foot end. You will be able to limit the bag's packing size by taking in the pouch until it is just barely big enough to accept the bag, and then sew it up in that size. Just don't store the bag tightly packed over longer periods between trips, especially if it is damp or

pattern

Fig. 7.6 Sleeping bag cover

pillow pouch

Fig. 7.4 Sleeping bag liner

8 ft (min.)

6 ft (min.)

Fig. 7.5 Ground sheet

guy lines

tent pegs

Fig. 7.7 Basic ground sheet shelters

dirty. Instead, hang it up draped over a coat hanger, making sure it is thoroughly dry first.

It may be a good idea to use a liner or sheet bag inside the down or synthetic filled sleeping bag. The liner keeps the latter clean and can itself be easily washed. Fig. 7.4 shows how such a liner can be made, using any lightweight cotton or comfortable synthetic material. The same liner can be used if you ever choose to stay in a youth hostel, where this design is prescribed for use under the blankets provided (except in countries like Germany, where many hostels demand you rent the peculiar mattress and blanket covers common there).

Tents and Shelters

It is quite possible to go camping without a tent. The easiest method, and indeed one of the greatest ways to sleep, is directly under the stars, providing you can keep insects at bay and protect your bag against moisture from above and below. From below, the problem is solved with the help of a ground sheet, shown in Fig. 7.5. Alternately, you can make or purchase a protective sleeping bag cover, as shown in Fig. 7.6. Make it big enough to allow you to turn around a little with the sleeping bag if you pitch the corners into the ground with tent pegs. The bottom should be of really water-proof material, such as rubber-coated fabric. The top should be water repellent material that allows water vapor to pass through, if it is to be comfortable at all. This extra sleeping bag cover will also keep you quite a bit warmer: even a thin one adds at least five degrees F to the comfort range of your bag.

The next more sophisticated solution is to use a larger ground sheet that can be pitched up to cover the bag from below and above. This can also provide an adequate shelter against the wind, assuming the wind does not turn around during the night. Fig. 7.5 shows how to cut and sew such a ground sheet. Fig. 7.7 illustrates some examples of pitching it with the help of trees, branches, or tent poles and pegs.

If you are camping in an area with mosquitos or other bothersome insects, as is often the case in areas where cycling is good, you will want to sleep in a closed tent. You probably want to do the same whenever using an official camp site, where adequate privacy would not be possible without having your own four walls. The simplest tent would be no more than the previously shown ground sheet with a piece of mosquito netting sewn on. I have camped with such an item, weighing no more than two pounds, quite satisfactorily when travelling alone.

The next step up is a real tent, of which there are numerous basic designs and even more variants. The most relevant basic tent designs are illustrated in Fig. 7.8. Tents have either one or more internal poles or external rods or hoops to support them. Basically, a distinction can be made between tent designs with one or more central poles, and those suspended from an external support. In the latter, the cloth is tensioned by means of bent rods, like in an umbrella.

all designs shown with fly sheet

dome tent

tunnel tent

ridge tent

single pole tent

Fig. 7.8 Basic tent designs

On the whole, the latter types are more space efficient, since the walls and roof of the tent are naturally curved out instead of hanging in, as is the case with the older tent designs. Amongst the various conventional tent designs with upright

All dimensions quoted are minimum requirements

Fig. 7.9 Ergonomic tent design criteria

poles, the models with a wide opening, in which you sleep across the width, rather than in the length, are by far the most spacious and practical, although they are usually both more expensive and more sensitive to the wind.

If you will be camping in rocky or sandy areas, where tent pegs either do not penetrate or hold, dome and tunnel tent designs, characterized by their external rod supports, are preferable. In areas with frequent rain, the tent, whatever design it is in other respects, should at least allow plenty of height to sit upright. Under those circumstances, you may have to spend a lot of time inside the tent,

where you will also have to cook and eat. Fig. 7.9 shows some of the ergonomic criteria for tent dimensions.

The ideal designs, especially for rainy weather or in a strong sun, are those with a very generously dimensioned, covered entrance. This allows you to live and work under cover at the entrance to the tent. Thus, your cooking gear will be outside the tent under the porch, while you can sit inside at the entrance. You will find this way of working much more enjoyable and efficient than it is to either close yourself off inside the tent or stand outside. Fig. 7.10 shows a few porch designs, while Chapter 18 contains some guidelines on how to 'furnish' your camp.

Tent Materials

Cotton, polyamide (nylon) and polyester fibers are used to weave the cloth for tents. Polyamide is generally the cheapest. Since it is very sensitive to ultraviolet light, it can not be recommended for the outside roof or the fly sheet of a tent or its porch, where either polyester or cotton will last much longer. If the tent is of double wall construction, consisting of an inner tent and a full size fly sheet, the inner tent may be of uncoated polyamide or a very light cotton, while the flysheet should be of water repellent cotton or polyester. The floor of any tent should be of rubber- or plastic-coated cloth, sewn to the tent proper. Only such truly waterproof materials keep out the moisture from the ground. Even in dry regions the ground gives off moisture at night, when the air is colder than the ground.

Whatever the material, the most densely woven fabric, made with the finest and most even filament, will be of superior quality: light, strong and more impervious to water than more loosely woven cloth. This criterion is particularly important for fly sheets and the roof section of single wall tents. The ground sheet should be coated on the side facing down. Coated, really waterproof material can also be used for the fly sheet, while the tent proper must allow air and water vapor to pass through.

For additional ventilation, a large window or even an entire door flap made of mosquito netting makes

Fig. 7.10 Tent porch designs

the tent more inhabitable and allows you to look out even when the tent is closed to insects. There should be an additional flap made of normal tent fabric to cover the mosquito netting, if necessary on account of the weather. As for the hardware, aluminum poles and pegs are stronger and lighter than fiberglass, while steel items are unnecessarily heavy.

The maximum size tent that can be carried on a bike is one that accommodates four people. Although most people prefer to use several two-man tents instead of one larger tent, the latter solution offers more useful space and may be lighter to carry. In addition to the occupants, there must be room to keep the luggage – either in the tent itself or next to it, protected under the fly sheet. Depending on the number of persons the tent must accommodate, the floor plan should

Table 7-I Required floor space

persons	length x width		additional luggage area
1	200 x 90 cm	(80 x 36 in)	0.4 m² (4 sq. ft)
2	200 x 120 cm	(80 x 48 in)	0.7 m² (7 sq. ft)
3	200 x 170 cm	(80 x 68 in)	1.0 m² (10 sq. ft)
4	200 x 220 cm	(80 x 88 in)	1.3 m² (12 sq. ft)

smooth side up

Fig. 7.11 Open cell sleeping pad

separate valves

Fig. 7.12 Air mattress with separate chambers

be dimensioned according to the sizes summarized in Table 7-I.

Even if you have a tent, it will be a good idea to also take a separate ground sheet. It will serve to cover the bikes, your luggage or other items around the camp site. A ground sheet also allows you to sit outside when the ground is wet. Buy or make something like the model illustrated in Fig. 7.5 for this purpose.

Sleeping Pad and Air Mattress
Whether you sleep in a tent or not, the bare sleeping bag is not really adequate for sleeping. If you use a down bag, the down gets compressed flat under your body weight, which reduces the comfort and insulating properties drastically. Synthetic materials do not compact quite as much, but even they may prove uncomfortable. A few manufacturers make bags that have down in the top and either synthetic filling or foam material in the bottom. The most universal way to assure comfort and warmth is by means of a separate pad.

Two basically different types of foam pads are in use: open and closed cell foam. Closed cell foam, of which Ensolite is a familiar trade name, is hard to compact. Consequently, it does not get flattened underneath the sleeper, even though these pads are usually very thin, namely less than an inch. This material comes in different thicknesses, widths and lengths. For comfort, I consider the minimum required size to be 2 cm (¾ in) thick, 55 cm (22 in) wide and 120 cm (48 in) long. Unfortunately, the insulating property goes hand in hand with a large package when rolled up, even though the weight is minimal.

The second type of pad, shown in Fig. 7.11, is made of much less resilient open cell foam of much greater thickness. Usually this is smooth on one side, while the other side has a pattern reminiscent of an egg carton. It should be at least 6 cm (2½ in) thick. Length and width should be the same as the minimum dimension for the closed cell material. Though a full length pad is more comfortable, it will be too big to carry on the bike.

Air mattresses are also popular amongst campers. They are quite comfortable, but only if it is not particularly cold, and even then only if they are designed with separate chambers, as shown in Fig. 7.12. The conventional one-piece air mattress allows so much circulation of air that it can be quite cold. A good air mattress is actually no lighter than either type of pad described above, though it can be packed up more compactly.

In addition to the mattress or pad, I carry a cushion made of open cell foam. This is my one piece of extravagant luxury away from home, serving both as a pillow at night and as a cushion to sit on by day. Many campers pack their spare clothes and towels together, some rest their head on their shoes or sleep on a rock, but I prefer to be comfortable. You will probably find, as I did, that it is easy enough to wriggle around long enough to get reasonably comfortable on the back or the side when sleeping, but the head only gets the rest it deserves when it is supported on such a soft, smooth cushion.

Fig. 7.13 Solid fuel stove

Cooking Equipment

Build a wood fire to do your cooking on whenever you get the opportunity. It adds greatly to the charm of outdoor living. But often you will not be able to do that. In most of Europe it is strictly prohibited, and firewood can be hard to find in any country. For that reason, I suggest you also carry a camping stove.

You will be well served with any of the various models intended for backpacking – what's light and small enough to be carried on the trail, also serves its purpose for bicycle camping. Stoves that operate on several different types of fuel are available. The lightest and smallest burn solid alcohol tablets (such as Esbit). Slightly heavier are models that run on white gas (petrol in England), kerosene (paraffin oil) or pressurized propane gas.

Fig. 7.14 Coleman Peak 10 stove

Fig. 7.15 Camping gas stove

If you travel alone and only rarely intend to use it, the solid alcohol stove is probably adequate, especially if your needs do not exceed the occasional cup of coffee or a boiled or fried egg. This type of stove, depicted in Fig. 7.13, can not be regulated and burns up its fuel rather fast. On the other hand, the fuel is light and convenient to carry. At a very modest price, you can get a set consisting of a stove, a miniature saucepan, a lid that also serves as a frying pan, and enough fuel to last

one person for one or two weeks. This kind of fuel can be bought at most drug stores (chemists to my British readers), and on the bike you will pass enough stores to make this a very convenient type of stove.

There are numerous camp stoves designed to burn either white gas or kerosene, my favorite being the Coleman Peak 10, illustrated in

Fig. 7.16 Water containers and wash basin

Fig. 7.14. Whatever make and model, this is the most cost-efficient kind of stove, burning cheap fuel efficiently. The problem with both is the inconvenience of fuel resupply: it is hard to get it in quantities of less than a gallon at a time. Fine if your trip is of modest length, if your group is small or if you don't do much cooking: you can carry a quart of fuel in a special metal or plastic sealed bottle, available at backpacking stores. That will last one or two people about a week if you cook a full meal each day. On longer trips with several people, you may have to consider installing a one gallon can on one of the bikes. With the exception of the Peak 10, all kerosene burning stoves must be pre-heated using methylated spirit or solid fuel. Don't forget to take a supply of the special fuel (solid or liquid alcohol) for that purpose.

Stoves powered by liquified pressurized propane gas, as shown in Fig. 7.15, are convenient and clean. The fuel is quite expensive and rather heavy to carry, since you have to carry the cartridges as well as the fuel they contain. In Britain and on the European continent these stoves are convenient, since the fuel cartridges are readily obtainable. In the US, where their distribution is much poorer, you would need an unreasonably large supply of these awkward cartridges, certainly if you intend to cook frequently on a longer trip.

Other Camping Equipment

Depending on the intensity of the camping experience and the comfort desired, you may want to take more or less camping gear in addition to the items listed above. Generally, you'll want at least a nesting set of cooking pots, cup, plate, bread board (essentially a lap-top table, made of a 12 x 18 inch piece of plywood or fiber board), cutlery, can and bottle openers, a foldable plastic water container and a similar wash basin (as shown in Fig. 7.16). Furthermore, I suggest you take some form of lighting, wind screens for light and stove, and a number of storage containers, as well as strong, sealed bags to carry food and other supplies. Finally, you'll need dish washing liquid, brush, scouring pad and dish towel to keep your pots clean. Most of the other items needed are the same whether you go camping or not.

For most of these things, you will find backpacking stores to have an astounding range of different types. You will also be able to improvise or make certain items yourself. Get things that are as light as possible and relatively insensitive to deformation. Select screw-on tops for large containers, plastic rather than metal, small and oval cross sections in preference to round and large ones. You may also appreciate that the simplest items will be the easiest to carry and maintain. To give but one example, a couple of candles is more effective and convenient than a much heavier electric light.

In the Appendix you will find a proposed packing list. Though you may find such a list helpful at first, the biggest secret to effective packing and camping is the art of leaving things home (or even in the store) selectively. Deciding what to buy and carry is even more important than selecting the lightest, smallest or best items. Before buying or packing anything, consider seriously whether you can not improvise somehow without it, or whether something else may serve its purpose as well without the weight. For further suggestions on this subject, you are referred to Chapters 13 and 18, which deal with the practical aspects of packing and bicycle camping, respectively.

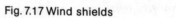

Fig. 7.17 Wind shields

Part II
The Art of Bicycle Touring

8
Bike Fit and Riding Style

The chapters of this second part of the book are primarily devoted to the skills and knowledge that are prerequisite to the safe and enjoyable practice of bicycling. Some of this material may also be found in general bicycle books. However, only here is the practical background of touring specifically considered. In addition, numerous subjects will be covered in this and the following chapters that are of particular relevance to bicycle touring. Many of these topics are not covered at all in conventional general bicycle books.

This particular chapter will first help you arrive at the adjustments that are necessary to cycle in comfort. This is followed by practical advice on posture, riding style and the methods that allow you to cover significant distances on a loaded bicycle. Excluded from this material will be the subject of gearing choice and pedalling rate, since these topics are covered comprehensively in the next chapter.

Bicycle touring in Utah. The lady in question took her foot out of the toe strap for the picture. (Photograph courtesy Backroads)

Riding Posture

To cycle long distances without exhausting, the conventional idea of a comfortable position may have to be reconsidered. Though bicycle racers have long known that they are most comfortable in a relatively low crouched position, most other cyclists – whatever kind of bike they ride – seem to feel that to be comfortable one has to sit upright. That may be fine for folks who travel only short distances in town or make minor excursions at low speed in easy terrain. However, the serious bicycle tourer has much more in common with the racer than he has with these occasional short distance cyclists. The fact that you probably have luggage on board and difficult terrain to handle makes this even more important.

Fig. 8.1 shows the three basic kinds of riding postures for comparison: upright, inclined and fully crouched. The cyclist who rides in the upright position may well be convinced this is the only comfortable way to ride a bike. As I look out of my window I see at least thirty people cycling by in this posture each hour. Those who are going north have a very slight uphill – only a 1% slope. All are working hard, you can tell by the strained expression on their faces, their cramped movements and their abysmally slow progress. Every now and again another type of cyclist comes by. Passing the others at twice their speed and obviously more relaxed, these are the ones who ride in either a deep incline or in a fully crouched position.

There are of course also other reasons why the latter are going faster and suffering less, but the first and most important step towards this more comfortable style is their different riding posture. In the lower

Fig. 8.1 Riding postures: upright, inclined, crouched

Fig. 8.2 Wind resistance as a function of posture

Fig. 8.3 Relaxed inclined position

position, the rider's weight is divided more evenly over handlebars, saddle and pedals. Firstly, this reduces the pressure on the rider's buttocks. Secondly, it allows the relaxed fast pedalling technique so essential for long duration power output. Thirdly, it enables greater restraining forces to bring more force to bear on the pedals.

Finally, it can reduce the wind resistance, which is a major factor in cycling, especially when travelling fast or against the wind regardless of riding speed. As you can tell from Fig. 8.2, the cyclist's frontal area is crucial to the wind resistance, and is much lower in the more inclined positions, which is reflected in the power required to ride the bike at the same speed.

Strangely enough, many people to whom the advantages have been demonstrated nevertheless insist on riding in the upright position. They bring all sorts of arguments, ranging from, "That's only for racing" to, "That is terribly uncomfortable" or, "You couldn't cycle any distance that way." The undeniable fact is that they are fooling themselves. In reality, they are less comfortable, whatever they think, and have to do more work to proceed the same distance or to ride at the same speed. Get accustomed to the right posture early in your cycling career, and you'll be a more effective cyclist, one who gets less frustration and more pleasure out of the pursuit.

Even within the general range of comfortable positions, there are enough different variants to allow changes and adaptations. This makes it possible to adapt to different conditions and gives you the chance to vary your position from time to time. The latter helps avoid the numbing feeling when pressure is applied in a certain position for a longer period. Especially the position of the hands may require some variation, certainly if the cyclist is not yet used to supporting a significant portion of his own weight on the arms.

The following sections will describe just how the saddle and the handlebars should be set to achieve the basic relaxed position that is shown in Fig. 8.3. This particular posture is worth looking into a little closer. Study the proportions, noting also that merely holding the handlebars in a different location allows adequate variation. This may be required to apply more force to the pedals or to reduce the wind resistance by lowering the front, or to get a better overview of the road or the scenery by raising the front by as little as perhaps 10 cm (4 in) either way. The following description is based on the assumption that you have a drop handlebar derailleur bicycle of the right size to match your physique and a crank length that equals one half the upper leg length, as described in Chapters 2 and 3, respectively.

Saddle Height

The height of the saddle, or rather the distance of its top relative to the pedals, is the most critical variable for effective cycling. It should be adjusted so that the leg can be stretched comfortably without completely stretching the knee, which would force excessive force and rotation on the joint. At the same time, the distance between the pedal in its highest point and the saddle must be such that the knee is not bent excessively. Once the former has been set, the correct crank length, as established above and in Chapter 3, assures that the latter condition is also satisfied.

Fig. 8.4 109% rule seat height determination

Here I shall describe three methods of establishing the correct seat height. These are all good enough for preliminary set-up and the first thousand miles of cycling. Your ultimate seat position may require additional individual experimental fine-tuning, based on your subjective long-term comfort. On the other hand, in the vast majority of all cases, each of these techniques will lead to a satisfactory seat position that is suitable for touring, without the need for subsequent fine-tuning.

The first method is referred to as 109% rule. It was developed at Loughborough University in England and is illustrated in Fig. 8.4 To use it, first measure your inseam leg length by standing with your back against a wall with the legs straight, the feet about 5 cm (2 in) apart, wearing thin soled shoes with flat heels. Make a pencil mark for the location of the crotch on the wall. This is easiest to do with the aid of a drawing triangle (oddly enough called a square in Britain) or a rectangular board held upright and pushed up against the wall between the legs. Measure the vertical distance between this mark and the floor.

Now multiply the figure so found, be it in inches or in cm, by 1.09. That is presumed to be the optimal distance between the top of the saddle and the pedal axle when the

Fig. 8.5 Practical seat height determination

Fig. 8.6 Hodges seat height determination

pedal is down, crank in line with the seat tube. Measure it out and set the seat accordingly with the plane connecting front and back of the saddle cover horizontal. How the saddle is raised or lowered will be explained under *Saddle Adjustments*, below.

Fig. 8.7 Foot orientation variation

The second method seems less theoretical and is illustrated in Fig. 8.5. It is a trial-and-error method and is easy to carry out without help. You must again wear cycling shoes with flat heels. Place the bike next to a wall or post for support when you sit on it. Adjust the seat up or down (following the adjustment procedure below) until it is set at such a height relative to the pedal that the heels of your cycling shoes rest on the pedals when your knee is nearly straight but not strained, with the pedal down, crank in line with the seat tube.

Sit on the bike and place the heels on the pedals. Symmetrical pedals can be merely turned upside down; on platform models the toeclips must be removed. Pedal backwards this way, making sure you do not have to rock from side to side to reach the pedals. Now raise the saddle 12 mm (½ in) above this height. Tighten the saddle in this position. Note that the heels-on-pedals style only applies to adjusting the seat height, not to riding the bike, as described below.

The third method is illustrated in Fig. 8.6. It was developed by the American bicycle racing coach Mark Hodges. It is probably the most accurate method, applicable to touring cyclists as much as it is to racers. You will need a helper to measure your leg length and a calculator to figure out the correct saddle height. Stand barefoot upright with your back against a wall, the feet 15 cm (6 in) apart. Now measure the distance from the floor over the ankle joint and the knee joint to the greater trochanter. That's the outwardmost bump on the femur or hip, which coincides with the hip joint's center of rotation: when you raise the leg this point does not move.

To establish the optimal seat height, measured between the top of the saddle near its center and the center of the pedal axle (crank pointing down in line with the seat tube), multiply the dimension so found by 0.96. If appropriate, add an allowance for thick soles, thick cleats or unusually shaped pedals.

Even after using any of these methods, you may have to do some fine-tuning to achieve long-term comfort. Riders with disproportionately small feet may want to place the saddle a little lower, those with big feet perhaps slightly higher. No need to get carried away: raise or lower the seat in steps of 6 mm (¼ in) at a time and try to get used to any position by riding several hundred miles or several days before attempting any change, which must again be in the order of about 6 mm to make any real difference.

When cycling, the ball of the foot (the second joint of the big toe) should be over the center of the pedal axle, with the heel raised so

much that the knee is never straightened fully. Not all cyclists incline
the foot equally, as suggested by
Fig. 8.7, where the foot orientations
of several European bicycle racers
are illustrated as they go through
the pedal cycle. Consequently, the
amount by which the saddle is
moved relative to the point determined may vary a little for different
riders – a matter of 6 mm (¼ in) one
way or the other.

Saddle Position and Angle

The normal preliminary saddle position is such that the seat post is
roughly in the middle of the saddle.
For optimal pedalling efficiency,
adjust the saddle forward or backwards after it has been set to the
correct height, as explained in the
preceding section. On any bike
designed on conventional lines,
sitting on the bike with the foot
under the toeclip and the crank
placed horizontal, the center of the
knee joint must be vertically aligned
with the spindle of the forward
pedal, as shown in Fig. 8.8. You can
locate the center of the knee joint at
the bony protrusion just behind the
knee cap.

The angle of the saddle relative to
the horizontal plane should initially
be set so as to keep the line that
connects the highest points at the
front and the back level, as illustrated in Fig. 8.9. After the handlebars
have been set to the correct height,
it may be necessary to modify this
angle to prevent slipping forward or
backwards. This too may not
become apparent until after some
miles of cycling. Adjusting procedures for both forward position and
angle are outlined below.

Fig. 8.8 Saddle forward position determination

Fig. 8.9 Saddle alignment

Fig. 8.10 Saddle adjustment

Saddle Adjustments

To do the actual mechanical adjusting work on the saddle, first take a
close look at the way it is installed on
the bike, comparing it with Fig. 8.10.
The saddle height is adjusted by
loosening the binder bolt behind the
seat lug, raising or lowering the
saddle with the attached seat post
in a twisting motion, and then tightening the binder bolt again at the

required height, making sure it is straight.

To change the forward position, undo the adjustment bolts (only one bolt on some models) on your adjustable seat post. These bolts are usually reached from under the saddle cover, though they can be reached from below or the side on some models. Once loosened, push the saddle forward or backwards until the desired position is reached; then tighten the bolts, making sure the saddle is held under the desired angle relative to the horizontal plane.

Handlebar Height and Position

Even for bicycle touring, the highest point of the handlebars should always be lower than the top of the saddle to ride efficiently. Just how low will be determined by the shape of the handlebars and the rider's physiognomy. It depends on the relative distribution of body weight and torso height, as well as on the upper and lower arm length. That's why only experiments can tell what will eventually be right for any particular rider. Here I shall merely tell you how to determine the initial position for a frame size check, followed by the adjustment for a relaxed initial riding style. After about a thousand miles of cycling, you should be able to fine-tune the handlebar height and stem length to match your needs perfectly.

The following description is again based on the use of a correctly dimensioned frame, as outlined in Chapter 2. In order to make sure it is not too high, first check whether the fully crouched position can be achieved. Place the handlebars in their lowest possible position and, sitting on the saddle, hold them in the lowest part of the bend (below the brake levers). With the lower

arms horizontal and the elbows under a slightly acute angle, the upper body should now lie almost horizontally. This is the fully crouched or 'full tuck' position. It may be necessary to choose a longer or shorter handlebar stem for comfort in this position. If this full tuck is not possible with any handlebar stem available, a smaller or (more rarely) a larger frame may be required.

To set the handlebars for a relaxed initial riding style, without sacrificing the advantages of the full tuck when conditions call for it, proceed as follows. First set the top of the bars about 3 cm (1¼ in) lower than the saddle. Sit on the bike and reach forward for the part of the bends between the straight top and the brake handle attachments. In this position your shoulders should be about midway between seat and hands, as shown in Fig. 8.3. The arms should feel neither stretched nor heavily loaded and they should run parallel.

If they don't satisfy the last criterion, your handlebar bend is too wide or too narrow; if you can not find a relaxed position, you will need a longer or shorter stem. If you should have a particularly long combination of lower arms and torso in relation to your leg length, you may not be comfortable even with a long stem. In that case, a slightly larger frame, which has a longer top tube as well as a longer seat tube, may be in order. Conversely, long legs combined with short arms and torso may require you use a shorter frame to achieve the right top tube length. In extreme cases of either variety, the right top tube length just cannot be achieved with a bike that fits in height. In this case, you may need a custom-built frame with the desired dimensions of seat tube and top tube. This would be the ultimate solution, although it is probably not quite so critical that you can't make do with a stock frame.

Finally, grab the handlebar bend at the ends, leaning forward on them while seated. The handlebar angle relative to the horizontal plane should be such that the hands don't slip either into the bend or off towards the ends in this position. If you initially have difficulties achieving this position, you may start off with the handlebars somewhat higher. In that case, the ends must also point down slightly. Lower and level them out as you develop the style that allows you to ride with the lower handlebar position after some practice.

Handlebar Adjustments

You are referred to the accompanying illustration Fig. 8.11. To vary the height of the handlebars, straddle the front wheel. Undo the expander bolt, which is recessed in the top of the stem. If the stem does not come loose immediately, you may have to lift the handlebars to lift the wheel off the ground, then tap on the head of the expander bolt with a hammer. This will loosen the internal clamping device. Now raise or lower the handlebar stem as required. Tighten the expander bolt again, while holding the handlebars straight in the desired position.

To change the angle of the handlebar ends with respect to the horizontal plane, undo the binder bolt that clamps the handlebar bend in the front of the stem. Twist the handlebar bend until it is under the desired angle, and then tighten the binder bolt again, holding the bar centered. To install a longer stem or a different bar design, you are referred to any bicycle maintenance book or your friendly bike store. The

Fig. 8.11 Handlebar adjustment

correct handlebar position often puts more strain on the hands than beginning cyclists find comfortable, especially when rough road surfaces induce vibrations. Minimize this problem by always keeping the arms slightly bent, never holding them in a cramped position. If you still experience discomfort, wrap the handlebars with cushioned foam sleeves (such as Grab-On) instead of normal handlebar tape.

Adjusting Special Bikes

For those who use a mountain bike or ATB for touring, most of the adjustments described above also apply as long as you ride on the road. Since most bicycle touring will be done on the road, whatever kind of bike is used, the only real difference is that the flat mountain bike handlebars do not allow the lower position for the full tuck. Consequently, I suggest you set the saddle and the handlebars so that the relaxed position described above is possible when holding the flat bars at the ends.

Once you do start riding off-road, especially in mountainous terrain, you may want to lower the saddle or to put it further back to cycle down a steep incline. Since the variation in geometry from one make and model to the next is quite significant, you may have to do a bit of experimenting to find the optimal positions for such special uses. Certainly the saddle adjustment is greatly eased for experiment and frequent change, due to the use of a quick-release binder bolt, as installed on virtually all mountain bikes, and sometimes an additional quick-release bolt to hold the saddle to the seat post. Further details will be given in Chapter 22, which is devoted to mountain bike touring.

Besides the users of off-road bikes, two other groups of cyclists also encounter different fitting problems: tandem riders and children. Advice to tandem riders will be found in Chapter 21, while Chapter 20 is devoted to the subject of touring with children.

Basic Bike Handling

Once saddle and handlebars are adjusted correctly, it will be time to take to the road on your bike. In case you are not yet familiar with the derailleur bicycle and the rest of your equipment, here's just a suggestion for getting on and off the bike. All other riding and handling techniques involve long learning processes that will be treated in separate chapters, but the simple act of starting the bike should be mastered immediately. Easy though this may seem, it is worth practicing, if only to avoid embarrassing or dangerous mishaps, especially when cycling with others or in traffic.

Of course, most cyclists are not entirely new to the game: you too may feel you've been cycling long enough to do without any additional advice or practice. It still does not hurt to follow the procedures described below seriously and consciously, so you become more efficient at handling the bike when touring. Your first experience will probably be on a bike without luggage, but it is a good idea to also load the bike with luggage and practice handling it that way before your first serious tour. When cycling with packs, take care to find the loaded bike's mass center, from which it is easiest to balance. Also note that getting on and off a loaded bike may require special precautions, depending on the extent to which the bags protrude.

Before you start off, make sure your shoe laces are tied and tucked in, or short enough not to run the risk of getting caught in the chain. Make sure the bike is set in a low gear, with the chain on the middle chainwheel (or the smaller one on a machine with only two chainwheels) and an intermediate or big sprocket. The bike should have been checked to make sure it will be operating properly and that the tires are well inflated.

Start off at the side of the road, after having checked to make sure no traffic is following closely behind. Straddle the top tube by swinging the appropriate leg either over the handlebars, the top tube, or the saddle. Hold the handlebars with both hands at the top of the bend. If you use toeclips, tap against the pedal with the toe of your starting foot to turn it around. This brings the toeclip on top, after which you can immediately place the foot under the toeclip. In case you use shoes with cleats, place the slot of the cleat over the ridge of the pedal. Pedal backward until the pedal is in the top position. Pull the toe strap, but not quite so tight as to cut off circulation in the foot, then pedal back three quarters of a revolution to bring the pedal to 2 o'clock, just above the horizontally forward position.

Look behind you to make sure the road is clear, then check ahead to establish which course you'll want to follow. Place your weight on the pedal, leaning lightly on the handlebars. Put the other foot on its pedal as soon as it is in the top position. The first few revolutions will be cycled with this second pedal upside down, either standing up or seated. When you have gained some momentum, tap the toe against the back of the free pedal to turn it over, and right away push the foot in under the toeclip. Pedal a few more strokes, then pull the loose toestrap taut, securing the second foot to its pedal as well.

To slow down, whether just to stop or to get off the bike, first look behind you again to make sure you are not getting in the way of cyclists or motorists following. Aim for the position where you will want to stop. Change into a lower gear, appropriate for starting off again later. Push against the buckle of the toestrap for whichever foot you want to have free first, meanwhile pulling the foot up and back to loosen it when that pedal is up. When using cycling shoes with cleats, the strap must be just loose enough to raise the foot to clear the pedal with the cleat.

Slow down by braking gently, using mainly the front brake to stop. When you have come to a standstill, or just before that point, make sure the pedal with the loosened strap is up, then pull the foot up and out. Place it on the ground, leaning over slightly in that same direction, while moving forward off the saddle to straddle the seat tube. Now you are in the right position to dismount or start again.

If you want to get off the bike at this point, bring the other foot up, pedalling backwards, and loosen the buckle of the toestrap to release the foot. Now you're ready to get off the bike. However, under most circumstances you will find that especially a loaded machine is most easily controlled when you remain on the bike, straddling the top tube. I suggest you only dismount completely if it is really necessary.

9
Selecting and Using the Gears

Touring bicycles, in the overwhelming majority, are equipped with a sophisticated derailleur system for multiple gearing. To change gear, the chain is shifted onto any chosen combination of chainwheel and sprocket with the aid of two derailleur mechanisms. Nowadays, fifteen and eighteen speed systems are generally used for genuine touring machines, although systems with ten, twelve and even five or six speeds may be quite adequate for many touring purposes. In the case of ten and twelve speed set-ups, two chainwheels are used in combination with five and six sprockets, respectively. Fifteen and eighteen speed systems have three chainwheels, combined with five and six sprockets, respectively.

The derailleur method of gearing allows minute adaptations of the gear ratio to the cyclist's potential on the one hand, and the terrain, wind resistance and road conditions on the other hand. All that is mere theory, because in reality the majority of people, including most beginning touring cyclists, plod along in the wrong gear for the work load. Indeed, learning to select the right gear may well provide the biggest single step towards improved cycling speed and endurance. That's the subject of the present chapter.

There is a sound theory behind the principle of gear selection, based on the optimal pedalling rate, which I have covered in several of my other books, such as the *Bicycle Racing Guide*. Interesting though this

FREEWHEEL WITH SPROCKETS

SHIFTERS

FRONT DERAILLEUR

REAR DERAILLEUR

3 CHAINWHEELS

Fig. 9.1 The derailleur system

LOWEST GEAR

HIGHEST GEAR

Fig. 9.2 Gearing as a function of chainwheel and sprocket size

theory is, one need not wait with applying the technique until it is thoroughly understood. That's why I shall outline the correct use of gearing to the extent you will need it as a touring cyclist at this point. Once you do develop an interest in the theoretical background, you will be all the more likely to appreciate the theory if you have already experienced the benefits of the technique in practice.

The Derailleur System

Fig. 9.1 shows and names the mechanical components of the derailleur system. The chain runs over two or three chainrings, also referred to as chainwheels, mounted on the RH crank, and any one of five or six sprockets mounted on a freewheel block at the rear wheel. As long as you are pedalling forward, the chain can be moved from one chainwheel to the other by means of the front derailleur or changer, and from one sprocket to another by means of the rear derailleur. Systems with seven sprockets are also available, but are not generally considered suitable for touring, since these offset the rear wheel too much for heavily loaded cycling.

Because the various chainwheels and sprockets have different numbers of teeth, the ratio between pedalling speed and the speed with which the rear wheel – and with it the whole bike – is driven changes whenever a different combination is selected. As illustrated in Fig. 9.2, bigger chainrings in the front and smaller sprockets in the rear result in higher gears, smaller chainrings and bigger sprockets give lower gears. Higher gears are selected when cycling is easy, so the available output allows a high riding speed. Select a lower gear when higher resistances must be overcome, such as riding uphill or against a head wind, or when starting off from standstill.

Each derailleur is controlled by means of a shift lever, usually mounted on the frame's down tube. Alternative   positions   are   less

downtube shifters

bar-end shifter

HANDLEBAR MOUNT (THUMB SHIFTER)

Fig. 9.3 Shift lever types

convenient on bikes with drop handlebars in the long run. Only mountain bikes, with their flat bars, allow the use of thumb shifters, mounted directly on the handlebars, within easy reach from the hand grips. The different types of levers are shown in Fig. 9.3. Make sure derailleurs and levers match and that both are suitable for touring use. They will be if they are intended for gears that are relatively widely spaced. The bike shop is the place to find out what is suitable hardware for your bike.

Most shifts are made with the rear derailleur, while the front changer is primarily used to move from one general range of gears to the other.

With the usual fifteen or eighteen speed set-up, all the gears in the high range are reached by means of shifts of the rear derailleur, while the front derailleur remains on the largest chainring. All the intermediate gears are reached by shifts of the rear derailleur, after the front derailleur has been moved once to engage the intermediate chainring. All the gears in the low range are again selected with the rear derailleur, once the front changer is used to put the chain on the smallest chainring.

Though it is also possible to select chainwheel and sprocket sizes in such a way that intermediate gears between rear derailleur shifts are always reached with a front changer shift, the above method simplifies the gear selection procedure considerably. This is certainly so for the typical touring bike set-up with fifteen or eighteen speed gearing. Intermediate gears may have to be engaged by means of double shifting on systems with ten or twelve speeds.

The rear derailleur is controlled from the RH shift lever. To put the chain on a different sprocket in the rear, move the RH shift lever, while pedalling forward with reduced force. Pull the lever back to change to a larger sprocket, which results in a lower gear; push it forward to reach a smaller sprocket, resulting in a higher gear.

The LH shift lever controls the front derailleur or changer, which simply shoves the cage through which the chain runs to the left or the right, moving it onto the smaller or the bigger chainwheel. Pulling the lever back engages the bigger chainwheel for the higher gear range on most models; pushing it forward engages the smaller chainwheel, to obtain the lower gearing range.

The Need for Gears

The reason for gearing lies in the possibility it provides to pedal at an efficient rate with comfortable force under a wide range of different conditions and riding speeds. If the combination of chainwheel and sprocket size were fixed, as it is on the single-speed bicycle, any given pedalling speed invariably corresponds to a certain riding speed. The rear wheel will be turning at a speed that can be simply calculated by multiplying the pedalling rate with the quotient of chainwheel and sprocket size (expressed in terms of the numbers of teeth):

$$v_{wheel} = v_{pedal} \times T_{front} : T_{rear}$$

where:

v_{wheel} = wheel rotating speed (RPM)
v_{pedal} = pedalling rate (RPM)
T_{front} = number of teeth, chainwheel
T_{rear} = number of teeth, sprocket

The actual riding speed depends on this wheel rotating speed and the effective wheel diameter. The effective diameter of a nominal 27 inch or 700 mm wheel is about 680 mm. This results in a riding speed in MPH that can be determined by multiplying the wheel speed in RPM by 0.08. These two calculations can be combined to find the riding speed in MPH directly from the pedalling rate and the chainwheel and sprocket sizes as follows:

$$MPH = 0.08 \times v_{pedal} \times T_{front} : T_{rear}$$

where:

MPH = riding speed in MPH and the other symbols are as defined above. To express riding speed in km/h, use the following formula instead:

$$km/h = 0.125 \times v_{pedal} \times T_{front} : T_{rear}$$

To give an example, assume you are pedalling at a rate of 80 RPM on a bike geared with a 42-tooth chain-wheel and a 21-tooth rear sprocket. Your riding speed, expressed in MPH and km/h respectively, will be:

$$0.08 \times 80 \times 42 : 21 = 13 \text{ MPH}$$

$$0.125 \times 80 \times 42 : 21 = 20 \text{ km/h}$$

Depending on the prevailing terrain conditions, that may be too easy or too hard for optimum endurance performance. If you are riding up a steep incline, this speed may require a very high pedal force, which may well be too exhausting and damaging to muscles, joints and tendons. On a level road the same speed will be reached so easily that you don't feel any significant resistance. All right for cruising, but not for serious touring if you have to cover a greater distance in a reasonable time.

The derailleur gearing system allows you to choose the combination of chainwheel and sprocket sizes that enables you to operate effectively at your chosen pedalling speed for optimal performance. You may of course also vary the pedalling rate, which would appear to have the same effect as selecting another gear. Indeed, with any given gear, pedalling slower reduces riding speed and therefore demands less power, whereas a higher pedalling rate increases road speed, requiring more power.

However, power output is not the sole, nor indeed the most important, criterion. Performing work at a given level of power output may tax the body differently, depending on the associated forces and speeds of movements. It has been found that to cycle longer distances effectively, without tiring or hurting excessively, the pedal force must be kept down by pedalling at a rate well above what seems natural to the beginning cyclist.

Whereas the beginner tends to plod along at 40–60 RPM, efficient long distance cycling requires pedalling rates of 80 RPM and more, while racers generally pedal even faster. That doesn't come overnight, because the cyclist first has to learn to move his legs that fast, but it is an essential requirement for efficient bicycle touring. Much of your early cycling practice should therefore be aimed at mastering the art of pedalling faster. That must be done in a rather low gear to ensure that training intensity is limited by the factor to be developed, namely muscle speed, rather than by power output or muscle strength.

Gearing Practice

Once you know that high gears mean big chainwheels and small sprockets, it's time to get some practice riding in high and low gears. First do it 'dry': the bike supported with the rear wheel off the ground. Turn the cranks by hand and use the shift levers to change up and down, front and rear, until you have developed a good idea of the combinations reached in all conceivable shift lever positions. Listen for rubbing and crunching noises as you shift, realizing a shift has not been executed properly until the noises have subdued.

Now take to the road. Select a stretch of quiet road, where you can experiment around with your gears without risk of being run into the ground by a closely following vehicle or get in the way of other cyclists. Start off in a low gear and shift the rear derailleur up in steps. Then shift to another chainwheel and change down through the gears with the rear derailleur, followed by the third chainwheel, assuming a fifteen or eighteen speed system.

Reduce the pedal force, still pedalling forward as you shift. Especially the front derailleur will not shift as smoothly as it did when the cranks were turned by hand. You will notice that the noises become more severe and that some changes just don't take place as you had intended. To execute a correct change, you may have to overshift slightly first: push the lever a little beyond the correct position to affect a definite change and then back up until the chain is quiet again. Get a feel for each gear and try to imagine which gear you should select for given conditions. Practice shifting until it goes smoothly and naturally.

Occasionally, it may be necessary to fine-tune the front derailleur posi-

This is what happens when you change gear with the rear derailleur: the chain is shifted sideways onto another sprocket.

Fig. 9.4 Gear number and development

tion after a change with the rear derailleur. That will be the case when the chain is twisted under an angle that causes it to rub against the side of the front changer. Some people never learn, quite simply because they don't take the trouble to practice consciously. Others take that trouble and learn to shift predictably and smoothly within a week. Half an hour of intensive practice each day during one week, and the continued attention required to do it right during regular riding, is all it takes to become an expert very quickly.

In recent years several manufacturers have introduced sophisticated derailleur systems with matching freewheel blocks that eliminate the need for fine-tuning. These indexed systems, such as the Shimano SIS and Sachs-Huret ARIS, work very well when new. However, a slight misalignment or a little wear can play havoc with the indexing of the various gears. Though they may be fine for team racers, who have mechanics with lots of spares and tools to take care of their equipment at their beck and call, I can not at this time recommend their use for touring purposes.

Gear Designation

Just how high or low any given gear is may be expressed by giving the respective numbers of teeth on chainwheel and sprocket engaged in the particular gear. However, this is not a very good measure. It may not be immediately clear that a combination designated 42 X 16 has the same effect as one designated 52 X 21, though they really do result in the same ratio, as can be verified mathematically. It will be clear that it becomes nearly impossible to compare gears on bikes with different wheel sizes this way.

To allow a direct comparison between the gearing effects of different gears and bikes, two methods are in use, referred to as gear number and development, respectively, and illustrated in Fig. 9.4. Gear number is a somewhat archaic method, used mainly in the English speaking world. It is the equivalent wheel size in inches of a directly driven wheel that corresponds to any given combination of wheel size, chainwheel and sprocket. It is determined by multiplying the quotient of chainwheel and sprocket sizes with the wheel diameter in inches:

$$gear = D_{wheel} \times T_{front} : T_{rear}$$

where:

$gear$ = gear number in inches
D_{wheel} = wheel diameter in inches
T_{front} = number of teeth, chainwheel
T_{rear} = number of teeth, sprocket

Returning to the example for a bike with 27-inch wheels, geared with a 42-tooth chainwheel and a 21-tooth sprocket, the gear number would be:

27 x 42 : 21 = 54 in

This is the customary, though rather quaint method used in the English speaking world to define bicycle gearing. The rest of the world expresses the gear in terms of development. That is the distance in meters covered by the bike with one crank revolution. Development is calculated as follows:

$$Dev. = 3.14 \times d_{wheel} \times T_{front} : T_{rear}$$

where:
$Dev.$ = development in meters
d_{wheel} = wheel size in m
T_{front} = number of teeth, chainwheel
T_{rear} = number of teeth, sprocket

The development for the same example would be:

3.14 x 0.680 x 42 : 21 = 4.30 m
In practice, you are not expected to figure this kind of thing out yourself. Instead you may refer to the tables in the Appendix. Just remember that a high gear is expressed by a high gear number or a long development. For touring purposes, very low gears in terms of gear number are in the upper twenties and the thirties (around 2.20–3.20 m in terms of development). High gears are those above 80 in (development of more than 6.40 m).

Gear Selection

Possibly the biggest problem for the beginning cyclist is to determine which is the right one out of the bewildering array of available gears. To generalize for most touring conditions, I would say it's whichever gear allows you to maximize your pedalling rate without diminishing your capacity to do effective work.

Perhaps you start off with the ability to pedal no faster than 60 RPM. That'll be too low once you have absolved some riding practice, but for now that may be your limit. So the right gear is the one in which you can reach that rate at any time, preferably exceeding it. Count it out with the aid of a wrist watch frequently until you develop a feel for your pedalling speed. If you find yourself pedalling slower, change down into a slightly lower gear, to increase the pedalling rate at the same riding speed. If you're pedalling faster, keep it up until you feel you are indeed spinning too lightly, and only then change into a slightly higher gear to increase road speed at the same pedalling rate.

Gradually, you will develop the capacity to pedal faster. As that happens, increase the limiting pedalling rate along with your ability, moving up from 60 to 70, 80 and eventually even higher pedalling rates. When riding with others, don't be guided by their gearing selection, since they may be stronger or weaker, or may have developed their pedalling speed more or less than you have.

It should not take too long before you learn to judge the right gear in advance, without the need to count out the pedal revolutions. You will not only know to change down into a lower gear when the direction of the road changes to expose you to a head wind or when you reach an incline, you will also learn to judge just how far to change down – and up again when the conditions become more favorable. Change gear consciously and frequently in small steps, and you will soon enough master the trick.

Derailleur Care and Adjustment

For optimal operation of the derail-leur system, several things should be regularly checked and adjusted if necessary. The derailleurs them-selves, as well as the chain and the various sprockets, chainwheels and control cables, must be kept clean and lightly lubricated. The cables must be just taut when the shift levers are pushed forward and the derailleurs engage the appropriate gear. The tension screw on the shift levers must be kept tightened to give positive shifting without exces-sive tightness or slack.

When the chain gets shifted beyond the biggest or smallest chainwheel or sprocket, or when certain combinations can not be reached, the derailleurs themselves must be adjusted. For this purpose they are equipped with set-stop screws, which can be adjusted with a small screwdriver, as illustrated in Fig. 9.5. If necessary, place the chain back on the sprocket or chainwheel, and select a gear which combines a small chainring with a small sprocket. To adjust the front or rear derailleur, proceed as follows:

1. Establish where the problem lies: front or rear derailleur, shifted too far or not far enough, on the inside or the outside.
2. Determine which of the set-stop screws governs movement limi-tation in the appropriate direc-tion. On many models these screws are marked with an H and L for high and low gear, respec-tively. If not, establish yourself which is the appropriate screw by observing what happens at the ends of the screws as you shift towards the extreme gears. The high range set-stop screw is the one towards which an internal protrusion moves as you shift into

Fig. 9.5 Derailleur adjustment

the highest gear with the appro-priate derailleur shift lever.
3. Unscrew the set-stop screw slightly (perhaps half a turn at a time) to increase the range if the extreme gear could not be reach-ed. Tighten it if the chain was shift-ed beyond that last sprocket.
4. Check all possible gear combina-tions to establish whether the system works properly now, and fine-tune the adjustment, if nec-essary.

Selecting Chainrings and Sprockets

All of the preceding is fine, assuming you are satisfied with the combina-tion of gears available on the bike as it is purchased. However, you may determine that you need lower or higher, more or fewer gears than what is installed as standard. Or you may want to determine the gearing range yourself for a bicycle that is custom built or adapted specifically for you. In either of these cases, you will want a convenient system of establishing the sizes of chainrings and sprockets needed to meet your requirements.

Table 9-I Suggested gearing ranges for touring bicycles

Terrain type	development	gear number
mainly level terrain, no wind	3.60 – 7.60	45 – 95
shallow hills or level with wind	3.20 – 8.00	40 – 100
hilly	2.80 – 8.40	35 – 105
very hilly	2.40 – 8.40	30 – 105
mountainous	2.20 – 8.00	27 – 100
off-road	2.00 – 7.20	25 – 90

To aid the selection process, you may find the graph Fig. 9.6 useful, even if it looks a little bewildering at first. Here I shall explain how to use it to determine the optimal sizes of sprockets and chainrings for any derailleur system.

First, decide what will be the maximum and minimum gears you want to have available. To do that, you need some experience. If you want to change your existing set-up, you'll have to establish which of the gears you now have are unnecessarily high or low for the conditions you will encounter or, alternately, which additional higher and lower gears you'll require. If you do not have the experience to decide that yet, ask for advice in a good bike shop or be guided by Table 9-I.

Once the range has been established, decide on likely combinations of chainring and sprocket for the extreme gears with the aid of a gear table, such as the one found in the Appendix. Keep in mind that the normal smallest sprocket is 14 teeth for a freewheel block with five

This is how you adjust a derailleur to make sure it reaches all the gears without dumping the chain.

Fig. 9.6 Gear selection graph

sprockets, or 13 teeth for models with six sprockets. Thus, in order to get a top gear of 100 inches, a 14 tooth sprocket should be combined with a largest chainring that has about 50 teeth. Alternately, the same gear can be achieved with a smallest sprocket of 13 teeth and a large chainring of 47 teeth. Other maximum and minimum combinations can be established from the gear table.

Next, consider over how many gears this range is to be divided: 10, 12, 15 or 18. When using a system with three chainwheels, you will almost certainly have a smallest chainring that has 20 teeth less than the biggest. From the gear table, check what will be the size of the largest sprocket required to arrive at the desired lowest gear when such a smallest chainring is used. In

our case, the use of a smallest chainring with 50 – 20 = 30 teeth would require a largest sprocket with 34 teeth to get a 25 inch lowest gear. This is a really low gear for hard climbing, and suggested here as an example only. Decide yourself what your lowest gear should be, to determine which sprockets you need.

Now establish the optimum distribution of sprocket sizes within the range that was determined this way (in the case of the present example: six steps from 14 to 34 teeth). This is where Details A and B of the graph come in. Cut out a copy of Detail B and place it on top of Detail A with the first arrow on the line corresponding to the smallest sprocket, and the fifth or sixth arrow (depending on the number of sprockets on the freewheel) on the line corresponding to the largest sprocket. In the illustrated example this is shown for the case of a 6-speed freewheel ranging from 14 to 34 teeth, resulting in sprockets of 14-17-20-24-28-34 teeth.

The ideal sizes of the intermediate sprockets can be read off opposite the arrows marked with the intervening numbers. You may have noticed that the resulting distribution of sprocket sizes gives values that are closer together at the low end (high gears) than at the high end (low gears). This results in steps between subsequent gears that feel similar, because they represent equal percentage differences relative to the respective preceding gears.

Helico-Matic rear hub with matching freewheel block from Maillard. Due to the special multiple spiral thread, the freewheel can be easily removed with the special tool, shown on the right.

Finally, we shall determine the ideal size for the intermediate chainring. This is done with Detail C and some simple arithmetic. From the appropriate scale of Detail C (for five and six speed freewheel blocks, respectively), you can tell what the approximate percentage step between sprockets is. This is determined on the basis of the size of the largest sprocket, e.g. 19 percent in the case of our example. The best middle chainring size will be one that differs half this much from the largest one. Thus, in our case, it should be 9.5% smaller than 50 teeth, which is calculated as 45 teeth.

Other Gearing Systems

It will be quite possible to make do with gears that are not determined as scientifically as what is outlined above. However, if you do have the opportunity to choose, I feel you should know how to do it for best results. On the other hand, do not get obsessive about things like this: learn to use what you have, even if it seems to be slightly less than perfect.

In fact, it is even possible to get by admirably with set-ups that have only five or six speeds, simplifying the whole gearing system by eliminating the front derailleur. In that case, all you have to do is make sure the lowest gear is low enough and the highest gear is as high as can be handled by the derailleur. To select the steps between sprockets for systems with five, six, ten and twelve speeds, the same method as described above may be used, once the highest and lowest gears have been established.

Not all derailleurs are capable of handling all possible combinations of gears. As this subject is very complicated, due to the vast array of different makes, models, sizes and combinations of front and rear derailleurs, sprockets and chainrings, it will be impossible to do more

than alert you to the problem. Before selecting any uncommon combination, ask in the bike store whether it will work with the equipment you already have or intend to install, or which modifications have to be carried out in order to make it possible.

In addition to the conventional systems with simple round chainwheels, there are some systems on the market that differ. Of the various types that have been introduced from time to time, so far the most promising is the Shimano Biopace system. This includes curiously shaped off-round chainwheels, available to match the same manufacturer's touring quality cranksets. Like all non-standard systems, the Biopace seems to bring an advantage only to those cyclists who have not learned to pedal at a high rate in a relatively low gear. The chainring sizes available for this system are very limited. Nice equipment, but it may be smarter to get used to spinning fast and smoothly using conventional equipment.

10
Bicycle Handling Skills

In the present chapter we will take a closer look at the skills needed to cycle effectively and safely. Though other cyclists – be they racers or commuters – also have to master similar skills, there are some special aspects to consider for bicycle touring. Handling a bicycle with luggage is a different matter altogether from dealing with the same bike unloaded. In addition, the touring cyclist will probably be forced to cycle under more adverse conditions from time to time. Finally, some of your touring may be on poorly paved roads or even off-road altogether. All these situations require special attention with regard to handling skills.

The first section of this chapter will deal with learning to ride the bicycle competently, with proper control over the steering and braking mechanisms This will help you cycle with minimal effort and maximum confidence. In the next section you will be introduced to the peculiarities of effective riding techniques for touring. Although an understanding of the theoretical background is helpful, I shall concentrate as much as possible on the practical aspects, making you practice what you learn. If you should be more than superficially interested in the material covered here, you are referred to John Forester's excellent manual *Effec-*

Curve radius, speed and lean are inter-related. At higher speed, more lean in the direction of the turn is required. The figure in the center follows the natural curve. To force a tighter curve at a low speed, lean the bike more than the body. To force a tighter curve at high speed, lean the body more than the bike.

Fig. 10.1 Balance and steering

tive Cycling. Better yet, you may follow a practical course on the subject, by contacting the Effective Cycling League at the address given in the Appendix.

The Steering Principle

Contrary to popular belief, a bicycle is not steered most effectively by merely turning the handlebars and following the front wheel, as is the case for any two-track vehicle, such as a car. Though bicycles and other single-track vehicles indeed follow the front wheel, they also require the rider to lean his vehicle into the curve to balance it at the same time.

If you were to merely turn the handlebars, the lower part of the bike would start running away from its previous course in the direction in which the front wheel is then pointed. Meanwhile, the mass of the rider, perched high up on the bike, would continue following the original course due to inertia. Thus, the center of gravity would not be in line with the supporting bike, and the rider would come crashing to the ground. Due to the effect of centrifugal force, the tendency to throw the rider off towards the outside of the curve increases with higher speeds, requiring a more pro-

nounced lean the faster you are going.

It is possible to steer by turning the handlebars, and then correct lean and steering to regain balance afterwards. In fact, many older people, especially women, seem to do it that way, succeeding quite well at low speeds only. As soon as imbalance becomes imminent, they have to make a correction in the other direction. After some more cramped and anxious movements, they finally get around the corner. This accounts for the tensioned and apparently impulsive riding style typical for such riders, even if they have practiced it so long that they don't realize their movements are awkward and their balance precarious.

The more effective technique for riding a curve at speed is based on placing the bike under the appropriate angle, where the centrifugal force is offset by a shift of the mass center to the inside, before turning off. Two methods may be used, depending on the amount of time and room available to carry out the maneuver. I refer to these two methods as natural and forced turn, respectively. To understand either, we should first take a look at the intricacies of balancing the bike when riding a straight line, after which the two methods of turning can be explained.

Bicycle Balance

What keeps a bicycle or any other single track vehicle going without falling over is the inertia of its moving mass. Rolling a narrow hoop will show that it is an unstable balance: once the thing starts to lean either left or right, it will just go down further and further until it hits the ground. That's because the mass is no longer supported vertically in line with the force. Try it with a bicycle wheel if you like. If the bike's front wheel could not be steered and the rider couldn't move sideways, he'd come down the same way very soon.

On the bicycle, the rider feels when the vehicle starts to lean over. Theoretically, there are two ways out of the predicament: either move the rider back over the center of the bike or move the bike back under the rider. In practice, the latter method is used most effectively, especially at higher speeds. When the bike begins leaning to the side, the rider oversteers the front wheel a little in the same direction, which places the bike back in such a position that balance is restored. In fact, this point will be passed, so the bike starts leaning over the other way, and so on.

This entire sequence of movements is relatively easy to notice when you are cycling slowly. When standing still, the balancing motions are so extreme that only a highly skilled cyclist can keep control. The faster the bicycle, the less perceptible (though equally important and therefore harder to master) are the steering corrections required to retain balance. To get an understanding of this whole process, I suggest you practice riding a straight line at a low speed. Then do it at a higher speed, and see whether you agree with the explanation, referring also to Fig. 10.1.

Clearly, both riding a straight line and staying upright with the bike are merely illusions. In reality, the bike is always in disequilibrium, following a more or less curved track. The combination of bike with rider leans alternately one way and the other. At higher speeds the curves are longer and gentler, while the amount of lean can be perceptible; at lower speeds the curves are shorter and sharper, with less pronounced lean angles for any given deviation.

The Natural Turn

Under normal circumstances, the rider knows well ahead where to turn off, and there is enough room to follow a generously wide curve. This is the situation of the natural turn. It makes use of the lean that results from normal straight path steering corrections. To turn to the right naturally, you simply wait until the bike is leaning over that way, while the left turn is initiated when the bike is leaning to the left.

Instead of turning the handlebars to that same side, as would be done to get back in balance to ride straight, you just leave the handlebars alone for a while. This causes the bike to lean over further and further in the direction of the turn. Only when the lean is quite significant, do you steer in the same direction, but not as abruptly as you would do to get back up straight. Instead, you fine-tune the ratio of lean and steering deflection to ride the curve out.

When the turn is completed, you will still be leaning over in the direction of the turn, and you would ride a circle without some other corrective

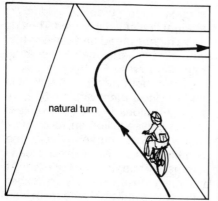

Fig. 10.2 The natural turn

Fig. 10.3 The forced turn

action on your part. You get back on the straight course by steering further into the curve than the amount of lean demands to maintain your balance. This puts your mass center back right above the bike or even further over, allowing you to resume the slightly curving course with which you approximate the straight line. This is illustrated in Fig. 10.2.

Unconsciously, you probably learned to do this when you were a kid, but never realized that you were doing all this. You could perhaps continue to ride a bicycle forever without understanding the theory. However, to keep control over the bike in demanding situations encountered while touring in difficult terrain with a loaded machine, you will be much better off if you have the theoretical knowledge and have learned to ride a calculated course, making use of this information. Get a feel for it by riding around an empty parking lot many times, leaning this way and that, following straight lines and making turns, until it is both second nature and something you can do consciously, knowing the relevant limitations.

While you are practicing this technique, as well as when riding at other

times, note that speed, curve radius, lean and load are all closely correlated. A sharper turn requires more lean at any given speed. At a higher speed, any given curve requires much greater lean angles than the same curve radius at a lower speed. Finally, the loaded bike tends to lean more than an unloaded machine. As you practice this technique, learn to judge which are the appropriate combinations under different circumstances.

The Forced Turn

You will often be confronted with situations that don't allow you to wait until you are conveniently leaning the appropriate way to make a gradual turn. Deficiencies in the road surface or the presence of other traffic in the road may force you into a narrow predetermined path, with only a few inches to deviate sideways. Or a sudden obstacle may force you to divert suddenly. Finally, you may have to get around a curve that is too sharp to be taken naturally at your current riding speed.

These situations require the second method of turning, which I call the forced turn. In this case, the turn must be initiated quickly, regardless which way the bike happens to be leaning at the time. You have to force the bike to lean over in the appropriate direction and under the right angle consistent with the direction and radius of the turn. And it has to be done quickly.

Do that by sharply steering away from the turn just before you get there. You and the bike will immediately start to lean over in the direction of the turn. You would risk a disastrous crash, as your bike moves away precipitously from the mass center, if you were to continue in a straight line. You have very quickly achieved a considerable lean angle in the direction of the turn. This must be compensated by steering quite abruptly in the same direction. Since this is the direction of the turn, you are set up just right to make a sharp turn. Once completed, steer back into the turn just a little further, to get the lean for regaining the roughly straight course, as explained for the natural turn.

The forced turn technique must also be practiced intensely and consciously, since it by no means comes naturally. Initiating a left turn by steering right will probably require the beginning cyclists to overcome all sorts of reasonable inhibitions and demands lots of practice. Take your bike to a grassy area or an empty parking lot a few days in a row, wearing protective clothing in case you fall: helmet, gloves, jacket and long pants.

Practice and experiment until you've mastered the trick, and refresh your skill from time to time, until this instant turning technique has become second nature. Figures 10.2 and 10.3 allow a comparison between the paths taken in the natural and the forced turn, respectively. The latter one will not only be helpful when taking a tight turn, but

is of equal benefit when you need to temporarily divert from your straight course for one reason or the other. In a subsequent section of this chapter you will be shown how to apply it to the difficult task of avoiding a suddenly appearing obstacle.

Braking Technique
The touring cyclist often has to use the brakes, though not always to make a panic stop. In fact, the sensible cyclist should hardly ever have to brake to a standstill. Instead, you will be using the brakes to control and regulate your speed. That may be necessary under touring conditions just as frequently as it does when riding in town or when racing, since the loaded bike and the sometimes less than perfect roads may dictate sudden changes in riding speed to remain safely in control of the bike.

Effective braking means that you can ride up fast close to the turn or the obstacle which requires the reduced speed, brake to reach the lower speed quickly, and accelerate immediately afterwards. So you will be using the brakes to get down in speed from 30 to 20 MPH to take a turn, or from 30 to 28 MPH to avoid running into the person ahead of you. Or you may have to get down from 50 to 10 MPH to handle a switchback or hairpin curve on a steep descent. To do that effectively without risk requires an understanding of braking physics. Though at times you may have to reduce speed quickly, you should also develop a feel for gradual speed reduction to prevent skidding and loss of control. In fact, most cyclists are more often in danger due to braking too vigorously than due to insufficient stopping power.

Braking amounts to deceleration or speed reduction, which can only take place gradually. The rate of deceleration can be measured and is expressed in m/sec^2. A deceleration of 1 m/sec^2 means that after each second of braking the travelling speed is 1 m/sec less than it was at the beginning of that second. A speed of 30 MPH corresponds to 13 m/sec. To get down to standstill would take 13 sec, if the braking deceleration is 1 m/sec^2; it would take 4 seconds to reach 9 m/sec or 20 MPH. At a higher rate of deceleration it would take less time (and a shorter distance) to get down to the desired speed.

Fig. 10.4 Effect of braking

The modern derailleur bicycle has remarkably effective brakes, providing it's not raining. A modest force on the brake handle can cause a deceleration of 4–5 m/sec^2 with just one brake. Applying both brakes, the effect is even more dramatic, enabling you to slow down from 30 to 15 MPH within one second. There are some limitations to braking that have to be considered, though.

In the first place, rain has a negative effect on the rim brake's performance, as the build-up of water on the rims reduces the friction between brake block and rim drastically. This applies especially if the thing is equipped with ordinary rubber brake blocks, as offered by most manufacturers as standard equipment. With any rubber brake blocks, I measured a reduction from 4.5 to 1.5 m/sec^2 for a given hand lever force (and to half that figure for bicycles with chrome plated steel rims, which should therefore not be used, even on the cheap bicycles on which they are installed). Lately, some special brake block materials have been introduced that are less sensitive to rain.

The second restriction is associated with a change in the distribution of weight between the wheels as a result of braking. Because the mass center of the rider is quite high above the road, and its horizontal distance to the front wheel axle comparatively small, the bicycle has a tendency to tip forward in response to deceleration. Weight is transferred from the rear to the front of the bike, as illustrated in Fig. 10.4. When the deceleration reaches about 3.5 m/sec^2 the weight on the rear wheel is no longer enough to provide traction, even when the rear wheel is loaded down with luggage. Braking harder than that with the rear brake just makes the rear wheel skid, resulting in loss of control.

In a typical riding posture, the rear wheel actually starts to lift off the ground when a deceleration of about 6.5 m/sec^2 is reached, whether using both brakes together or the front brake alone. Consequently, no conventional bicycle can ever be decelerated beyond this limit, regardless of the kind, number and quality of the brakes. This is a very high deceleration, which you should not often reach, but it is good to realize there is such a limit and that it can not be avoided by using the rear brake either alone or in addition to the front brake, but only by braking less vigorously. During a sudden speed reduction or panic stop, such high decelerations may be reached. On a downslope the effect will be even more pronounced, since it raises the rider even higher relative to the front wheel. In all such cases, reduce the toppling-over effect by shifting your body weight back and down as much as possible: sit far back and hold the upper body horizontally.

Since about twice as great a deceleration is possible with the front brake as with the one in the rear, the former should be preferably used under most conditions. In most circumstances short of a panic stop, you can brake very effectively using the front brake alone. When both brakes are used simultaneously, the one in the front can be applied quite a bit harder than the one in the rear. If you notice the rear brake is less effective if pressed equally far, it will be time to check, and if necessary adjust, lubricate or replace the brake cable.

Of course, most braking is not done abruptly. Gradual braking must also be practiced. In particular when the road is slick, in curves or when others are following closely behind, gradual deceleration and the ability to control the braking force within narrow limits is of vital importance. Practice braking consciously with utmost attention to the complex relationship between initial speed, brake lever force and deceleration, to become fully competent at handling the bike when slowing down under all conceivable circumstances.

Braking becomes a different kettle of fish in hilly terrain. On a steep downhill, the slope not only increases the tendency to tip forward, it also induces an accelerating effect, which must be overcome by the brakes even to merely keep the speed constant. A 20% slope, which is admittedly rarely encountered, induces an acceleration of about 2 m/sec^2. Obviously, you will encounter big problems in wet weather on such a downhill stretch if you don't keep your speed down to start with. So it will be necessary to reduce the speed by gradual, intermittent braking. This will help wipe most of the water from the rims, retaining braking efficiency a little better. This way, the brakes are not overtaxed when you do have to reduce the speed suddenly, as may be required to handle an unexpected obstacle or a sharp turn.

Effective braking must be practiced, to achieve complete control of the bicycle under normal and difficult cycling conditions. In particular, the dramatic difference between the bike's behavior when braking on the straight and in a curve must be experienced to be appreciated. Again, this is a matter for conscious practice in a place without traffic. Include braking in your regular exercises during the first weeks of cycling preparation. Even after you have been riding for some time, you may be well advised to repeat practice sessions, as outlined for steering and braking control in this chapter, from time to time. It will pay off when touring.

Basic Riding Techniques

Riding a derailleur bicycle with total confidence requires hands-on experience. That might be considered a good reason to ride lots of miles before you go on your first tour. But some of the associated skills can be learned faster and more thoroughly when you understand the principles that are applied. Building up on the information about posture, gearing, steering and braking provided in the preceding sections, you will be shown here what to do under various typical riding situations. The many miles of experience will come soon enough when you start touring. However, the handling practice is gained more effectively when applying these techniques consciously.

Getting up to Speed

Though the touring cyclist is not into cycling for speed alone, he should learn to reach an acceptable speed quickly and smoothly in order to ride enjoyably and effectively. In Chapter 8 you have been shown how to get on the bike and start off smoothly. The next trick is to reach the ultimate riding speed as quickly and efficiently as possible. The idea is to waste as little time and energy as possible during this process of getting up to speed. Tricky, because acceleration demands disproportionately high levels of power and consumes energy correspondingly. And the faster it's done, the more demanding it is.

Clearly, you have to strike a balance here. Accelerating faster than necessary wastes energy that will be sorely needed later. Done too slowly, it may become a plodding affair. It will be your decision to find the right balance between speed and power, but the way to reach it is easy to describe: start in a low gear and increase speed gradually but rapidly. No fast and slow spurts but a gradual build-up of speed.

Either keep pedalling faster and faster in the low gear, changing up only as you reach a significant speed, or be prepared to do some short duration hard work, standing on the pedals, pulling on the upstroke, as well as pushing on the downstroke. As soon as speed is reached, sit on the saddle and select

a good gear for spinning at a comfortable but high pedalling rate.

Riding a Constant Speed

With a small measuring device called accelerometer one can follow the changes in riding speed of a cyclist travelling at speed. It has been found that the most effective riders tend to be those whose speed varies least over time. Not only does a good cyclist ride the same number of miles one hour as the next, he travels as many yards one minute as the next, as many feet with one crank revolution as the next, and indeed ideally as many inches during each section within any revolution. If you slow down during one short section, it will take disproportionately more time and energy to make up for the loss.

Pay attention to this at all times while cycling. As long as the external conditions don't change drastically, you should make every effort to keep a constant speed and movement. Gauge your speed by comparing it to that of your companions, or use your watch, counting out pedal revolutions and milestones when cycling alone.

Accelerating

However efficient a constant speed may be, sometimes you will still want to accelerate to a higher speed. This may be necessary to catch up with riders ahead, so you can take advantage of the wind-breaking effect by riding immediately behind them, or to avoid getting dropped behind. In traffic, you may have to accelerate in situations like getting across an intersection before the light changes or to avoid running into another vehicle.

As with getting up to speed in the first place, it is most efficient to increase the speed as gradually as

Fig. 10.5 Group cycling against the wind

Fig. 10.6 Group cycling with cross wind

Riding Against the Wind

At higher speeds or whenever there is a head wind, the effect of air drag on the power needed to cycle is quite significant. Economize on your effort by avoiding the wind resistance as much as possible. Keep your profile as low as possible when cycling against the wind. Especially when riding alone, try to seek out the sheltered parts of the road wherever possible, without exposing yourself to danger.

When you ride in a group, try to exploit the wind shelter effect of riding immediately behind another rider, or staggered appropriately when there is a cross wind. This technique is referred to as drafting in the US or pacing in Britain. Figures 10.5 and 10.6 show the resulting configurations for situations without and with cross wind, respectively.

Hill Climbing

Climbing uphill by bike is not just another skill that can be learned equally well by all, it also requires a certain physique for greatest effectiveness. With some conscious effort, everybody's climbing skills can be improved up to a point; yet some riders are born climbers, while others may have to go uphill slowly all their lives. What it takes is a high power to weight ratio. To put it differently, you need a big heart and voluminous lungs relative to the total body mass. In general, a low body weight will be advantageous. Just the same, it is an ability that can be learned and developed well enough by the average rider to at least handle all hills you encounter, even if you go up slowly.

Again, a regular motion is most efficient, and that is best mastered by staying seated in a rather low gear. For a hilly tour, you should take the trouble to equip the bike with

possible. Unless you are already spinning at your highest possible rate, you will find accelerating by increasing pedalling speed more effective than by increasing pedal force in a higher gear. In other words, as long as you can spin faster, it is best to shift down into a slightly lower gear and increase the pedalling rate vigorously. Once you are gathering momentum and are getting close to your maximum spinning speed, shift up and continue to gain speed in the slightly higher gear.

wider ratio gearing than for level riding. Just what sizes of sprockets should be installed is up to you, but I'd say 90% of all beginners tend to pick gear ratios that are too high (or, to put it differently, sprockets that are too small). There should be nothing embarrassing about a rear sprocket with 34 teeth and a chainwheel with 36 or even fewer teeth in the back for mountainous terrain. Many touring bikes, and particularly mountain bikes, are equipped with such extreme gears, which are low enough to tackle almost any hill without having to get up from the saddle.

weight on left leg   weight on right leg

Fig. 10.7 Honking uphill

Climbing out of the Saddle

When the lowest available gear is too high to allow a smoothly spinning leg motion, it is time to shift to another technique. Some riders try to increase the length of the power stroke by means of some hefty ankle twisting, really pushing the leg around at this point. That is an unnecessarily tiring technique, requiring long muscle work phases and short recovery periods. A better method of high gear, low pedalling speed climbing is referred to as honking in Britain, and seems to be a mystery to most American cyclists.

Honking makes use of the rider's body weight to push down the pedals, whereas the body is pulled up after each stroke very quickly by standing up. In this mode, the muscle work is done each time the body is raised, rather than when pushing the pedal down and around. To do it effectively, hold the tops of the brake handle mounts in the front of the handlebars. You can either take quick snappy steps or throw your weight from side to side in a swinging motion, as illustrated in Fig. 10.7. I suggest you practice honking as well as spinning: the one

VERY BRIEFLY STEER IN OPPOSITE DIRECTION TO INDUCE LEAN

STEER BACK TO CORRESPOND TO INDUCED LEAN

CORRECT COURSE

Fig. 10.8 Avoiding an obstacle

in a high gear at pedalling speeds below 55 RPM, the other in a low gear at 65 RPM or more. Avoid pedalling rates of 55–65 RPM by choosing the gearing range to stay within either the one range or the other.

Avoiding Obstacles

Oftentimes, you will be confronted with some kind of obstacle right in your path. This may be anything from a pothole or a broken branch to a discarded can or bottle. Even when travelling at speed and with little room to maneuver, you can learn to avoid running into such things by using the technique of the forced turn described in a preceding section. This maneuver is illustrated in Fig. 10.8.

As soon as you perceive the obstacle ahead of you, decide whether to pass it to the left or the right. Ride straight up to it and then, before you reach it, briefly but decisively steer into the direction opposite to that of your chosen avoidance (to the right if you want to pass on the left). This makes the bike lean over towards the other side (to the left in this case). Now steer in that direction just as quickly, which will result in a very sharp forced turn. As soon as you've passed the obstacle, oversteer a little more, to cause a lean that helps you put the bike back on its proper course.

This too is something to practice on an empty parking lot, wearing a helmet and two long sleeved shirt (the double layer of fabric is much easier on the skin, since the one layer will just slip off the other, rather than removing chunks of your flesh). Mark phoney obstacles with chalk or place foam pads or sponges on the road, and practice passing them abruptly on both sides until you've mastered the trick.

Jumping the Bike

Another weird but useful act for hard riding situations is the skill of making first the front, then the rear wheel jump over or through an obstacle. You may have to do that when there is an unavoidable obstacle ahead of you. It's a matter of shifting your weight back or forth to lift the appropriate wheel off the ground. To jump up, first throw your weight backwards, while pulling up on the handlebars to unload while lifting the front wheel. At the same time accelerate vigorously, by pushing hard on the forward pedal. With some practice, you'll soon be able to lift the front end of the bike at least a foot up in the air.

Next, try to do the same with the rear wheel, throwing your weight forward while pulling up your legs and bottom at the same time. This is harder, but it can also be mastered. Finally, practice coordinating the two shifts, so that you first lift the front and then, as soon as you've reached the highest point, start raising the back. After some time, you should be able to actually make the bike fly: lift both wheels in such short sequence that the rear wheel comes off the ground well before the front wheel comes down.

One variant of this technique is the art of jumping up sideways, which may be needed to handle obstacles like curbs, ridges and tracks that run nearly parallel to the road. To do this, the bike has to be forced to move sideways in a short and snappy diversion just preceding the jump. Do that by combining the diversion technique described above under *Avoiding Obstacles* with the jump. Fig. 10.9 shows how this can be done.

Get close to the ridge you want to jump, riding parallel to it. Then briefly steer away from the ridge. This

Fig. 10.9 Jumping sideways

immediately causes the bike to lean towards the obstacle. Now catch yourself by steering sharply in that same direction, lifting the front wheel when you are close to the obstacle, immediately followed by the rear wheel. Practice is all it takes, and the empty parking lot with a chalk line as a substitute ridge will be the best place to do that.

Sometimes, you will have to ride through a big pothole or any other depression in the road surface. To do that with minimal risk to bike and rider, you can use something akin to the jumping technique. Enter the depression with your weight near the front of the bike. Then unload the front wheel by throwing your weight back and pulling up the handlebars, just before the front wheel hits the lowest point of the depression.

Fig. 10.10 Traversing a depression

Finally, ride up the other side and pull up the rear, while shifting your weight to the front of the bike to climb back out. This technique is particularly useful when cycling off-road. In open terrain, select your route through the depression so as to avoid too abrupt a drop and subsequent climb, as illustrated in Fig. 10.10.

11
Bicycle Safety and Health

Bicycling is not an entirely riskless undertaking. Neither are many other pursuits, but what scares off potential cyclists most is probably the danger of being involved in a collision with a motor vehicle. Yes, that chance exists in bicycle touring, as it does when crossing the street in front of your own house. Actually, this is but one of several kinds of possible injury causes in bicycling. You can learn to avoid most of the risks and minimize the impact of

these and other injuries or other health hazards. That is the subject of the present chapter.

Considering the various risks, ranging from those to your own body and equipment to the harm or loss you may cause others, it may be smart to take out some kind of insurance. Personal liability insurance is perhaps the most important one of these. In addition, you may want to make sure you have adequate health insurance to cover the dangers of the road as well as whatever may happen to you while travelling, especially if you go abroad.

Cycling on the South Island in New Zealand, you may have to wait a while to let several thousand sheep cross the road. (Photograph courtesy Backroads)

If you are used to a society like the British, where a National Health Service takes care of your health needs, you may be astonished what a little health care can cost you abroad – and that many of those who administer such services expect to be paid on the spot when dealing with a foreign traveller. Finally, you may like to take out a travel insurance, making sure your bike and other equipment is covered.

In addition, it would be a good idea to learn how to deal with accidents, injuries, sickness and other health related emergencies while touring. Do you really know what to do when you are bleeding, when you think you may have broken something, when one of your companions faints or is seriously hurt? Take a first aid course to be prepared for dealing with the unanticipated. That is a lot smarter than shutting your eyes, hoping nothing serious will happen. Even if you are spared yourself, you may be able to save someone else's life. If you can't for some reason follow a first aid course, at least read up on the subject – appropriate literature is included in the Bibliography.

The Risks of Bicycling

Quite a lot of research has been done in recent years on the subject of bicycle accidents and injuries. Some of these studies were specifically oriented to bicycle touring, such as the survey by Jerrold Kaplan of the injuries reported during the first year of the Bikecentennial program. Other reports are largely based on either day-to-day cycling experiences typical in an urban environment or on the accidents reported by club cyclists, racers or students. To summarize the available evidence in a nutshell, the majority of bicycle accidents are attribut-

able to a very limited number of typical mistakes, most of which can be either avoided or counteracted by intelligent cycling techniques.

Of course, accidents, collisions and falls are not the only forms of injury to the cyclist, even though they are the most obvious. When talking to experienced bicyclists, you will soon find out that other forms of injury causes are often of more concern in those circles. Saddle sores and torn tendons, inflamed knees and numb hands rank higher than broken collarbones and cracked skulls in their conversation about injuries, even though they get their share of broken bones too. We will take a look at both categories.

Perhaps the most important lesson to learn from the investigations dealing with the safety of touring cyclists concerns the correlation between risk and trip length. Put simply, the likelihood of getting hurt – be it as a result of a traffic accident or a fall – increases dramatically after a daily distance of 70 miles. That applies especially to cyclists carrying luggage and handling difficult terrain, and most dramatically to inexperienced riders. Hence the following advice: certainly if you are new to bike touring and carry luggage, keep your daily distance down to no more than 70 miles to minimize the risk.

Another significant finding is that the more experienced cyclists have markedly fewer accidents, and can go longer distances before being exposed to the greater risk. This is one good argument to try and gain experience and skills as quickly as possible. Following the advice contained in the preceding chapters not only increases the joy, satisfaction and effectiveness of your cycling, it also drastically reduces the risk to which you are exposed when touring.

Traffic Hazards

In the Bikecentennial survey of long distance touring cyclists, only two fatal accidents occurred, which is sad enough. However, fatal accidents are only a small percentage of all injuries, and numerous quite serious accidents do occur. Though the majority of all injured cyclists themselves are largely to blame for their injuries, there always will be some accidents that are directly attributable to bullying and inconsiderate motorists.

Unfortunately, this type of accident forms a high proportion of those that experienced cyclists encounter. These riders have learned to handle their machines rationally and safely in traffic, thus virtually eliminating their risk concerning the more common kind of accidents to which the incompetent are exposed. Having practically eliminated the latter, they are just as vulnerable to the remaining irrational dangers of the road.

The only defense against inconsiderate road users is not to provoke them. Give in, even if that seems highly unfair. It's an unequal battle and sometimes it's just smarter not to insist on justice. You will encounter fewer of these particular risks if you avoid the kind of situations where they are most likely: Sunday afternoons and late evenings, when boisterous drunks are many on the road. Oddly enough, these accidents are also more likely on relatively lightly travelled roads near smaller towns. Though I realize that busy roads near big cities do not make the ideal bicycle touring environment, you may try to avoid the quiet roads near smaller towns at high-risk times.

Most accidents, of course, are not of this type. They simply happen while two people make a mistake each: one initiates a wrong move, and the other fails to react in such a way that a collision is avoided. Keep that in mind when cycling. Remain alert for the possible mistakes others may make, and try to avoid doing the unexpected or unconsidered yourself as much as humanly possible. Anticipate not only the predictable, but also the unexpected: the motorist looming behind the next corner or intersection, the dog appearing from a driveway, or the bicyclist suddenly crossing your path in the dark without lights.

Ultraspec: stylish and functional eye protection from Rhode Gear, to keep sun, wind, dust and insects out of your eyes. Available to fit directly or over the top of prescription glasses.

The latter subject deserves special attention, but the only way to arm yourself is to make sure you do not cycle out after dark without lights yourself, so at least *you* can be seen. Proper lighting on the bike is needed in addition to the curiously ineffective array of reflectors that is increasingly prescribed by law in various countries. The gravest danger of reflectors lies in the inappropriate impression they transmit of your visibility, whereas in reality several of them only make you visible to those who do not endanger you anyway. A bright light in the front and a big rear light or reflector facing back are essential, while all the other goodies won't do a thing that the former wouldn't do more effectively.

Most accidents occur by daylight, even though the relative risk is greater at night. Whether by day or at night, cycle with all your senses alert. In general, ride your bike as you would drive your car, always verifying whether the road ahead of you is clear, and taking particular care to select your path wisely at junctions and intersections. As a relatively slow vehicle, you must look behind you, to ascertain that nobody is following closely, before you move over into another traffic lane or away from your previous path.

Forget anything you ever heard about bikes being different from motor vehicles. As a wheeled vehicle, your bike answers to the same laws of physics as does your car. Adhere to the most basic rules of traffic as you learned them to handle a car as well, and you'll be safe on a bike. No doubt the worst advice ever given to cyclists in many parts of the US is to ride on the side of the road where a pedestrian would go, namely facing traffic. On a bike you *are* the traffic, and you belong on the same side as all other vehicles travelling the same way.

The rules of the road as applied to motor vehicles are based on a system that has gradually evolved. This system works the way it does because it is logical. If it is dangerous for motorists to do certain things, then it will be at least as dangerous on a bike. This applies equally when travelling abroad, although it will be smart to prepare for the peculiar kind of laws that have been instituted in some societies which discriminatorily relegate bicycles to an inferior (and invariably more dangerous) place on the road.

In general, whatever you may be inclined to think, the most dangerous societies are those where bicyclists are offered many separate bicycle paths and where different laws apply to cyclists than to other road users. France, Italy and England are wonderful cycling countries, whereas Holland, Belgium, Germany and Denmark are high-risk societies to rational bicyclists.

Thus, for example, in Denmark the bicyclist is expected to carry out the most dangerous maneuver when turning left, turning from the RH side of the road, crossing the path of all traffic continuing straight or turning right. I can not possibly give you full instructions on the kinds of superhuman skills you have to master in order to satisfy such peculiarities of the laws in every country. Get this information from the host country's motoring organization, touring club or tourist office before leaving.

In any traffic system, don't hug the curb but claim your place on the road. Your place is about 1.80 m (6 ft) to the right of the centerline of the path normally taken by cars on a wide road. Keep at least 90 cm (3 ft) away from the inside edge, even if

Fig. 11.1 Correct path at intersection

the road is too narrow to stay clear to the right of the normal path of motor vehicles. Don't dart in and out around parked vehicles and other obstructions along the side of the road. When making a turn, adhere to the method outlined in Fig. 11.1 (assuming RH traffic). Thus, to go straight at an intersection, make sure you will not be overtaken by vehicles turning right. To turn right, get close to the RH edge. To turn left, choose a path near the center of the road or the middle of a traffic lane marked for that direction well before the actual intersection, after having established that you will not be cutting across the path of vehicles following closely behind.

Excessive attention is often paid to hand signals in traffic education for cyclists. Yes, you should signal your intention before you do things like diverting, turning off or slowing down. That applies particularly when cycling with others in a group, where the first person also should point out and audibly identify obstacles or hazards in the road. But avoid the dangerous habit of assuming a hand

signal will ward off danger. Your hand is not a magic wand, and if somebody is following so closely that you can signal to him your intention of turning across his path, you should not do that. Instead, wait until your maneuver does not interfere with traffic following closely behind.

The most feared type of bicycle accident is the one that involves being hit from behind. These accidents do happen, and both the fatal accidents that occurred during the Bikecentennial survey were of this type. Though there is hardly any defense possible to ward them off, it is worth considering that they are characterized by a number of common factors. They invariably occur on otherwise deserted roads, where the attention of motorist and cyclist alike are at a low, since both feel perfectly secure.

Inconspicuous clothing, a low sun, blinding one or both participants, and a lack of the cyclist's awareness, due to tiredness at the end of a long day, are also common features. It may be smart to increase your conspicuity. Wearing brightly visible colors, such as yellow, pink, orange or bright green, may well help others spot you in time to avoid this type of accident.

Falls and Collisions
Whether or not a motor vehicle is involved, virtually every injury to the cyclist in all falls and collisions results from the impact when the cyclist falls off the bike. He either hits the road surface, an object on or along the road, the colliding vehicle or the bike itself. The same skills necessary to prevent traffic accidents involving cars will keep you from experiencing most of the other types of falls and collisions. Be watchful, consider the effects of your own actions, and use the tech-

Fig. 11.2 Collision avoidance maneuvers

nical skills described in the preceding chapter to divert when the situation becomes threatening. Four types of falls and collisions can be distinguished: stopping, diverting, skidding and loss of control. Here I shall first describe these accidents, followed by a few hints about preventing and treating the typical injuries that may result.

Stopping Accidents

In a stopping accident, the bicycle runs into an obstacle that halts its progress. Depending on the cyclist's speed, the impact can be very serious. As the bicycle itself is stopped, inertia keeps the rider going forward, throwing him against or over the handlebars. The kinetic energy of the moving mass will be dissipated very suddenly, often in an unfortunate location. Your genitals may hit the handlebar stem or your skull may crash onto either the road surface or the object with which the bike collided.

The way to guard yourself against these accidents is to look and think ahead, so you don't run into any obstacles. If necessary, control your speed to allow handling the unexpected when a potential danger may be looming up behind the next corner. Learn to apply the diverting

technique described in the preceding chapter, and as illustrated here in Fig. 11.2. The way to minimize the impact of the most serious form of stopping accident is by wearing an energy absorbing helmet, which will be discussed more fully below.

Diverting Accidents

A diverting type accident occurs when the front wheel is pushed sideways by an external force, while the rider is not leaning in the same direction to regain balance. Typical causes are railway tracks, cracks in the road surface, the edge of the road, but also touching another rider's rear wheel with your front wheel. The effect is that you fall sideways and hit the road or some obstacle by the side of the road. Depending how unexpectedly it happened, you may be able to break the fall by stretching out an arm, which seems to be an automatic reflex in this situation.

Characteristic injuries range from abrasions and lacerations of the hands and the sides of arms and legs to bruised hips and sprained or broken wrists. More serious cases, usually incurred at higher speeds, may involve broken collarbones and injuries to the face or the side of the skull. The impact of the lesser injuries can be minimized by wearing padded gloves and double layers of clothing with long sleeves and legs. Wearing a helmet will minimize damage to the side of the head, especially at elevated speeds.

Diverting accidents can often be avoided if the cyclist is both careful and alert. Keep an eye out for the typical danger situations. Don't overlap wheels with other riders, don't approach surface ridges under a shallow angle. A last second diversion can often be made along the lines of the diverting technique described in Chapter 10. In the case of a ridge in the road surface, use the technique of sideways jumping, also described there. When your front wheel touches the rear wheel of another rider, or if your handlebars are pushed over by an outside force, you may sometimes save the day if you react by immediately leaning in the direction into which you were diverted, and then steer to regain control.

Skidding Accidents
When the bicycle keeps going or goes in an unintended direction, despite your efforts to brake or steer, it will be due to skidding between the tires and the road surface. This kind of thing happens more frequently when the road is slick on account of moisture, frost, loose sand or fallen leaves. Especially under these conditions, sudden diversions or movements, hard braking and excessive lean when cornering may all cause skidding either forward or sideways.

Skidding accidents often also cause the cyclist to fall sideways, resulting in abrasions, lacerations or more rarely fractures. Avoid them by checking the road surface ahead and avoiding sudden steering or braking maneuvers and excessive

leaning in curves. Cross slick patches, ranging from wet or greasy asphalt or railway tracks, from sand or leaves on the road to the white lines used as road markings, with the bicycle upright. Achieve that by carrying out the requisite steering and balancing actions *before* you reach such danger spots.

If you can not avoid it, once you feel you are entering a skid, try to move your weight towards the back of the bike as much as possible, sliding back on the saddle and stretching the arms. Follow the bike, rather than trying to force it back. Finally, don't do what seems an obvious reaction to the less experienced, namely getting off the saddle to straddle the top tube with one leg dangling. As with so many cycling techniques, skidding can also be practiced in a relatively safe environment on an empty parking lot.

Loss of Control Accidents
At higher speeds, especially in a steep descent, loss of control accidents sometimes occur. In this case, you just can't steer the bike the way you intend to go. This happens when you find yourself having to steer in one direction at a time when you are leaning the other way, or when speed control braking initiates unexpected oscillations. Often this situation develops into a collision or a fall along the lines of either one of the two accident types described above.

Prevention is only possible with experience: don't go faster than the speed at which you feel in control. The more you ride under various situations, the more you will develop a feel for what is a safe speed, when to brake and how to steer to maintain control over the bike. Once the situation sets in, try to keep your cool. Don't panic. Follow the bike, rather than forcing it over. The worst thing you can do is to tense up and get off the saddle. Stay in touch with handlebars, seat and pedals, steering in the direction of your lean. This way, you may well get out of it without falling or colliding, though your nerves may have suffered.

Treating Abrasions

Abrasions, referred to in club cycling circles as road rash, are the most common cycling injury resulting from any kind of fall. They usually heal relatively fast, though they can be quite painful. Wash out the wound with water and soap, and remove any particles of road dirt to prevent infection. There may be a risk of tetanus if the wound draws blood. If you have been immunized against tetanus, get a tetanus shot within 24 hours only if the last one was more than two years ago.

If you have never been immunized before, get a full immunization, consisting of two shot within 24 hours, followed by two more after two weeks and six months, respectively. Apply a dressing only if the location is covered by clothing, since the wound will heal faster when exposed to the air. Avoid the formation of a scab by treating the wound with an antibiotic salve. See a doctor if any signs of infection occur, such as swelling, itching or fever.

Sprained Limbs

In case of a fall, your tendency to stick out an arm to break the impact may result in a sprained or even a fractured wrist. In other accident situations this can also happen to the knee or the ankle. Spraining is really nothing but damage to the ligaments that surround and hold the various parts of a joint together. Typical symptoms are a local sensation of heat, itching and swelling.

Whenever possible, keep the area cold with an ice bag. If you feel a stinging pain or if fever develops, get medical advice, because it may actually be a fracture that was at first incorrectly diagnosed as a sprain. This may be the case when the fracture takes the form of a simple 'clean' crack without superficially visible deformation of the bone.

Fractures

Typical cycling fractures are those of the wrist and the collarbone, both caused when falling: the one when extending the arm to brake the fall, the other when you don't have time to do that. You or medical personnel may not at first notice a clean fracture as described above: there may be one without any outward sign.

If there is a stinging pain when the part is moved or touched, I suggest you get an X-ray to make sure, even if a fracture is not immediately obvious. You'll need medical help to set and bandage the fractured location, and you must give up cycling (except perhaps on the windload simulator or home trainer, if you are into fitness maintenance at all) until it is healed, which will take about five weeks. Sad if that happens during a bicycle tour, but better than continuing in agony.

Brain Injury

If you fall on your head in any kind of fall or collision, the impact may smash the brain against the inside of the skull, followed by the reverse action as it bounces back. The human brain can usually withstand this kind of treatment without lasting damage if the resulting deceleration does not exceed about 300 G or 3000 m/sec^2. Look at it this way: the head probably falls to the ground from a height of 1.5 m (5 ft).

This results in a speed of 5 m/sec^2 at the time of impact. To keep the deceleration down below 3000 m/sec^2, this speed must be reduced to zero in no less than 0.002 sec.

Neither your skull, nor the object with which you collide is likely to deform gradually enough to achieve even that kind of deceleration. That's why energy absorbing helmets with thick crushable foam shells were developed. Neither flexible nor rigid materials will do the trick by themselves. It's not a bad idea to have a hard outer shell cover to distribute the load of a point impact, and it is nice to get some comfort inside from a soft flexible liner, but the crushing of about ¾ inch of seemingly brittle foam is essential to absorb the shock. The minimum requirement for a safe helmet is the American standard ANSI Z-90.4.

Even the best cyclists sometimes fall. The Soviet racer Oleg Logvin practicing impromptu head protection. (Photograph John Swanda)

Other Health Problems

The remaining part of this chapter will be devoted to the health hazards of cycling that have nothing to do with falling off the bike. We will look at the most common complaints and discuss some methods of prevention, as well as possible cures. This brief description can not cover the entire field. Nor should most of the issues discussed here be generalized too lightly. The same symptoms may have different causes in different cases; conversely, the same cure may not work for two superficially similar problems. Yet in most cases the following remarks will apply.

Saddle Sores

Though beginning bicyclists may at first feel uncomfortable on the bike seat, they have no idea what kind of agony real seat problems can bring. In bicycle touring, much more than in racing, you have the opportunity to avoid the most serious seat problems by taking it easy for one or two days when symptoms start to develop. Racers – and long distance touring cyclists in a hurry – often have a much harder time at it. What happens during the many hours in the saddle is that the combined effect of perspiration, pressure and chafing causes cracks in the skin where bacteria can enter. The result can be anything from a mild inflammation to the most painful boils.

There is of course little chance of these things healing as long as you continue riding vigorously. As soon as any pressure is applied, when you sit on a bike seat, things will get worse. Prevention and early relief are the methods to combat saddle sores. The clue to both is hygiene. Wash and dry both your crotch and your cycling shorts after every day's ride. Many bicyclists also treat the affected areas with rubbing alcohol, which both disinfects and increases the skin's resistance to chafing, or with talcum powder, which prevents further damage.

You'll need at least two pairs of shorts on a longer tour or when going on frequent day rides, so you can always rely on a clean, dry pair when you go out. Wash them out, taking particular care to get the chamois clean, and hang them out to dry thoroughly, preferably outside, where the sun's ultraviolet rays may act to kill any remaining bacteria. Treat the chamois with either talcum powder or a special treatment for that purpose. I prefer to use a water soluble cream, such as Noxema, since it is easier to wash out.

The quality of your saddle and your riding position may also affect the development of crotch problems. If early symptoms appear in the form of redness or soreness, consider getting a softer saddle, sitting further to the back of your saddle, or lowering the handlebars a little to reduce the pressure on the seat. If the problem gets out of hand, take a rest from cycling until the sores have fully healed. In the meantime, consider another touring activity, such as hiking or sightseeing.

Knee Problems

Because the cycling movement does not apply the high impacting shock loads on the legs that are associated with running, it's surprising that knee problems are so prevalent. They are mainly concentrated with two groups of cyclists: beginners and very strong, muscular riders. In both cases, the cause seems to be pushing too high a gear. This places excessive forces on the knee joint, resulting in damage to the membranes that separate the moving portions of the joint and the ligaments holding the bits and pieces together. In cold weather the problems get aggravated, so it will be wise to wear long pants whenever the temperature is below 18°C (65°F), especially if fast descents are involved.

Prevent excessive forces on the knee joint by gearing so low that you can spin lightly under all conditions, avoiding especially climbing in the saddle with pedalling speeds below 60 RPM. Equip your bicycle with the kind of gear ratios that allow you to do that, and choose a lower gear whenever necessary. Once the problem has developed, either giving up cycling or riding loosely in low gears will aid the healing process. I suggest you continue cycling in very low gears, spinning freely. That will probably prepare you to get back into shape, while forcing you to avoid the high gears that caused the problem in the first place.

Tendonitus

This is an infection of the Achilles tendon, which attaches the big muscle of the lower leg, the gastrocnemius, to the heel bone. It is an important tendon in cycling, since the pedalling force can not be applied to the foot without it. It sometimes gets damaged or torn under the same kind of conditions as described above for knee injuries: cycling with too much force in too high a gear. The problem is aggravated by low temperatures, which explains why it generally develops in the early season.

To avoid tendonitis, wear long woollen socks whenever the temperature is below 18°C (65°F). It may also help to wear shoes that come up quite high, maximizing the support they provide. Get used to riding with a supple movement in a low gear, which seems to be the clue to preventing many cycling complaints. Healing requires rest, followed by a return to cycling with minimum pedal force in a low gear.

Numbness

Especially beginning cyclists, not yet used to riding longer distances, sometimes develop a loss of feeling in certain areas of contact with the bike. The most typical location is the hands, but it also occurs in the feet

Cycling over a bridge crossing the waterfall near Logan Pass in Montana. (Photograph courtesy Backroads)

and the crotch. This is caused by excessive and unvaried prolonged pressure on the nerves and blood vessels. The effects are usually relieved with rest, though they have at times been felt for several days.

Once the problem develops, get relief by changing your position frequently, moving the hands from one part of the handlebars to the other, or moving from one area of the seat to the other if the crotch is affected. To prevent the numbness in the various locations, use well padded gloves, foam handlebar covers, a soft saddle in a slightly higher position, or thick soled shoes with cushioned inner soles, laced loosely at the bottom but tightly higher up, depending on the location of the numbness.

Back Ache

Many riders complain of aches in the back, the lower neck and the shoulders, especially early in the season. These are probably attributable to insufficient training of the muscles in those locations. It is largely the result of unfamiliar isometric muscle work, keeping still in a forward bent position. This condition may also be partly caused or aggravated by low temperatures, so it is wise to wear warm bicycle clothing in cool weather.

To avoid the early-season reconditioning complaints, the best remedy is not to interrupt cycling in winter. Even two longer rides a week at a moderate pace, or extended use of a home trainer with a proper low riding position, will do the trick. Alternately, you may start off in the new season with a slightly higher handlebar position and once more a low gear. Sleeping on a firm mattress and keeping warm also seems to either help alleviate or prevent the problem.

Sinus and Bronchial Complaints

Especially in the cooler periods, many cyclists develop breathing problems, originating either in the sinuses or the bronchi. The same may happen when a rider used to cycling at sea level gets into the mountains, where the cold air in a fast descent'can be very unsettling. It's generally attributable to undercooling, the only solution being to dress warmer and to cycle slowly enough to allow breathing through the nose.

After a demanding climb in cooler weather, do not strip off warm clothing, open your shirt or drink excessive quantities of cold liquids, even if you sweat profusely. All these things cause more rapid cooling than your body may be able to handle. You will cool off gradually and without impairing your health, if you merely reduce your output and allow the sweat to evaporate naturally through the fibers of your bicycle clothing. This works best if you wear clothing that contains a high percentage of wool.

Sun Burn

When bike touring, you will be exposed to the sun for many hours at a stretch. Unless you have a naturally high resistance to ultra violet light, exposed parts of the body are likely to suffer sun burn. To prevent it, use a sun tan lotion with a protection factor of 15. This means that only one fifteenth of the ultra violet rays reach the skin. Even more effective is zinc oxide based protection, applied in selected locations such as the nose the ears and the neck.

Sun burn is just that: a burn, and that means it should be treated like any other burn. Cold water and perhaps a light dressing such as baby oil are all you can do, apart from waiting for it to heal. In really severe cases, sun burn can be serious enough to justify professional medical care. There are substances that suppress the pain, but there is little chance of healing a burn with any kind of treatment.

Overtraining

Though this phenomenon is more commonly associated with the pursuit of bicycle racing, it can occur amongst ambitious touring bicyclists as well. While it is not usually recognized as a cycling injury, it should be treated as one. There are certain symptoms associated with overtraining and there are real hazards in ignoring these. It is simply a matter of having pushed your body beyond its present limits by cycling too far and too fast.

Two types of overtraining syndromes may be distinguished. Be-ginning cyclists, preparing for great feats or participating in tours for which they are not adequately prepared, are most likely to suffer from the sympathicotonous condition. It is due to inadequate preparation: too rapid an increase of workload from one week to the next. The symptoms include excessive nervousness, tension and perspiration, as well as a rapid pulse. The treatment is relatively easy, since all you have to do is slow down for one week, and only increase your workload very gradually.

More experienced riders sometimes suffer from the parasympathicotonous condition. This is caused by an excessive total work load, often exceeding the body's capacity to take in food for a prolonged period. Symptoms include listlessness, weight loss and what

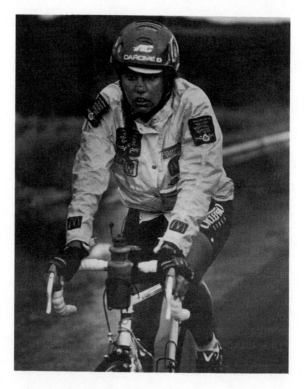

Long distance cycling is hard work – especially if you try to do the ultimate. Here Susan Notorangelo battles exhaustion during her 3000 mile ride across the American continent in 1985. Unless you set out to break a record, I suggest taking it a little easier.

seems like incurable tiredness. Here too, the answer lies in a reduction of the workload, though a doctor must definitely be consulted if the feeling of fatigue persists despite a drastic reduction in work load.

The morning pulse is a convenient indicator that can warn you of either type of overtraining condition. If it increases more than it usually does between lying in bed and just after getting up, you'd better take it easy for a day. Perhaps equally useful is to ask yourself how you are feeling in general. If you have difficulty sleeping and tire more than usual, if you feel listless, have a poor appetite, perspire more than usual or feel unjustified anxiety, it will be time to suspect overtraining. Go see a physician if a couple of days' relative rest does not solve the problem.

12
Cycling in any Weather

Bicycle touring must not be limited to warm and sunny days. Admittedly, it does seem to be more enjoyable to cycle when the weather is nice. However, all seasons have their particular and characteristic charm. Once you learn to cope with bad weather spells, you will probably also find many more opportunities to enjoy the fair weather periods in between.

Rain gear on, rain gear off. In changeable climates you will waste much of your time getting changed, unless you have rain garments of a material that lets perspiration pass through.

I grew up in a climate where sunshine and 'real' summer weather are very rare indeed, yet we never hesitated about taking the bike. The first group ride I organized in California, many years later, was a different experience altogether. At seven in the morning the phone rang, with a prospective participant suggesting I call off the ride, since the forecast included a twenty percent chance of rain. Only three of our group of twelve finally showed up and had a wonderful ride. Not a drop of rain fell, but even if it should have rained for a while, we would still have had a fine day's ride.

The moral is twofold: don't let uncertainty of the weather stop you from cycling, and prepare well enough to cope with poorer weather, if necessary. Adequately dressed, equipped and prepared, cycling can be enjoyable in almost any weather. Even if we agree that bicycle touring is better in favorable weather, and even if you do feel a little miserable at times, a ride in bad weather can still be a lot more enjoyable than sitting at home under the same conditions. I have also included some useful references on instant weather forecasting in the Bibliography, which may prove useful to make the most of the good spells, as well as to prepare for whatever weather is coming up.

On a longer tour, when good and bad days follow one another, you may be able to restrict actual touring to the better days if time allows. Or you may have to ride whatever the weather, if your time is more restricted. In a nutshell, students, teachers and the independently wealthy can perhaps afford to pick their cycling weather, while the rest of us will just have to keep cycling. Yet you may establish soon that with the right preparation, riding a bike in supposedly inclement weather is actually better than you thought, even if you could also have afforded to postpone the trip.

Hanging around a camp site or a motel on a rainy day is not necessarily that much fun either. You'll also find that sightseeing in a strange city is better done on days with favorable weather. Once you're cycling, you can keep reasonably warm and dry, but getting on and off the bike, going in and out of buildings, changing from rain gear into regular clothing, may well make such a sightseeing day more miserable than it would have been on the bike.

Then there are times of the year or parts of the world for which supposedly bad weather is on the order of the day. Of course, it all depends on what you're used to. If you've lived in the American Southwest all your life, you may find it hard to imagine that people two thousand miles North cycle at all, where it even rains in summer, and where it gets pretty cool in the off-season. And what to think of those poor souls who grow up in places like Britain, where even the summers are nippy, and rain can be expected in any season? I suggest you learn to handle any kind of weather, in order to experience bicycle touring as intensely and as frequently as possible. You will probably most enjoy some of the rides in the kind of weather you would at first not have considered suitable.

Four things have to be kept in mind to handle unfavorable weather conditions, which will all be discussed in some detail below:

- ☐ clothing;
- ☐ other equipment;
- ☐ riding style;
- ☐ touring technique.

Clothing

I shall be brief on the subject of clothing, since it was covered adequately in Chapter 6. The secret is to consciously choose the kind of clothing that suits all the various types of weather you can reasonably expect to encounter on any one ride. In summer that will include some different things than at other times of the year, and on an extensive tour you will want to be prepared for more changeable conditions than you have to be on a one-day trip.

Also consider the difference of elevation in this respect. I shall not forget two exceptional tours in my own experience that showed me the importance of that. The first time was when I was seventeen years old and rode my trusty three-speed from my native city of Rotterdam all the way to the Swiss Alps. At 2000 m (6000 feet) above sea level, I had to put on every fiber I could find and stuff old newspapers under my cycling shirt as well. Even so, I caught an awful cold on the descent.

The second such experience was twenty years later on the Hawaiian island of Maui. All the way up to the top of Mount Haleakala it was warm and pleasant, as it would be the next day for the descent. Just the night was a little rough, with temperatures around freezing. Equipped with only sheet sleeping bags for the night, we hid under old newspapers and

Excellent light weight rain suit from Bike-a-Lite. Made from a material that allows perspiration to pass through, while keeping the rain out.

cuddled up as closely as we could, without feeling even remotely comfortable. Still, experiences like this are perhaps the spice of bicycle touring: you tend to remember with some fondness even the little mishaps. As long as your health or safety is not seriously implicated, the charm of coping with the unexpected is undeniable.

When packing your gear, decide what range of temperatures and what kind of precipitation you are likely to encounter. Dress for the most immediate, but in such a way that you can convert to another kind of predictable weather without great ado. If rain is likely, make sure the rain gear is easily accessible, and if the temperatures may change, make sure you can accommodate by simply putting on or removing subsequent layers of clothing, rather than being forced to take items off before you can put other items on. Dressing in layers, with the coolest and lightest closest to the skin, will be best in changeable weather.

On the other hand, if the weather is expected to be and remain cold, you'll find it advantageous to wear warm woollen garments closest to the skin. If additional warm and long underwear is required, remember that your physical activity places specific requirements on your underwear that do not apply to those who are more inactive. Light but slightly bulky fabrics that are flexible and close fitting will be ideal, polypropylene scoring highest when it comes to long underwear.

Not only cold and rain, but even extremely hot or dry weather has to be considered specially. Though it may seem nice to wear as little as possible, keep in mind that you will be out on the bike in the direct sunlight for quite some time.

Besides, especially in hilly terrain, sections of great exertion, where your effort keeps you very hot, may be followed by downhill or windy sections, on which your body may get undercooled due to wind chill, even if the air temperature is quite high.

Certainly at higher elevations, I suggest covering up your tender skin. If you haven't a naturally high resistance to ultraviolet rays, wear the kind of cycling clothing that regulates the body's temperature and use an effective sun screen. Refer to Chapter 11, *Bicycle Safety and Health*, for some additional comments on protection against sunburn. To keep covered enough in the sun, you may wear relatively light cotton items with long sleeves and a helmet.

To provide the best temperature control effect, wool is definitely the best material, especially if it is closely knit of a relatively thin, soft and stretchable fiber. Your companions will also be pleased to note that wool does not smell anything like as offensive as most synthetics and cotton once it is or has been soaked with perspiration.

Other Equipment

Cycling in cold or rainy weather is best done on a bike that is equipped with those conditions in mind. That applies even if you encounter such weather only occasionally. On the other hand, the use of removable gadgets, or even some inconvenience in doing without optimal equipment, may be appropriate in some cases. I shall leave it up to you to decide how much suffering you want to put up with. Similarly, it will be a matter of your own inventiveness to produce the handy quick-release attachments and improvised weather protection gadgets that some technically inclined people find a challenge to invent and construct. As for regular equipment to withstand the elements, that will be described in this section.

Particularly in rainy weather, the bike itself must be equipped appropriately. As far as most components are concerned, that means getting high quality gear. To give an example, high quality bearings, as used on the most expensive hubs, bottom brackets and headsets, are much better sealed and more resistant to water than superficially similar items sold for half the price.

Three particularly important major items are brakes, tires and lights. All caliper brakes of reasonable quality work admirably well if used in conjunction with the right brake blocks and wheel rims, provided they are adjusted properly. Even though heavy loads and bad roads may suggest the use of presumably stronger steel rims, only aluminum rims provide an adequate coefficient of friction in conjunction with most brake block materials.

The brake blocks should be of any material that provides adequate friction even when wet. Though synthetic materials are widely advertised as being superior in the rain, only one type really lives up to its promise, namely the sintered material used by Modolo in their D-0015 brake blocks, which unfortunately doesn't fit on many touring bike brakes. And contrary to popular prejudice, longer or larger brake blocks do not provide better braking action than short ones – neither wet nor dry. If you should still choose steel rims, make sure they are not chrome plated but stainless and are used in conjunction with special brake blocks intended for use on steel rims.

Tires for touring in wet or cold weather should probably have a more chunky tread profile than the skinny thin things recommended for easiest cycling. Even on a wet road, perfectly smooth tires, such as the recently popular slicks, provide adequate grip for propulsion and braking, as long as the road is not slick, and as long as you are going straight. However, a little snow, ice, mud or fallen leaves on the road, which is hard to avoid in the rain, can be handled much better if the tire has a well defined tread profile. And to maintain traction in curves, you will find a roughened or profiled tread area wrapped relatively far around the tire's circumference to provide much more predictable road holding properties.

In wet and cold times of the year, you will probably more often find the need for lighting on your bike. This subject was covered in Chapter 4. Just make sure lights and reflectors are properly installed and maintained, and switch on your light whenever other road user's visibility may be impaired enough to justify lighting. In wet and snowy weather, a generator may more easily slip off the tire, and a battery may get soaked and ruined; so check up on these components more frequently. Proper adjustment, the use of a rubber cap over a generator wheel and removing batteries when not in use will prevent the most serious problems.

Other equipment-related points include a more frequent need for bike maintenance and the installation of some auxiliaries that may not otherwise rate very high. Lubrication is the major consideration here: cables, bearings and especially the chain will need regular cleaning, followed by lubrication, using a waxy spray can lubricant, oil or grease.

Amongst special equipment, fenders or mudguards rate high, as does a mud flap at the end of the forward one, to keep the water off your body and out of your luggage. In weather that is both wet and cold, a pair of shoe covers on the pedals is very worthwhile.

Riding Style

In cold, windy and rainy weather, you may benefit from an appropriate riding style. Try to become aware of the effect any particular condition may have on your bike's behavior. In the rain you'll want to ride so as to stay as comfortable as possible, while retaining maximum stability and balance. In cold weather you'll want to avoid exposing yourself too much and – when temperatures get down to freezing – you should make

Rainy weather shoe covers. Though shown here worn over rather heavy foot wear, these items can just as well be worn over proper cycling gear.

Fig. 12.1 Shift of weight

sure you don't skid on ice or snow. In very windy weather it will make sense to minimize your exposure to the wind, so as to reduce wind resistance and minimize the negative effect of the wind on your bike's balancing. The latter applies particularly in the case of a strong side wind, especially if the wind or its effect varies strongly during the ride.

To avoid spills on wet, muddy or icy roads, you should try to adjust your center of gravity, as shown in Fig. 12.1. The more weight you transfer from the front wheel to the back, the less likely a sudden move will be to result in a skidding or diverting type of disturbance, as described in Chapter 11. For the same reason, try to avoid excessive lean in corners: ride a natural, rather than a forced curve whenever possible. Read through the explanation in Chapter 10 again and practice the techniques recommended there on dry and wet roads to become really competent and confident.

In windy situations, it will generally pay off to keep your upper body low, in order to minimize wind resistance. When riding in a group, try to stay in some such formation that minimizes the individual riders' total exposure to the wind. That's done by riding directly in line closely behind each

other when the wind comes from straight ahead. In the case of a side wind, fan out the group into a staggered formation as shown in Fig. 10.6 in Chapter 10. Either way, the strongest rider should maximize his time in the front, while the weaker ones should be granted maximum shelter. If all are more or less equally strong, take turns at the front. Lead changes are carried out as shown in Fig. 12.2.

Touring Technique

Special touring techniques may be called for in inclement weather, although some people manage to solve all their problems by merely wearing appropriate clothing and having a properly equipped bike. One of the things to keep in mind is the long-term chilling effect, due to relative air movement, even if the temperatures do not seem quite so low. Keep especially your extremities warm and comfortable: feet, hands and head.

Additionally, there is the luggage, spare clothing and any camping gear to consider. Whenever the weather is or may become suboptimal, you should have packed everything in such a way that vital items remain dry and are accessible without getting wet – including especially those things on which you have to rely later to keep you dry, warm and comfortable. That's a matter of packing and wrapping your equipment and luggage with due thought and consideration. It is not possible to give you precise guidelines on how to do it, but a warning to consider these points should suffice the intelligent rider.

The way you plan the overall tour or the day's ride is also critical. In certain kinds of weather, you won't be able to cover big distances between stops. At other times,

Fig. 12.2 Lead change in group riding

getting off the bike frequently may actually make the ride more uncomfortable. In an enduring rain, you will probably find it beneficial to attack the day as much as possible in just one or two long continuous stretches. By the time you are changed and getting about off the bike, you will be grateful if you don't have to start all over again after the interruption.

On the other hand, in particularly cold weather you should probably ride several shorter sections. Try to find a warm and sheltered place and something warm to eat or drink between these stages. Don't return to the bike until you feel comfortable. Though I shall probably never enjoy cold weather, I have at times covered quite significant distances this way without getting really miserable. Some people actually enjoy a brisk ride in the cold, being able to cover quite impressive distances without either harm or discomfort.

Even camping can be done with some success in temperatures around or below freezing. It will be a matter of adequate clothing and overnight equipment, as well as technique. Don't do it until you have experienced camping under easier weather conditions first. Until you can make yourself really comfortable in and around a tent in summer, there's little hope of your being at ease doing the same in winter. Make sure tent, sleeping bag and cooking gear are up to the task,

Plastic shoe covers, like these, have the advantage of light weight and absolutely minimal packing size. Unfortunately, they get damaged rather easily, especially if you get on and off the bike frequently. (Photograph VK International)

and don't hesitate to transfer to a motel or some other form of solid housing if it gets too cold, wet or miserable.

In this context, I suggest there should be no compulsion to combine bicycle touring with life under canvas. Hotels, motels, hostels and the like are fine places to spend the night, and riding a less loaded bike will pay off in winter as much as it does in summer. Throughout this book I have included references to camping, since there is both a significant interest and a corresponding need for accurate information. Besides, it is a field in which I myself have a lot of experience. Just the same, I regard a night under a solid roof, in a ready made bed and with a private bathroom, a blessing every cyclist should grant himself from time to time. That applies especially when the weather is less than perfect for a night under the stars.

13
What to Take
and How to Pack it

We now reach perhaps the most neglected subject in the field, the one thing that can not be solved with either money or direct instruction alone. How to select the items you take along, and how to stash them inside the bags or on the bike, is indeed so inadequately known and considered that it is reasonable to devote an entire chapter to what is in other books usually covered in a few lines. In addition to this chapter,

Heavily loaded bike used for rough trail touring. Generally, I recommend taking less luggage: you can probably get by admirably with half the load shown here.

you are referred to the packing list in the Appendix, but the basis of sensible packing is the thought that goes into it, which is covered here.

Consider for a moment that my parents went bicycle touring in the late 'twenties with forty-pound bikes, in an age when aluminum, lightweight synthetic fibers, wash-and-wear clothing, plastic cups, containers or bottles and freeze-dried food were all equally unknown. Even so, they carried everything they needed without much suffering. Compare that with today's situation, with bikes weighing barely more than half as much and a nearly unlimited choice of specially designed lightweight gear available. Yet most of today's touring cyclists are loaded up to the point of approaching the limit of material endurance, if not personal bodily collapse. Today, more than ever before, you should be able to travel light if you pack it right.

The secret, it seems, lies not so much in the quality of the equipment, but more in the selectiveness of the cyclist who packs it on the bike. What to leave at home is more important than what to buy. And knowing how to pack what you do choose to take along is at least as important as deciding which bags are bought and how they are installed on the bike.

Of course, choosing the right luggage racks and bags is still important, and you are once more referred to Chapter 5, where this subject was covered. In the same chapter you will find solid advice on the distribution of weight and the attachment of bags to the bike. I do suggest you go over those remarks once more after you have covered the material here presented, before you set out on your first serious tour.

What to Take

As in virtually all other bicycle touring manuals, you will find a number of suggested packing lists in this book, contained in the Appendix. But such lists must be used with great caution. Neither I nor anyone else can know just what you will need on a particular tour over a given distance at a certain time with a specific purpose in mind. And those are only the most basic variables. Your personal interests and your limitations, both physical and material, are additional and less tangible factors that affect what you should pack and carry.

Eventually, you yourself will have to compose the list of things to take, even if it is only by modifying one of the suggested packing lists found in this book or elsewhere. Whether you use a pre-printed list or one you thought up yourself, you will find it necessary to revise that list as you go along. You will probably find certain things inadequate, missing or incomplete, other items unnecessary, superfluous, too big or small, or expendable altogether. Many more items will turn out to be useful in some situations, in certain areas, at particular times only. And finally, there will be some items that you may never use, yet should not be left behind because your life or health may depend on them in extreme situations.

It is not my job to tell you just what these things are, especially when it comes to the hard-core emergency supplies. I can merely suggest you consider such factors. Some people carry enough medicines to put an elephant out of his misery, others will feel totally secure with a copy of the Bible or some other work on religion or philosophy. And like so many other supplies, their importance varies with the different factors, ranging from the time of the year and the duration of the trip to the terrain encountered and the degree of your accumulated experience.

It will be easiest to keep track of the things you pack with the aid of simple 4½ x 6 inch note books. Make one of these up for each touring season, to take notes before and during your trips. A second note book is used for packing lists and other pre-tour notes, and is kept at home. I find my packing list gets longer and longer from year to year, yet I seem to be taking less and less as time and experience progress. That is due to the selective remarks about the usefulness of particular items and the desirability of others. Also see the remarks about record-keeping in in Chapter 23, *Keeping a Record of Your Tour*.

Over the years the packing list not only grows in length, it also expands in depth and detail, as remarks about the particular items are inserted. After each tour, the smartest thing to do is to unpack at least as systematically as you had packed before you left. Make four distinct piles:

1. Items you couldn't have done without whatever the situation.
2. Things you will only need under certain situations, or on particular tours.
3. Items you used on this tour, though they could be replaced by others that would also serve an additional purpose or that are smaller, lighter or otherwise more suitable.
4. Ballast, i.e. things you carried for no useful purpose or could have left at home with impunity whatever the situation.

In addition, by way of fifth category, put down your note book, in which you can write down those items you really missed and had not packed but would have liked to have along. At the same time, update the note book to shorten or expand the list, as may be appropriate on the basis of your findings regarding the four piles of gear.

Not only the nature, but also the number of these items is of significance. To give but one example, I have since my early youth limited the number of shoes, socks and undies to the absolute minimum. Whatever the duration of the tour, I take the stuff on my body when I leave home, and just one set of spare socks, undies and tops. When I started touring again with other people many years later, my companions always rejected this technique, carrying one or two pairs of additional shoes and enough other clothes to last at least a week without washing.

Whereas I cycled lightly packed and only spent a few minutes washing the day's socks and underwear at night, the others had loaded themselves up and were forever rummaging in their bags to separate the clean from the dirty from the not

Done correctly, following the instructions in Fig. 4.23, even a normal wired-on tire can be rolled up quite small. This handy package can either be stuffed in a bag or tied to the outside. In the latter case, make sure you install it in such a location that it does not have to be removed each time you need access to the bag on which it is attached.

quite so dirty. Finally they finished up doing a major laundry operation, and next day had to carry a week's supply of wet clothes around with them, that could not be dried conveniently. It took my companions one trip to limit the number of shoes they carried, and another one before they reduced their underwear supplies, until finally, after several years, they had learned how much more convenient it is to travel as lightly as I do.

The dictum of travelling light if possible should be paramount. Be selective in the materials you take, even if the particular kind of thing is very important to you. Thus, an avid photographer may be tempted to take a full stock of camera equipment, complete with several camera bodies, lenses, tripod and flash – nothing but the best. That makes sense if photography is the specific objective of the trip. If, on the other hand, you go for the bike ride, even the keenest photographer will find that he can get by admirably with one small camera. I know one accomplished photographer who never takes more than a pocket tripod and a Minox or the old Rollei 35 S, to take photos that were accepted for the covers of major pictorial periodicals.

You are of course free to take what you want. If you are like everybody else, you'll probably also learn to limit yourself to taking only the essential quantities after a few years of conscientious note taking and shaving off your packing list. On the other hand, you can take my advice right off on your first trip and be at least two years ahead of the others. Remember, though, that if you feel like chucking the whole bike touring business after your first trip, since you find it all too much of a burden, because of the laundry and the

packing and carrying, you can return to this chapter and learn how to make life easier.

Different Loads
for Different Trips

Many factors affect the number and type of items you should take along on a tour. I suggest you start off with some simple trips where you don't need to take too much along and where it doesn't matter very much if you do forget something that seems essential. Clearly, if you stay in hotels and eat in restaurants, you will need less than when camping, providing you are in a part of the world where restaurants and hotels are close enough to avoid hunger marathons and long rides in the dark to find accommodation.

If you cycle near towns and on weekdays, you will find it easier to purchase certain things along the way. In most European countries, where shops and most other facilities are closed evenings, Sundays and one or two afternoons each week, this can be particularly problematic. But even in regions with more liberal closing hours, I recommend starting with a simple day trip on a Saturday, followed by some midweek or weekend trips with overnight stays. If you start the latter on a Friday, you will have had the first night's experience to suggest what else you need while most shops are still open. The advice not to undertake your early trips in the outback is just as valid in Europe as it is in the US or Canada, even if towns and shops are so much closer together in the Old World, where you rarely have to worry about being really stranded far away from civilization.

Take not only the right kind of clothing and overnight or other camping gear, but also the most elementary supplies for the maintenance of your bike and your own body, as well as adequate aids to orientation. A trip without a map is as frustrating as one without food or the appropriate clothing may be. And being stranded because you lack the tools or the pump to carry out a minor repair can turn a perfectly pleasant trip into a nightmare. Once more, it's up to you to decide what to take and what to leave at home, but try to systematically think of everything that may be needed.

Conversely, remember that the problem of taking too much may be just as serious. Before packing each item, consider what will happen if you don't take it. Leave anything home if its absence will not significantly detract from the enjoyment of the trip. Sounds simple, but it takes an astonishing amount of self discipline to execute. Also take the weights of the various items into consideration. Compare the weights of several similar items, and choose the lightest consistent with the purpose. As you pack and decide, keep updating your packing list, so

you are saved the same decision making process for the next trip.

The Art of Packing

In addition to the remarks pertaining to the selection of bags and their attachment and distribution, as covered in Chapter 5, *Luggage Carrying Equipment*, you may benefit from some basic hints on how to fill these bags and how to attach the various pieces of luggage to the bike. That's what we'll cover in the present section.

The first thing to keep in mind is that whatever has to come out first or fastest must be most easily accessible: somewhere near the outside. That means these items must be packed last and preferably in outside pockets or even outside the bags altogether. Thus, your money and essential documents should be so easily accessible that you can immediately grab it and carry it on your body whenever you leave the bike.

Similarly, rain gear or a sweater and jacket in rainy or cold climes, or sun glasses and sun lotion in sunny

Handy off the bike as well as on your luggage rack. These luxurious pannier bags from Rhode Gear can be easily removed from the rack, strapped together and carried by the top handle.

regions, your camera, the current map and your note book, should all be very easily accessible. These items must be located, accessed and used without getting off the bike. For most of these instant access items, you will find a handlebar bag most convenient. Personally, I don't like even the best handlebar bags, carrying the same kind of things divided over the pockets in my clothing, the saddle bag and a small pack on the front luggage rack. Rain gear should be strapped to the outside of the saddle bag or a pannier bag, so it is both easy to reach and will not make the contents of the bag wet when you put it back.

But let's look at the sequence of packing, rather than only considering the most urgent items. The first thing to go in should be the last thing you'll need: spare laundry, sleeping bag, future supplies. Whether you pack big things first or last, often recommended in some apparently logical order, should solely be determined by the answer to the question when you'll need to gain access to the various items. A big package like the tent is not best kept underneath a lot of small items, if that means you have to unpack all these things before you can set up camp.

Similarly, consider what is most sensitive to damage or to getting wet. A sleeping bag is a nice big package, that can be conveniently removed in one piece, but if you have to do that in order to reach something more immediately needed, it may be getting wet in the rain or it may get torn if it is manhandled too much. Again, I can't prescribe a secret sole correct method. Instead, you will have to take my remarks and suggestions to heart, thinking and deciding for yourself.

Items that belong together are best kept together. That applies

Fig. 13.1 Shape of well packed and poorly packed bag

even if it means that one side of the bike will perhaps be loaded noticeably heavier than the other. Thus, the cooking gear and food, heavy though they are, are best put in one bag, while sleeping bag and sleeping gear, generally much lighter in weight, should go in another bag. That saves wild rummaging and searching, whereas the laterally unequal weight distribution does not affect the bicycle's stability. In fact, it prevents oscillations that are more likely to occur when the bike is packed equally heavy on both sides.

Items that are attached outside the bags or directly to the bike, as well as some of the bags that do not have their own integral means of attachment, are generally best held with webbing straps or leather belts. Either of these is far preferable to the inexplicably popular elastic bungee or shock cords. Since they retain their length even when force is applied to them, they do not encourage sagging and slipping of the luggage. When using leather belts, treat them with the same

Velcro

Fig. 13.2 Pouch for maps, books or stationary

waterproofing also used on leather saddles, such as Proofide or neat's foot oil. Webbing straps must have the kind of buckles that do not slip, yet are easy to tighten or loosen: try them out before you buy.

Food and other supplies bought along the way on your tour may be carried in rather provisional bags for a short time. I like to use an additional light backpack for this purpose. In the back of it I place a solid light fiber board (such as a clip board with the clip removed), which maintains the bag's shape. This prevents hard and bulky items, such as cans of food, from causing excessive discomfort. If you have a few spare straps or belts, you may also be able to attach this bag to the bike over the top of another bag temporarily. Whatever you do, make sure everything is secured adequately safely, so you neither lose anything, nor risk the bag's getting caught in the bike's moving parts or brakes, nor interfering with your movements.

When packing the various bags, consider the final shape they should take on when full. Their ultimate shape is more or less defined by the way they are sewn: never spherical but relatively long, flat and even. They are designed that way to remain compact and to interfere minimally with bike, rider and other objects, while protecting the

contents optimally. Try to achieve that by stuffing the contents in such a way that the intended final shape is approached. Roll together the items that go inside in packages that each do not exceed the width of the bag. Put smaller and narrower items in last, stuffing them into the ends, filling up the length of the bag. Consult Fig. 13.1: if the packed bag takes on an almost spherical shape, as shown in the RH detail, you've gone about it the wrong way. This would make it hard to close the bag properly and may cause damage to bag and contents.

The Inside Package
Finally, consider the question of packaging the items that go inside the bike bags. Their size and shape, as well as the form of protection they offer, are all significant. Wherever hard and undeformable items are concerned, you'll find two smaller packages easier to store than one large item. So, though the soft and deformable package containing the sleeping bag is no problem to stack in one piece inside a bag, your camp stove fuel, beverages and other supplies are best divided up over several smaller containers.

As far as the shape is concerned, long and narrow packages are more easily stashed than bulky items of the same volume. In addition, flat packages are handier than more nearly round or square cross sections. Thus, bottles should be long and of oval cross section, rather than short and round. You will not always get an opportunity to determine the shape of things to pack yourself, but in many cases you do have the choice when buying packaging materials. No need to keep things in the packages in which they are sold in the first place. You can easily get appropriate bottles and other containers from a backpacking or other outdoor supplies store.

Special items need special forms of packaging. All printed and written materials must be kept flat and dry. Thus, maps (excepting the current one, which should be kept handy), books and writing paper are best kept in flat rigid cases, as shown in Fig. 13.2. They are made of cardboard and fabric, and wrapped in a polythene bag to keep them dry. Since maps, books and writing paper are not all the same size, you may have to make several of these, keeping items of similar size together. Put these cases in such a place that they are not bent or damaged by other things in the same bag.

The weight of packaging materials is as important a factor as is their size. With regard to the latter, make sure you don't waste space in your luggage on empty or unnecessary packaging. Estimate or even measure out how much of any one supply you will need for the duration of a particular trip, then take a container to match just that volume whenever possible. As concerns weight, choose the lightest materials and the lightest construction consistent with the amount of abuse received. The conscientious use of household scales, capable of weighing anything up to about 2 kg (4– 5 lbs) is highly recommended when it comes to selecting the packaging, as it is when comparing several items serving the same purpose. Mark each container with its volume and tarre weight, using an indelible marking pen, for future reference. Use a different color marker to indicate the contents.

You may be able to scrounge quite suitable packaging materials for many purposes. I find an ample

Fig. 13.3 Storage bag

Fig. 13.4 Utensil pouch

supply of bottles and boxes amongst the annual household supply of supposedly one-way packaging materials. These things range from swivel top shampoo bottles, useful for drinks and other liquids, to photographic film cans, suitable for keeping salt and matches dry, to simple polythene bags and sheets used to wrap moisture-sensitive items.

Easily spilt items, such as flour and sugar, may not be adequately protected by a plastic bag alone, though a rigid canister is not very space-efficient. The optimal protection of things like that is provided by a double bag, made up by sewing a cloth bag with draw-cord closure around a polythene bag, as shown in Fig. 13.3. Knives, forks and spoons should be stored and kept together in a pouch. If you can't buy a suitable item, make your own, sewn from any sturdy fabric, as shown in Fig. 13.4.

14
Planning Your Tour

When I first proposed writing a bicycle touring book, the reaction of many non-cyclists was that it should contain mainly descriptions of routes to follow. That is not what you will be getting here. You may appreciate how useless that would be, if you consider how slender the chances of any one rider are of living close enough to most – or even any – of the rides described that way.

Instead of the cook book approach, telling you where to start and where to turn off, I will make

Fellow travellers in the Canadian Rockies. (Photograph courtesy Backroads)

every effort to help you in the intelligent planning of your own tour, following your own inclination in the area you have chosen. That, I feel, will be more useful, and will prepare you to use the same skill for any tour in any part of the world.

How to get about once you have selected your route will be covered in some detail in Chapter 16, *Finding Your Way*. In the present chapter you'll learn how to go about planning your tour in advance. This encompasses all the preparatory work required to successfully pull off a tour of any length, with respect to both the selection of the general route and other planning details. In addition to the remarks in the present chapter, you will find some practical advice in several of the books listed in the Bibliography.

A few rules should probably be observed to assure the greatest chance of success. Each one of these rules may be individually broken under certain circumstances, without necessarily spoiling the entire trip. However, if you are on a limited time budget, their observation is quite critical. Oddly enough, it is probably less dangerous to start a grand tour improperly prepared than a weekend trip or a two-week vacation. The planning mistakes made in the first case can all be corrected or compensated as time goes by, whereas the short tour just doesn't give you enough time to learn from your present mistakes and correct them until it is too late. Here are the basic criteria for successful tour planning:

☐ Inform yourself adequately about the area ahead of time, to make sure you know what to expect and that it is what you want, both in terms of scenery, terrain, weather, type of accommodation, strenuousness of the trip, and in a more general cultural sense.
☐ When touring with others, agree in advance on what all participants expect. Decide ahead of time what you will be doing and seeing, what to expect of each other, and what each participant wants to do, so you avoid conflicts along the way.
☐ Do not tackle terrain more difficult or remote than what you know from experience you can handle.
☐ Preferably select beginning and end points for the route that can be conveniently reached by public transportation, or make arrangements to leave a car at some place to which you are sure you can return at the conclusion of the trip.
☐ Ascertain that your equipment is suitable for the terrain and that you can carry enough spares and tools wherever help may not be readily available.
☐ Obtain the best mapping material available, consistent with the length of the trip, the remoteness of the region and the nature of the terrain.
☐ For a longer tour, inquire in advance about overnight accommodation facilities, restaurants and stores along the route.
☐ Allow contingencies for emergencies, such as cutting the trip short and returning from some place along the route by public transportation if that should be necessary.

Taking all these points into consideration would be perfect planning, and no doubt you will at times be somewhat in the dark about one or the other aspect. In fact, a little uncertainty is perhaps the spice of life, and it will generally be no disaster if one item or the other is not fully secured. It is important, though, to have considered each of these aspects, even if you check off some of them as being of no serious concern for a particular trip. In fact, I have occasionally found myself insufficiently prepared in one or more areas, but I have made an effort to weigh their relative significance and risk during the planning stage, before starting the trip, which is exactly what I recommend you do.

In general, it is probably smartest to start on a small scale. Go on some relatively short trips, starting with half-day rides close to home. Subsequently, work your way up via day trips to weekend tours over increasing distances. Gradually increase their complexity, from trips without food or overnight problems, via picnics and motel stays, to short camping trips in easy terrain, finally to longer tours that present a combination of many of the problems you can expect to encounter anywhere. Progress from carrying little luggage to touring fully loaded, and from riding in familiar surroundings to well mapped areas farther away to the relatively unknown. Expand your experiences until you are confident under most conceivable circumstances.

Where and When to Go

The selection of suitable touring terrain is not really as difficult as it may seem. Not so long ago most bike books included the recommendation to investigate a likely area by car first, and then go out the next weekend with the bike. That is not what I propose, since I consider essentially all roads in most parts of the world basically suitable for cycling. Just the same, most people will agree that certain factors make cycling more enjoyable in certain areas. You are probably familiar enough with your own area to be able to guess at suitable terrain, yet you should consider that the world –

Cycling in the Grand Tetons. The gentleman in the picture doesn't have much luggage on the bike, since he is participating in an accompanied tour. The sag wagon daily carries the luggage to the next stop. (Photograph courtesy Backroads)

even your little corner of it – looks different from the bike than it does from behind the wheel of a car.

Some of the things that make cycling particularly enjoyable in certain areas and on particular roads are:

☐ Terrain or specific roads with minimal differences in elevation.
☐ Areas with little wind and sheltered roads that do not expose you to strong winds.
☐ Scenically pleasant areas with large areas of public lands, especially if these are not quite so popular as to attract excessive motor traffic.
☐ Roads that are well paved and relatively wide for the volume of motor traffic they carry.
☐ Roads that avoid built-up commercial, industrial and housing areas.
☐ Roads that lead through or past points of interest and small towns, especially if the latter have character of their own and offer facilities you might want to use.
☐ For longer trips, roads that are served at suitable intervals by convenient facilities for overnight stays and shopping for food.

This list may seem a bit of an eye-opener to the less experienced. It has virtually no similarity with the list of points proposed by a class of inexperienced cyclists I taught several years ago. These people all placed as their first preference that there should be separate bike paths on or along the road, closely followed by the desire for narrow roads far away from the nearest town. My list was drawn up in consultation with a number of experienced touring cyclists, and I feel the advice contained here is valid for all beginning and advanced cyclists alike.

At the same time as deciding where to go, determine when your trip shall be. You may be restricted either one way or the other. If you have little money or time to travel, you will have to select an area close to home. In that case, select a time when cycling conditions are favorable in your part of the world. If, on the other hand, you are restricted to a certain time, you may have to select a destination that offers good conditions at that particular time of the year.

With respect to the season, remember that good does not necessarily mean hot: milder weather is generally more favorable for cycling, and the most popular vacation time in any one area is rarely the best time to ride your bike there. Any touring cyclist chased off the road along the Pacific coast or in the vicinity of any National Park by a stream of incompetently and inconsiderately driven motorhomes can confirm that.

Of course, with suitable equipment, some of the points on my list may be overcome, if not ignored. Thus, unpaved paths and trails may lend themselves wonderfully for mountain bike touring, especially over distances short enough to allow the return to the civilized world, should you need help or supplies. Similarly, you may purposely choose a mountain tour for its scenic character, where there is little point in shying away from differences in elevation.

Once you have decided in which part of the world or of the country to tour, define the area more precisely. The overall pre-tour planning is perhaps best done with the aid of a simple geographic map, such as the state or country map contained in a school atlas. You will be able to get a feel for the terrain, since hills and rivers, towns and major geographical features determine the picture more than the roads, which dominate conventional road maps. This way, you will be able to select one or more likely regions within the larger area selected. Comparing carefully with the scale of the map, you can roughly set out the distance you should be able or willing to cover. In general, it will be best to seek out a more or less circular route, which can be started and discontinued at any point that turns out to be suitable in the next step of preparation.

For that next step, get down to a more detailed road map. How to select a suitable map, and how to glean a maximum of useful information from it, will be shown in the section entitled *Reading the Map* below. Now define the towns, the points of interest, the roads and the geographical features along your route on the road map. Done with a modicum of imagination, you should

(Photograph Darryl Skrabak)

be able to judge many aspects of importance by merely interpreting the map intelligently and critically. With the aid of this map, supported by guide books or other literature about the area selected, decide on a suitable route to follow.

To give but one example, a road connecting a suburb with the nearest major town will not be a quiet one. If the tour starts or ends too far from your home to cycle there, take into particular consideration the problem of getting there and back. In America, railway stations and bus depots are often not in very nice parts of town. Airports are generally served only by freeways or similar roads that are generally not legal to ride and which make it very hard to find another way into the nearest town. Long distance busses and trains, and especially ferries in those parts of the world where water is a characteristic feature, on the other hand, are often very suitable for accessing important points on your route by bike.

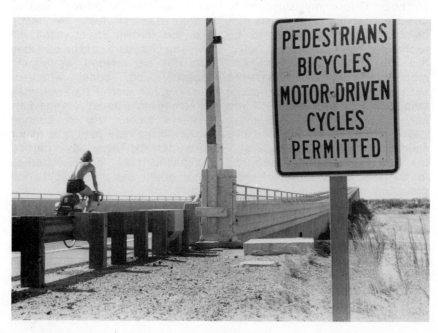

When travelling to the starting point on public transportation, consider that major towns and cities – I'd say anything with more than 60,000 inhabitants – can be very frustrating to cyclists from elsewhere. Finding your way in or out of such a place can be a veritable nightmare in almost any country. For that reason, I suggest you do not book your trip to such a place but to a minor town nearby that is served by the same line of public transportation, even if that means taking a slower train or bus that stops where the express line does not.

It is of course possible to reach virtually any area by car, carrying the bike. However, there are two hitches. Firstly, you will have to return to the same point for the return journey. Secondly, there is a significant risk to the car. What will happen to it when you leave it overnight or for a couple of weeks? I've once had the experience myself. Having left the car at a gas station for a weekend, I was forced to return after less than an hour. Guess my surprise to observe how the engine was just being removed, obviously to be exchanged for an older and defective one of the same make and model. Just make sure you leave the car with someone you can trust, or take adequate precautions if you can't.

Whether this will be a long tour or a short one, consider such factors as the wind direction. There are maps for all parts of the world that show prevailing winds. With the help of these, you should be able to select your route in windy parts to benefit from them as much as possible. Remember that in most regions the winds tend to increase in strength as the day progresses. This means that riding against the prevailing wind in the morning or at night will

be a lot easier than it is late afternoon. On the coast, the wind tends to be directed towards the sea in the morning and inland in the evening. Use this kind of knowledge to your benefit when deciding which route to follow.

Reading the Map

There are three different types of maps that are suitable for your purpose at different times, as shown in Fig. 14.1: topographic maps, road maps and street maps. The former show the geographic features most accurately but lack a lot of information pertaining to roads and other man-made features. The road maps emphasize just these aspects, while the street maps show even more detail about roads and buildings in built-up areas, including specifically street names and traffic details such as one-way systems.

For cycling on regular roads in or near populated areas, the road map will generally be the most suitable, whereas topographic maps are more suitable for off-road use or other trips in less frequently travelled terrain. Street maps will help you find your way in cities if they can not be avoided, as should probably be done wherever possible. For shorter trips you may be able to make do with a singe map, while a longer trip in strange surroundings may require a minor library of maps. These may in part be purchased back home, whereas some others can only be obtained locally.

Next to the type of map used, its scale will be the most important feature. That is the ratio between the distance as measured on the map and the corresponding distance in the terrain. For shorter trips in populated areas the most useful one for cycling will be a road map to scale

1 : 100,000, where one cm on the map corresponds to one km on the road (or one inch equals about 1.6 miles). Longer tours will be best covered on road maps to scale 1 : 200,000.

Other scales do have their uses for the cyclist as well. For off-road touring you will need even more detailed topographic maps, say to scale 1 : 50,000 (one cm equals 0.5 km or one inch equals 0.8 miles). Street maps may have a scale like 1 : 25,000, where one cm equals 0.25 km or one inch equals 0.4 mile. The large scale geographic map used for initial planning will have a scale totally unsuitable for cycling, representing large distances in the field by tiny distances on the map, which makes it impossible to show useful details *en route*.

The most important things on any map are its date of last revision and the legend. Before using any map, first check whether it is reasonably up-to-date, and then get familiar with the particular legend and the symbols used. The legend varies from one series of maps to the other, and any time spent studying it before the trip will save you no end of frustration and errors later on out on the road. For the same reason, I suggest you rely as much as possible on maps from the same series.

For road maps to cover any place in the US, those published by the various state or regional automobile associations are often highly suitable, though their scales vary quite a bit, depending on the size of the state or the region they cover. In other countries you will find various series of maps, such as the rightfully

Fig. 14.1 Topographic map, road map, street map

famous Michelin maps used in many European countries or those published by Bartholomew for Great Britain and Ireland.

Some important features for cyclists shown on some maps but not on others include elevations and railway lines. Elevations may be either given in the form of figures or contour lines. Contour lines are most useful to cyclists if they show intervals no greater than 20 meters or 50 feet. This generally means the corresponding maps are to scale 1 : 50,000 or less. The principle is shown in Fig. 14.2: contour lines represent imaginary slices at elevation intervals, each connecting all points at the same height. The more lines are crossed by a road, the

(Photograph David Epperson / Bicycle Sport)

Fig. 14.2 Contour lines

greater the elevation difference; the closer they are together, the steeper the climb or descent.

When planning your route, keep the elevation differences in mind and avoid them as much as possible. When unavoidable, you may actually find steeper sections easier to climb than to descend, given the same elevation difference. The short steep section can be taken off the bike, while a very steep descent may actually force you to get off, since it could be too dangerous to stay on the bike if the bike is heavily loaded and you are not perfectly in control.

To give you an idea of the effect of elevation differences on your cycling performance, refer to Fig. 14.3. It shows the equivalent distances that can be covered at different speeds with the same energy needed to surmount certain differences in elevation. In effect, you may be able to travel a little further in hilly terrain than this graph would suggest, since you will usually benefit from the elevation difference on the downhill sections. However, the benefit on the way down is always less than the hindrance on the way up. There is no doubt that progress is slower in the hills than one would estimate just looking at the map without considering the differences in elevation.

The effect of elevation difference on continuous performance. The various curves show how many miles could be covered during one hour on level ground and at any incline up to 15% with the same output.

Fig. 14.3 Climbing v. distance

Elevation markings are not the only characteristic features, but they are quite important. If the map contains no other aids, learn to estimate by other features whether a road will be steep or not. Snaking roads and suddenly decreasing building and road density are often indicative of mountains. Rivers generally flow relatively gently downhill, while artificial waterways tend to follow the contours of the terrain. Railways often get up and down the hills by the easiest route, as does a road closely parallel.

On the other hand, watch out for the tricks the designers of roads, railways and canals may have played on you: you can't follow the trains through tunnels or over bridges and viaducts. Though any canal has a tow path for maintenance, it may be barred to the public and it may be interrupted or unsuitable for cycling in critical places, such as aquaducts, locks and tunnels. Similarly, beware of nature's tricks: though all rivers flow downhill, there may not be enough room for a road right next to it.

To get a good idea of the distance involved, even at this early planning stage, an additional aid in the form of a curvimeter can be recommended. This device, shown in Fig. 14.4, is used to figure the length of the trip by making its little wheel follow exactly the route on the map, starting after you've set it to zero. The dial is calibrated in a number of different scales, so make sure you read it off at the correct one, as verified by checking with the marked distance in the legend block.

zero setting button

Fig. 14.4 Curvimeter

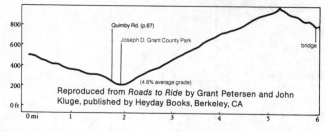

Fig. 14.5 Road profile

Other Sources of Information

Though the map is no doubt the most useful planning device, it should by no means be the only one. Certainly for areas with which you are not yet fully conversant, I recommend getting some background information from regular touristic guide books. This way, you will get more out of a tour, since you are generally better informed. In addition, there are special bicycle guides, some of which are quite attractive, though I rarely found them really useful. One useful feature often contained in such manuals is a road profile, such as the one shown in Fig. 14.5. This makes it clear very quickly what kind of elevation differences a certain road section has in store for you.

Getting maximum information from maps and guides is not only a matter of studying them ahead of time, it is also a matter of regular use while travelling. Only if you frequently consult the map while travelling, rather than blindly following the road and the signs, will you develop a true appreciation of the benefits offered by various kinds of maps. Consult it frequently and consciously to really benefit from the specific map used, and to appreciate the features that make one map more useful than another. These abilities will greatly help when it comes to finding your way and when planning the next tour.

Part III
The Practice of Bicycle Touring

15
From Day Trips to Long Tours

The chapters of this third part of the book are all concerned more directly with the practical aspects of various forms of bicycle touring. In the present chapter I shall describe the various ways of bike touring in some more detail, suggesting how you may progress from simple trips to more challenging rides. You will be encouraged to expand your experience to whatever form of touring you choose. Subsequent chapters will deal quite specifically with the various aspects and day-to-

Taking a break *en route*, cycling the Kaibab Plateau in Arizona. (Photograph courtesy Backroads)

day experiences in the many different situations encountered when touring by bike.

As is the case with so many things, even the most demanding type of bike touring can be done without much preparation. On the other hand, it is the consensus of most cyclists with limited time budgets that the instruction gained from talking to others or reading a book like the present is worth every minute, as is a modicum of preparation and the attention to equipment covered in the preceding parts of the book. It will be more enjoyable if you set out adequately prepared.

Getting Ready to Tour

No need to overdo the preparation bit, especially if it is physical fitness you are worried about. I recently read an article in one of the US cycling magazines, in which a woman cyclist describes the agony she went through to work up to her long bike tour. Before going on her journey, this lady desperately tried for months to get fit by spending literally hours each day punishing herself on a home trainer. That's quite ridiculous: except for the utterly feeble, every normal human being is fit enough to go on even quite extensive tours without a special training program. I'm not saying you'll be able to race or keep up with crack athletes, but you should definitely be able to cover distances long enough to give you the sensation of real touring without any special preparatory exercising.

One of my friends set out many years ago on a continental crossing. He astonished all by completing the tour without all the special fitness aids suggested before departure. On the first day he covered a modest distance, and he felt a little sore the next day. But within a week he was daily covering distances that compared favorably with those achieved by much more experienced and trained riders. You don't have to go on a tour from coast to coast, but even a two or three week vacation is long enough to allow you to get into the proper shape as you go along.

Even if you do feel the desire to prepare yourself physically, the obsession with home trainers and wind load simulators, used by some to prepare for their big tour, is totally superfluous. It's simply the wrong way to go about it. A thirty minute exercise bout on one of these machines is a deadly bore, and yet the training benefit for the average person intent on touring is virtually nil. Sure enough, these devices can be used to advantage within an athletic training program. However, the practice it takes to participate in individual or organized bike tours is much more quickly, effectively and enjoyably gained riding a real bike on a real road.

Whereas on a home trainer you can at best train the few muscles that directly affect the pedalling motion, real life cycling involves the entire process of movement, force, balancing, steering, orientation, fresh air and interest. Who, short of a few nervous crackpots, would feel so insecure as to forego this much wider experience for fear of being physically insufficiently up to the task? Of course, you may be one of those, but I recommend going about it more practically. It is both more effective and more satisfying.

Of all the forms of preparation that are appropriate for bike touring, bicycle commuting is perhaps the most effective. Instead of a twenty minute car trip or a thirty minute bus commute, getting to work on the bike will take a little longer. Don't see that as commuting time lost, but rather as cycling time gained. Even if the commute takes ten or twenty minutes longer, at the same time you'll be gaining perhaps 40 minutes or so of true cycling experience. Possibly the beginning cyclist does not feel up to doing this, yet it's a lot more enjoyable and practical than sweating madly on a home trainer will be. You'll be much better prepared for your touring and you'll probably feel fitter and happier all year. It not only strengthens your heart and muscles more effectively than can be done on the home trainer, it also improves your bike handling skills.

From Casual Rides to Cycle Trips

Even though it is quite possible to start a long tour without extensive cycling experience, it may be smarter to start off with relatively short rides close to your home. This way you will develop an appreciation of the bicycle and the feeling of riding continuously before starting on more demanding tours. It is worth noting in this context that the typical casual ride by people who are not dedicated cyclists is less than two miles in length, while even a one hour continuous ride will cover about six to ten times as much, depending on the speed of travel. Clearly then, continuous cycling presents a different experience to those who are used to riding a bike only casually.

Don't set out on what shall become your first real trip without some defined plan of where to go and how to get there. Choose the distance on the basis of the time available, the points worth cycling to and your ambition. Having a destination is far preferable to just cycling aimlessly. Visiting a beach, a restaurant, a picnic site, a winery, a park, a zoo or a museum – all are likely goals, as are a hundred other places you can probably come up with that are located within reasonable cycling reach even for an out-and-out beginner.

Even on a short trip like this, taking perhaps only an hour there and another hour back, go through the entire planning and preparation process recommended in the various chapters of Part II. Decide when and where to go, which roads to follow, what to take and what to do once you get there. Plan your timing, and consider the contingencies in case one thing or the other does not go according to plan. Pack the food, equipment and supplies you want to take along properly, dress right, plan your route and take the appropriate map. If you get into the habit of doing this consistently and systematically right from the start, it will enable you to get ready for longer tours just as systematically and effectively.

You may choose to go on rides of this type alone or in groups. It is my observation that it is probably more enjoyable to first gain some experience alone, and then ride with others that are at least equally experienced. Riding with a whole group of greenhorns may seem like a lot of fun, but often becomes extremely frustrating, since you will probably spend disproportionately many hours waiting for all the other yoyos to get their act together. No need to feel superior, since they'll spend as much time waiting for you. It's just that you all seem to delay one

Typical well-constructed handlebar bag from Eclipse. It is supported at the top from a handlebar bracket and held down by means of elastic shock cords. The top map compartment is removable.

another at different times. When starting out alone, you only have to deal with your own inefficiency.

Once you have been on a few excursions like this under the most favorable conditions – selecting nice days, easy terrain and modest distances – start venturing further afield. Go on some rides in more challenging terrain, in less friendly weather, over longer distances or at a higher speed. Then extend the duration of your rides, moving up from trips taking a few hours to half day and whole day tours. As distances and terrain get tougher, you may have to start carrying more luggage, and invest more thought into planning and preparation. If all is well, you will also start noticing that cycling becomes both more natural and more enjoyable as your level of experience increases.

Overnight Trips

The next stage, for which you may be ready anytime from one to three months after you start bike touring, will be tours that take you over such distances that overnight stays have to be considered. That will also involve more luggage and more preparation. To the insecure it may be a good idea to try a dry run first, taking the kind of luggage needed for an overnight trip, pretending to stay overnight but returning the same day just the same. Some people camp out in their own back yard before they go out on a camping trip, and I see nothing wrong with it.

If your dry run works out, and you establish that you haven't forgotten items that would be essential if it were for real, it will be time to start doing some real two-day tours. The less insecure rider will have little inhibition doing this kind of thing with less practice. It should be easy

enough, considering you probably live in a society where real hardship can be avoided with the aid of a credit card or a telephone call.

Decide whether you want to stay in a hotel, motel or hostel, or whether you want to camp out. Consider whether there will be any need to make advance reservations, which may well be the case in some popular areas. In addition to the regular kinds of accommodation just mentioned, you may consider some of the alternatives geared specifically or in part to touring cyclists. In this vain, it may be smart to join a national touring organization, such as Bikecentennial or Bicycle USA in the US, or the CTC in England. Many of these organizations operate either organized systems of overnight accommodations or a referral service that allows you to find cheap accommodation, or in some cases a free place to roll out your sleeping bag.

Then there is the question of where to go in more general terms. I suggest you do not choose the kind of destination where everybody else also seems to go, since those areas are invariably overrun with motorists and other tourists. Just the same, destinations booked out for people travelling by car may offer accommodation to those who arrive on a bike. That's not unreasonably, since in many cases the facility's capacity is not limited by the number of persons, but rather by the number of cars that can be accommodated. So when making reservations or inquiries, be sure to mention that you will be travelling by bike.

Go on a number of weekend tours like this. Better yet, if you should have the opportunity and the time, two or three day tours at mid week, when fewer people are competing for a place on the road and at the popular destinations. First get to know the areas within the range of sixty miles or so from your home that can be conveniently reached by bike in a half-day ride, while allowing a return trip in comfort the next day. This eliminates a lot of the time consuming and potentially trouble-some decisions regarding transportation to and from the starting point of the tour.

Even if you live in an part of the world that doesn't rate high as a cycling paradise, you are quite likely to find plenty of good touring opportunities on these rides. You will get to know the area well through cyclist's eyes. This experience will also greatly help you think of suitable shorter rides in your home region that do not require overnight stays. By and by, you may start venturing out on longer tours, tackling greater distances and perhaps starting further away, interfacing with public transportation systems or using some kind of car pooling technique if you travel in a group. This latter method can also be used with one car accompanying the cyclists or following them at some distance. This way, you may either take turns

driving or perhaps one member of the group may actually prefer driving a car to bike touring.

Vacation Tours

Once you have got to know the area around your own home base, venture out further afield. First expand your radius to perhaps a hundred miles or more on day and weekend trips of one, two or three days. Next, you may want to travel in remoter areas. Of course, all this assuming you want to expand your bicycling horizons: be my guest if you prefer to stay closer to home. Again, this can be done without all this gradual preparation, but I feel it is advantageous to combine your progress in bicycle touring with the experience of getting to know your own region as a present or potential cycle touring terrain.

In my native Holland, I could not ride more than 100 miles in any one direction without leaving the country, and I went on literally hundreds of day and weekend rides before I felt obliged to venture abroad. Perhaps your area is less bicycle oriented than the low countries, where a thousand towns and a

Bicycle transportation the luxury way in a reinforced plastic case. Being rectangular and sturdily constructed, this box is perhaps the ultimate bike carrier for transporting the bike on public transportation, whether bus, train or plane. The problem is that you have to find a place to keep the empty box once you arrive at your touring destination. (Photograph VK International)

hundred thousand miles of various types of roads are contained in a compact area free from really insurmountable natural or man-made bicycle barriers. But even if paradise seems to be far off, suitable bike touring conditions are more prevalent than most people realize.

Your first vacation tours, therefore, must not necessarily take you very much further afield either, although you may prefer to try more distant destinations right away. It will be up to you. But, whether going far or staying near, the type of planning and preparation should be similar. Use the guidelines in the preceding chapters for selecting the route, choosing what to take along and learning how to pack it on the bike.

Well designed Karrimor Overlander panniers. Due to the use of heavy materials, generous overlaps and cinch straps, these bags are probably more durable and practical than many of the more elegant looking fully zippered American bags.

Once you've started, simply expand upon your own experiences to progress from a greenhorn to a confident and competent touring cyclist.

In the remaining chapters of the book, it will present many of the particular aspects that apply most specifically to the longer tours. That is the reason I shall not expand on these subjects in this context very much more here. It will make some difference whether you travel alone or in a group, with adults or children, whether you use a regular bike and travel on well paved roads or a mountain bike cross-country. There will be different things to consider when touring abroad or at home, when cycling in summer or in the off-season.

In connection with all vacation tours further away from home, you will be confronted with the problem of reaching your destination with your machine. Some more remarks on the subject of transportation – specifically with respect to getting the bike to your destination – are contained in the section entitled *Getting There With Your Bike* in Chapter 19, which deals primarily with foreign travel. The remarks about bike rental there should also be regarded as a suggestion for domestic travel, assuming you can find out in advance whether adequate equipment will be available for rent.

Bike Touring as a Way of Life
All these situations are merely variations on the same theme, and the basic skill of bike touring is not lost on any of these options. Perhaps you will go camping on one tour, whereas you may decide to stay in hotels, motels or hostels at other times. On one trip you may travel in a

familiar society, where it is both easy to find your way and remains reasonably safe, even if you do get lost. Another tour may take you to another scene or another country, where getting lost is on the order of the day and the problem of survival may be very real.

Another, though very modest variation on the general bicycle touring theme is the mid-week evening ride. Certainly in summer and spring, the days are generally long enough to allow plenty of time for quite extensive bike rides after completion of a typical working or studying day. Plan your time properly, know where you want to go and pack your stuff ahead of time. You can go on a ride of thirty, forty miles or more. It can be combined with an evening picnic, a trip to the beach or a game of baseball. Not very ambitious, but one of those additional treats that makes life so much more enjoyable than merely following the same old routine.

That is the one extreme, the simple bike trip that can be conducted without much planning or special equipment. On the other extreme are those really long tours that most people dream of but never actually carry out. I have experienced both types, and can't honestly say whether the one is necessarily superior to the other. Of course, I still have the most vivid memories of some of my early really long foreign tours. However, the little trips that are easily conducted and involve nothing more exciting than many of our other leisure activities perhaps contribute quite significantly to our general feeling of living a meaningful and enjoyable life. Don't neglect those little rides, assuming they don't compare to real bicycle touring.

Accompanied bike touring. Organized tours from organizations like Backroads, shown here, are an excellent introduction to bicycle touring and provide more opportunity to socialize than individual tours.

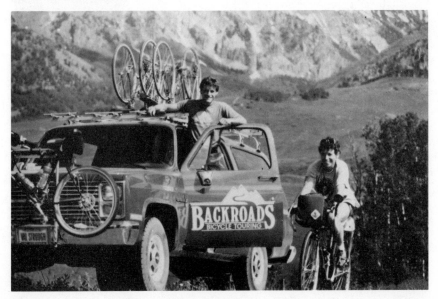

On longer tours you may learn to get around in countries where languages are spoken that you will never even begin to understand. You may encounter customs and opinions that seem strange or threatening. But all of these situations can be mastered even by normal mortals, providing you take the trouble to think about what you are doing and how it affects the options available. You can become a really experienced cyclist, whether you travel far or near. You may choose to become a veritable globetrotter, or you may prefer instead to restrict your cycling to more accessible regions and congenial societies. Whatever your choice, you'll enjoy almost any bicycle touring experience if you are well prepared and remain conscious of the problems and advantages offered by the bicycle as a means of getting around.

16
Finding Your Way

In addition to the information imparted in Chapter 14 about planning the route ahead of time, you probably need some practical advice on the subject of orientation. Having mapped out the route is only one aspect of this complex: you will also have to carry out those plans. And, what is perhaps at least equally relevant, you have to find your way once you get out there on the bike. Or you may have to get back when you do get lost despite your gallant efforts to plan ahead and follow the map. These will be the subjects covered in the present chapter.

For most people the problem occurs relatively infrequently in familiar terrain, unless you happen to be punished with the same abominable lack of sense of orientation from which I suffer. In fact, I may be the best guide to the subject, precisely *because* I have so much

trouble finding my way myself. As you move further and further away from the straight and narrow, venturing out into remote regions and indeed in foreign lands, you will experience an ever increasing need for a systematic approach and some additional aids to orientation. In addition to the following remarks, you may find some of the references on the subject that I have included in the Bibliography to be helpful.

Preliminary Orientation
The time to start your orientation work is before you set out on any ride. It will be best if you make an effort of always deciding ahead of time where you intend to go. Before setting out, consult a map and call up before your mind's eye where the various landmarks and points of reference will be relative to your route at different places along your

Consulting the map. You may have to fold the thing in a complicated pattern to fit it into one of those presumably handy pouches on the top of the handlebar bag. At least this one by Eclipse is big enough to take a fair size map and can be reversed to consult another section of the map.

path. Go over the remarks about maps and route planning in Chapter 14 again, so you know how to choose the right map and get the greatest benefit possible from its use.

If you make a habit of doing this work even on relatively simple trips close to home, you will soon develop the systematic approach that allows you to do the same work effectively when you really have to depend on it. Only the person who has frequently gone through the process of consulting a map and planning his route will be able to do it almost unconsciously when it really matters whether you do or not, particularly when travelling in more remote or difficult terrain.

Of course, remote and difficult are not necessarily the same. Very often, it will be much easier to find your way in an area with only few roads than it is in regions that are criss-crossed by roads leading in all conceivable directions. On the other hand, you should not underestimate the potential difficulty of orientation in areas with only few roads, especially if these few roads wind their way around, up and down and along the slopes of hills, without clear views and devoid of easily recogniz-able landmarks. You could be travel-ling down the wrong road for many miles before you find out.

In the pre-tour planning stage, estimate the distances of the vari-ous sections of the ride and the nature of the terrain for each section, on the basis of the informa-tion gleaned from the map. Also try to see ahead of time whether one landmark or another should be to your left or your right, close by or far away, clearly visible or mostly hidden. Establish whether you should be going uphill or down, travelling through open terrain,

woods or built-up areas in particular sections of the ride. Use the position of the sun as a major rough guide if you don't carry a compass, which indeed seems superfluous for tour-ing in most accessible areas.

Especially try to envision the signi-ficant points directly along the road: railway crossings, bridges, intersec-tions and outstanding buildings. All this may seem trivial, and indeed it probably is – as long as you are travelling in familiar or well serviced terrain. After all, in those areas there will probably also be signs telling you which way to go, or there may be people to ask. However, only by consciously taking notice of these features on the basis of your map and pre-tour planning before you leave, will you be able to orient your-self independently once you are travelling. And if that is not signifi-cant on your first rides close to your home, it certainly will become more important once you venture out further afield.

If you have a good memory, you may be able to store all the informa-tion pertaining to the pre-planning so done in your mind. I don't, so I can't. If you should be anything like as uncoordinated as I am, you will do well to write a list, summarizing the plan of your route. Keep a systemat-ic list of the directions, landmarks, distances and major reference points in their relative positions on a sheet of paper that can be consult-ed as you go along. With enough experience – a dozen trips is all it takes – you should be able to write so systematic and comprehensive a list, that you can usually find your way without constant reference to a map. Just the same, don't go out without one.

By way of orientation for longer trips, especially abroad or in other areas further away from home, I

Fig. 16.1 Map clip

Fig. 16.2 Map roll

suggest also consulting an overall map of the particular region, state or country. Such a map will not be much use when actually cycling – a typical scale for such a map will perhaps be around 1 : 1,000,000, whereas good cycling maps are at least five times as detailed. However, this rough scale map will help you get a feel for the general picture, making you aware of the relationships between towns and mountains, roads and railways, mountains, shores and rivers, forests and plains. Prepare the overall route on this map, and refer to the more detailed one for each daily section.

In addition to one or more maps, you may want to use another simple planning tool at this preliminary stage, namely the curvimeter, illustrated in Fig. 14.4 in Chapter 14. Set it to zero and make the little wheel follow the planned route as accurately as possible, reading out the distances from the appropriate scale on the dial for each section and the overall trip length. It will probably show about 10% less than the distance in the field will register, but it is a convenient guide to the distances to be covered. If you don't use such a tool, you may be able to achieve an adequately accurate estimation with the aid of the map's printed scale and such rough tools as a match stick. If you add 15–25%, depending on the relative directness of the roads, the result will be accurate enough for a rough preliminary estimate.

Reading the Map
Of course, reading the map starts as early as the preliminary planning stage. However, the practical problems are more relevant once you get out on the road. Certainly if your route plan is less than firm in your mind, or imperfectly summarized on a sheet of paper, you will need frequent consultation of the map. Keep it easily accessible, for example in a clip on your handlebars, as shown in Fig. 16.1, or in the transparent pocket that is provided on the top of many handlebar bags. Or you may make up a reference roll, attached to the handlebars, around which the map is wrapped, along the lines of Fig. 16.2. If nothing more convenient is available, carry the map in the back pocket of your cycling shirt and don't forget to pull it out frequently for consultation. Keep it folded with the currently relevant section facing out, and protect it against dirt, rain and perspiration by means of a transparent pouch – a plain polythene bag, closed off with adhesive tape, will do the trick.

Take the characteristics of the map used for planning into consideration. Pay attention to the scale, so you get a feel for the distance or the corresponding travelling time represented by a particular distance on the map. If you have no other guide, measure the scale and the distance in terms of match stick lengths. Also note that road maps tend to overemphasize the roads, representing them and other road-related information so much that often more significant features are in danger of being overlooked. Thus, the actual configuration of a curve or an intersection, or the relative widths of supposedly minor and major roads, may vary quite a bit from the actual situation in the field. In that respect, topographic maps are much more realistic.

Remember also that each series of maps follows some conventions that are typical for that one only. Consequently, it will be smart to try and adhere to maps from the same source as much as possible. If you will be travelling for several days or long one-day rides, and ride on regular roads rather than on minor unpaved cross-country trails, I suggest choosing maps drawn to a scale of about 1 : 200,000. Some people prefer them even more detailed, except that you'd need a trailer full of printed matter to keep up a longer tour.

Also check the date of last revision on the maps you intend to use. If it is too old, you may run into difficulties, especially near built-up areas, where man's industry often outpaces the geographer's pen. Typical examples are the ferry service that has in the mean time been discontinued, or the regular road that has been expanded into a freeway, making it off-limits to cyclists.

Though some people like to keep their map looking fresh as the day they bought it, I find it handier to use it for making some of my notes. Certainly the points of interest you definitely want to visit can be marked in on the map at an early stage. This makes it much easier to plan your route so as not to miss them, even if your route is changed on account of other events. I also like to mark the locations of my overnight stays and longer stops, indicating the appropriate date. This will help you gauge your progress as you are travelling. It also helps greatly at a later stage, when it is time to gather the mementos of your tour, as described in Chapter 23.

Practice is the key to effective map use, as it is to so many other aspects of bicycle touring – or any other of life's challenges, for that matter. And though it may seem trivial, you will be best prepared for tricky situations if you start consulting the map well before you badly need it. That means several things. In the first place, you can make frequent use of the map, even in areas where you could also find your way around without it, so you are familiar with the specific map and conversant with orientation when the need arises. Secondly, you should consult the map frequently as you are travelling, so you always know where you should be on the map to avoid getting lost.

The latter point is a quite useful. It will generally be easy enough to find your way, if you can immediately define up to where your position had been verified with the map. But once you realize that you are lost and have no idea how long or how far you have been erring, you may have a very hard time indeed retracking your paces. Conscious cycling is the secret in this respect too. Know during each stage whether you are still where the map suggests you should be. If the next crossing on the map is supposed to be within a mile, you can conclude you went the wrong direction at the last junction if you haven't reached a crossing after two miles.

In the latter case, you only have to go back the two miles to the last junction where you know you must have gone wrong. If you don't know where you took the wrong turn, you may be forced to aimlessly search for many miles before you have even established where you went wrong, let alone how to get back on the correct and proper course. All in all, you will be less likely to get lost and more likely to find your way back if you are thoroughly familiar with the use of your map.

Other Orientation Aids

Maps are not the only tools that may be used to find your way around when bicycle touring. The curvimeter, described in Chapter 14, is of some limited use in orientation, as well as in planning. To keep track of the distances in the field and how they compare to the map, it will be handy to install a speedometer or merely an odometer on the bike, particularly if you can make a habit of keeping track of distances

between landmarks and road junctions as you go along. Remember though, that the rougher the map's scale and the hillier the terrain, the greater the discrepancy between the distance measured on the map and the actual distance, which will usually be quite a bit more in such cases.

Two other useful devices are binoculars and a compass. The former can help you locate or identify landmarks further afield. Nowadays, small binoculars of very high quality that are light enough to be taken on the bike are readily available. The compass will do a lot more useful things than merely show which way is North. It usually comes complete with an instruction manual, which is worth working your way through before setting out on your first tour, so you get the maximum benefit.

If you don't carry a compass – and I know of very few cyclists who do – there is another simple way to guess the direction. South is where the sun is around twelve noon in the Northern hemisphere, and for each hour earlier the sun is 15 degrees further East, for each hour later it is as much further West. Of course, this guideline is most reliable when the sun is relatively low, that is in the early or late season or further away

The modern electronic speedometer and mileage counter is a handy gadget that can also be useful to aid with orientation in the field. This IKU model is particularly suitable, since it is easily operated, with only two simple and easily handled push buttons.

from the equator. And in a rainstorm it may be little consolation to know you could find your way – if only the sun would come out.

In addition, you should establish where you are in your particular time zone, relative to its center. That can make a difference of up to 7 degrees either way. Finally, in this regard, make an allowance for daylight savings time, called summer time in most parts of the world that use it. It can make an additional difference of 15 degrees. Figure these deviations out before you leave, and summarize the total deviation in a note on your map.

An even simpler aid to orientation is often provided at the state's expense: road signs. In some parts of the world all the preceding advice will seem superfluous, due to society's generosity in putting up adequate directional signs along most roads at virtually all junctions. Even so, you will need a map, since that same thoughtful society may not be aware of your particular short-term destination. As a cyclist, you may not be aiming quite as far as what seems practical to the typical motorist, and your plan may include taking the road in the direction of A only a few miles, followed by a detour in direction B, before finally reaching the road marked for your immediate destination C.

Then there is that other useful orientational institution: asking the way. For the cyclist, there are certain risks involved when following this simple method. One obvious drawback is that most of the potential suppliers of such information are either motorists or pedestrians. The former don't mind making a little detour of twenty miles or so, or they don't realize that the shortest way goes over the top of a mountain pass that will take you all day on the bike. The latter, by contrast, often have a very limited perspective on the world. Many pedestrians have no idea how to get to places that are at some distance, and the response, "you can't get there from here" is indeed not as unlikely as you may think.

Whether questioning motorists or not, there is the risk of being sent linea recta to the nearest freeway, which is off-limits to cyclists in most countries. You can't go that way, even if you should be competent enough and willing to put up with the kind of traffic encountered on such a less than rustic road. Another potential problem is that locals often don't know anything about some of the goals that may be of interest to a touring cyclist, which do not necessarily coincide with the places other people want to reach.

Finally there are those areas where most of the passers-by are tourists, who have no idea at all, although most of them at least carry some kind of map. Whatever you do, don't ask anybody the way without consulting the map at the same time, and don't follow any advice without verifying it on the map first. In Chapter 19 you will find a few more remarks that are particularly relevant when trying to find your way abroad.

17
Food for the Road

Compared to the demands of a sedentary lifestyle, bicycle touring is a strenuous affair, and a lot of food is needed to keep you going. Consequently, the questions of what to eat and how to go about it are often raised in cycling circles. Considering that most bike tours are not really all that monstrous in their energy demands, and that most people have acquired an impressive store of body fat, the chance of literally

Roadside stop for a snack and drink. Even with younger children – ours were 8 and 11 years old at the time – long distance cycling is no problem, providing you interrupt the trip occasionally and make sure there is enough diversion along the way and between rides. The children develop an incredible appetite during this kind of trip.

running out of energy supplies is quite remote for the average touring cyclist. What does need to'be said will be covered here.

Before getting hung up about the subject, realize that there is hardly a topic about which more nonsense has been written and about which more people hold preconceived notions than that of food and diet. So, at the risk of being accused of adding more of the same, here's my limited view as a touring cyclist. In cycling circles you will encounter staunch vegetarians and veritable carnivores, carrot munchers and pill poppers, all claiming the key to their fitness, endurance or peace of mind lies in the way they fill their bellies. Though the subject is not without interest, I would suggest considering it more soberly: forget about fad diets and concentrate on selecting your food consciously instead.

Especially in America, cyclists typically seem to stem from the same ranks as health food freaks and other diet conscious people. Nothing wrong with that, but many of the theories propounded in those circles are only relevant for people with a sedentary lifestyle. However, it makes a great difference whether you spend the day lounging about in office, car and home, or spend a good part of each day burning up calories on a loaded bicycle. What the touring cyclist needs is not a diet but a clear understanding of the function of food as it applies to his performance and overall health. Most of all, active cyclists should consider the following facts:

☐ Endurance activity requires much more in the way of calories and allows the kinds of food that would be fattening or otherwise undesirable to the inactive person.

☐ On the other hand, a two or three-week tour does not determine a permanent life style, so your diet should vary, reflecting the energy level required during active and inactive periods, respectively.

☐ As for the supposedly superior nutrients, such as proteins, vitamins and minerals, an active person does not necessarily require more of these than an inactive person of the same weight.

☐ More is not necessarily better: if X grams of protein or Y milligrams of some vitamin or mineral are required, then it does not follow that twice these quantities will improve your health, strength or endurance even one bit.

The Tasks of Food

Your body, including every individual organ, muscle and bone, needs food to function properly. The tasks that must be fulfilled by the things you eat and drink boil down to providing the following:

☐ Energy to keep the body's temperature at the necessary level for the various systems to operate.

☐ Energy needed to perform mechanical work by means of muscle action.

☐ Liquids to conduct heat, to control body temperature and to allow various physiological processes to function.

☐ Building materials needed to grow and replace cell structures.

☐ Enzymes that allow the other processes to operate efficiently.

The most important substances to ingest so these functions can be carried out are listed as follows:

☐ Water
☐ Carbohydrates
☐ Fats
☐ Proteins

☐ Vitamins
☐ Mineral trace elements
☐ Fiber bran

In the following sections, each of these major substances will be briefly described, followed by an analysis of the tasks for which the body needs the various types of food and drink. I'll show how the different food substances fit into the complex of functions that must be fulfilled for the human body to operate effectively, especially under such physically demanding conditions as presented by long distance bicycle touring. Finally, I will give some practical suggestions for solving the food problem *en route*.

Water

About 70% of your body weight is water. It is the major carrier for other substances in the body and is essential for the process of temperature control. Water must be replenished as it evaporates or is excreted. It need not always be taken in the form of plain water, since it is contained in most foods, especially in fruits, vegetables and meat. And of course almost any beverage provides it quickly.

Many substances needed within the body, such as sugars and minerals, are dissolved in water and pass into the cells by means of osmosis. That is the process of filtering an aqueous solution through a thin membrane. In osmosis, the transfer is always from the side with the higher concentration to the side where it is lower. Consequently, the concentrations of essential substances (such as sugar and in some cases table salt) in the water you drink should be at least as high in the liquid as it is in the body cells. Thus, the way to introduce sugars is to bind them in what is referred to as

an isotonic solution, meaning it has at least the same concentration of dissolved materials as the liquid in the body cells.

Water is particularly important for regulating the body's temperature. During vigorous cycling in hot weather, the cyclist may lose water faster than the rate at which his system can possibly absorb it. Half a liter, or about one pint, per hour is all the body will absorb, while it may evaporate at twice that rate. To keep the body at the optimal temperature for muscular and mental work, water is required. Whenever the temperature threatens to get too high, the pores and sweat glands are opened and perspiration is excreted, the natural evaporation of which cools the body.

Especially in hot weather and on long exhausting rides, you may need more water than you can carry in bottles on the bike. Start drinking well before the start, and drink frequently in moderate quantities during the ride. Allow perspiration to evaporate, rather than wiping it off. Since water is also an excellent medium to tie up sugars and electrolytes isotonically, it is frequently suggested to carry two bottles on a hot and exhausting ride: one with plain water for cooling, the other with a water-based mixture containing 2–2.5% sugar and up to a teaspoonful of table salt per pint. Personally, I prefer natural fruit juice over this man-made mixture. It serves the same purpose but tastes a lot better.

Carbohydrates

This predominant energy source, comprising both sugars and starch, is present in virtually all foods. The difference between sugar and starch is that the latter takes about two hours longer to provide energy, as it must be turned into usable sugar first, while most sugars can be taken up in the blood stream very shortly after they are consumed. However nice it may seem to get something that works quickly, starch-rich foods are preferable over sugars, since they also provide other nutrients and keep the body's digestive system in better trim. They should be the staple of the active cyclist's diet.

Particularly rich sources of starch are all grain products and potatoes. Yet starches are also contained in virtually all other vegetable and carnivorous foods. Natural sugars are contained in most fruits and honey, while refined sugars are provided only too generously by just about all ready-made foods and drinks. Whether natural or refined, they provide energy equally efficiently – ordinary refined sugar at the lowest cost. Though you may want to take a sugared drink for quick energy on the road, try to avoid sugars in your everyday diet, except in the form of fruits and natural juices, which also contain other valuable nutrients and digestive aids.

Fat
Although justly derided as a no-good in the inactive person's diet, fat is the most energy-efficient nutrient. However, fat as consumed is very slowly digested and converted to energy only indirectly. In the body, fat is used as a store of energy and an insulator. The body converts excess nutrients of any kind into body fat. Nutritive fat is present in meats and dairy products, but also in many nuts, seeds and various other vegetable sources. The distinction between polysaturated and unsaturated fats is probably not as significant to the active cyclist as it is to the sedentary person.

Fat can be used as an energy source in the form of free fatty acids (FFA), dissolved from the stored body fat. These are carried in the blood stream and are used for energy much like sugar. After it is consumed, the fat first builds up as padding in various places, to be released in the form of FFA as needed to supply energy when work must be done at a certain level. This will be covered in more detail under Food for Energy below.

It is probably true that the majority of people in the western world have accumulated too much body fat. But it is very hard to avoid eating it altogether, since it is tied up with proteins in so many products that we have grown fond of. The tender American steak contains twice as much fat as the tougher stuff consumed in the rest of the world, and it is hard to convince most people they don't need to eat as much meat as they do, or that tougher meat would be better for them.

Protein
Protein comprises various combinations of a group of aminoacids. These are contained in meats and dairy products, as well as – though in lesser concentrations – in legumes and grains. For the body to use proteins for cell building, the aminoacids must be present simultaneously in a particular ratio, which is most closely approximated by egg white, fish and meat. Other forms of protein foods are only adequately efficient if eaten in some combination of various types, for instance legumes with potatoes, bread with milk, or beans with rice.

Contrary to popular belief, cyclists don't need more protein than other people of the same age and body weight. Only about 1 g of protein is required per day for each kg of body weight. Slightly more may be needed by growing youngsters, pregnant women and during the initial building-up phase when a previously inactive person first takes up cycling, developing new muscle tissue. Most American adults get enough protein to allow for these instances. On the other hand, protein deficiency may become a problem on a long tour, especially in other countries, when you rely too much on food that is either simple to prepare or easy to find ready-made.

Excess proteins – those that are not used for cell building – are simply burned up to provide energy or stored in the form of body fat, much like carbohydrates. A crying shame, since proteins are on average five times as expensive and considerably harder to digest. For the latter reason, protein rich meals should not be eaten during or shortly before really hard trips. Breakfast and lunch should be heavy on starches, minerals, vitamins and bran, whereas they should be low on fats and protein. The best time to eat meals containing more protein is perhaps about 6–7 PM: late enough not to interfere with demanding physical activity, yet early enough to be digested before the night.

Vitamins

Vitamins are primarily a group of acids, required in small quantities to provide the enzymes necessary for operation of various functions. They are distinguished into water soluble and fat soluble types. The water soluble vitamins (B and C) leave the body fast with the urine, so they must be replenished daily, while the fat soluble ones (A, D, E and K) can be stored in the body over longer periods. Various vitamins are contained mainly in fresh fruits and vegetables, organ meats and whole grain products. A well balanced and varied diet provides all the essential vitamins you ever need.

Consequently, there is probably no need for vitamin supplements if you have an adequate variety of vitamin-containing foods in your diet, and there is no need to take vitamin tablets even during the toughest rides. Especially the fat soluble vitamins should be taken in moderation to avoid large build-ups with questionable effects on your health. The water soluble vitamins B and C, being necessary for energy production in the body, may have to be supplemented if performance falls off and no other cause is evident. Since any excess of these is excret-

Very handy handlebar bag attachment on Ultimate model from Cannondale. The fiber-reinforced plastic bracket on the bag latches in place on a corresponding part permanently installed on the handlebars. Extremely convenient to carry valuables, since you can easily take the bag with you when leaving the bike.

ed, there's no risk of getting too much. In some cases you may benefit by taking modest doses of multi-vitamin tablets on a regular basis, certainly if you are for some reason not able to adhere to a properly balanced food intake during a prolonged tour.

Minerals

Also referred to as electrolytes, some minerals are required in small quantities for enzyme functions. Those that are only required in the minutest quantities are referred to as trace elements. Most are present mainly in vegetables, fruits and grains. The most familiar of these elements is the sodium that becomes free when ordinary table salt dissolves in water. Others, such as potassium, calcium, and iron (the latter needed as a carrier of oxygen in blood and certain muscle fiber cells) are equally needed. Since these electrolytes are water soluble, their excess is excreted with urine and perspiration. Consequently, after a very long and hard ride in hot weather, a case may be made for their replacement if heavy perspiration depletes their level below their required minimum concentration in the body.

Back in the early 'seventies a medical layman analyzed perspiration, assuming all substances lost in it should be replaced. No medical evidence has ever been presented to support this assumption, but that has not stopped dozens of manufacturers from introducing similar potions. They are all expensive and taste awful, containing too much sugar and useless electrolytes. Totally unnecessary of course: the water and sugar can be provided in a more appetizing form and better balanced proportions, while the only electrolytes that matter (sodium

and potassium) can be replenished by adding some table salt in hot weather and by eating a banana, respectively. Beyond that, eating a reasonably balanced diet will take care of all your electrolyte needs.

Fiber Bran

Fibrous materials, which are contained largely in unprocessed vegetable and grain products, are necessary to stimulate the digestive cycle. With the exercise of your cycling, you will not need it as much as most inactive people, but you may not get enough to feel well. Cycling with clogged intestines is not very enjoyable. Again, the famous balanced diet, with whole grain bread instead of the white pulp usually dished up in most households, cooked and raw vegetables and various fruits, will keep you well supplied. If not, use bran cereals or add bran flakes to other foods. Going for a walk after the main meal also works wonders.

Food for Energy

The overwhelming majority of the food you eat will be used to provide energy – both the heat energy to keep your body warm and the mechanical energy that allows you to do muscle work. Carbohydrates, fat and proteins all lend themselves to that purpose. They can all be converted to the glucose that is transported in the blood or the glycogen that may be stored in the liver and muscle tissue. Thus, they can ultimately all be burned to form the ATP that constitutes the raw material for muscle work. However, these three foods are not all equally efficient, and they require different proportions of oxygen to perform their task. Furthermore, different kinds of foods – even with similar constituents – require longer or

Table 17-I.
Characteristics of carbohydrates, fats and protein as energy sources

food type	energy content		respiration quotient	typical time to digest
	(kJ/g)	(kcal/g)	RQ	hours
carbohydrate	17.2	4.1	1.0	
sugars				0.1−2
starch				2−3
fat	38.9	9.3	0.7	6−8
protein	17.2	4.1		6−8

shorter digestion periods before they can be used effectively. Table 17-I summarizes the major differences between the three basic energy sources, while Table 17-II may help you get some feel for the time it takes the body to digest certain foodstuffs.

The amount of work expended and the food energy consumed can best be measured in kJ (kiloJoules). To relate this to more familiar units, 4.2 kJ = 1 kcal, which is what's really meant when calories are referred to in older works about nutrition. An average person leading a quiet life needs about 7,000 kJ of energy per day. A hard day's cycling will add anything up to 4,500 kJ of mechanical energy.

Considering the human engine's efficiency of approximately 25%, that means an additional 18,000 kJ must be provided, adding up to a total daily energy requirement of about 24,000 kJ. That is also just about the maximum your body can take up in a day. Any energy expended in excess of this (that happens in a tough mountain tour or a double century, which is bicycling jargon for a 200 mile ride) will go at the expense of your body weight. On the other hand, eating more than enough to supply that food will not even make you fatter: it goes straight through your system.

As you can tell from Table 17-I, fat is easily the most energy-efficient nutrient, offering twice as much

Table 17-II. Digestion times in hours for various food types

time in stomach	food types
1−2 hours	water, coffee, tea, boiled rice, soft boiled egg, fresh water fish
2−3 hours	milk, coffee with cream, boiled or baked potatoes, low-fiber cooked vegetables, fruit, white bread, hard boiled egg, omelette or fried egg, salt water fish, veal
3−4 hours	whole grain bread, fried or French fried potatoes, fried rice, fibrous vegetables (e.g. spinach), salads (without dressing), beef, ham, boiled tender chicken
4−5 hours	beans, high-fiber vegetables, boiled or fried meat, poultry and game
6−8 hours	mushrooms, bacon, sardines in oil

energy per gram as either carbohydrates or protein. The fat you burn passes into the system as free fatty acids (FFA). That's not the fat you have just eaten. Rather, it derives from the stuff that has accumulated in various places on the body. These fat stores are formed by all excess foods not needed for immediate energy supply, which is always converted into fat, except if it exceeds the maximum digestive limit mentioned above. At most levels of output the body uses a combination of free fatty acids and glycogen for aerobic energy production: mainly fat at low levels, mainly glycogen at higher levels, as represented in Fig. 17.1.

It is possible to determine what proportions of the energy comes from fat and carbohydrate metabolisms, respectively, at any time. This is done by comparing the volumes of exhaled carbon dioxide and inhaled oxygen, called the respiratory quotient RQ. If RQ iṣ 1.0, all energy comes from carbohydrates; if it is 0.7, all comes from fat. Any intermediate ratio allows the physiologist to determine how much fat and how much carbohydrates are being burned. On really long exhausting rides, such as mountain tours, the supply of carbohydrates is in danger two ways. At high output levels it is used up first and fastest, and its supply is limited to what can be taken up by the body in a day. You may run out before your destination is reached.

No such problems at low output levels, such as relaxed touring rides, where free fatty acids are preferably burned. The supply of fat on even the leanest body will probably suffice to cycle half way around the world at a modest speed. But to the mountain touring cyclist, who has to keep up a high output all day, the supply

problem may become evident. Anywhere beyond 75% of his maximum output level, he'll be burning virtually only carbohydrates, as evidenced by an RQ close to 1.0. The glycogen in liver and muscles, the glucose in the blood and the food in the belly are the only energy supplies available. Once these are gone, it's all over.

The obvious way to prolong your energy supply is by reducing the pace to a level below 75% of the maximum, whenever possible. That's one good reason to take it easier by riding sheltered, which may be achieved by taking turns in the front with your companions. This reduces the wind resistance enough to make all the difference on a long fast ride. This tends to shift the balance more towards the fat metabolism. Finally, there is some evidence that the fat metabolism can be stimulated by taking caffeine.

Everything in moderation though: probably not more than 4 mg per kg of body weight (2 mg per lb). That is the equivalent of about two small cups of strong coffee at the beginning of a hard ride for the average person. Even when used as suggested, there is a problem with caffeine, since it works as a diuretic. That means it encourages liquids to leave the body in the form of urine. Consequently, in hot weather, particularly for tours involving a lot of climbing, the excessive use of caffeine may be dangerous: you will need all the water you can drink to act as a cooling medium.

Carbohydrate loading is a technique used by some cyclists who want to perform well in a duration activity only once in a blue moon. It's no use for short or really long rides, nor for vacation tours, and dubious at best even for its intended purpose. The idea is to exercise to

The respiratory quotient RQ is used as an indicator to establish to what extent energy is generated by burning carbohydrate and free fatty acids (FFA), respectively. Up to about 75 % of VO_2max the low value for RQ indicates that most energy is provided by the fat metabolism. To maximize endurance, try to stay within that range as long as possible during a long race.

Fig. 17.1 Fat v. carbohydrate consumption

exhaustion several days well before the big events, after which you start eating carbohydrates in generous supplies, without doing very much in the way of hard work. The assumption is that the muscles will absorb lots of carbohydrates in the form of energy carrying glycogen. For bicycle touring it is a highly questionable technique. Don't fool around with it.

Weight Reduction
The quickest, easiest, healthiest and cheapest way to cycle more effectively may well be by reducing your body weight. That's assuming you are like most people in the industrialized world, who carry unnecessary ballast in the form of excess fat. The body fat percentage can be accurately determined by means of several techniques, most simply by measuring certain skin folds, which any sports physician or paramedic can do. For a touring cyclist, looking in the mirror will probably suffice. To limit your weight, use a combination of various techniques: eat less and differently, taking more fibrous matter and less fats and sugars; do more physical work in addition to your cycling – walk or use your bike

instead of the car, the stairs instead of the elevator.

Only on a very long tour is there any risk of running out of body-stored supplies. Typically, the touring cyclist, however big his appetite, eats a little less than the energy he consumes each day during a longer tour. You can easily verify that by comparing your weight before and after any tour of a week or more. On really long tours – say four weeks or longer – it is conceivable that you eventually use up essentially all the stored body fat. This may lead to symptoms similar to those described for the overtraining syndrome in Chapter 11. If you should develop these symptoms, take it easier for a couple of days and make sure you get a varied and adequate diet.

A Touring Cyclist's Meal Planner
It is possible to eat adequately without any other advice than that contained in the preceding sections. If you follow those suggestions, you'll be adequately prepared for even the toughest bicycle tours. However, for those who prefer some additional guidance, here are some

specific hints on how one might divide the required food intake over a touring day.

☐ *Breakfast:*
Aim for a high starch intake, combined with vitamins, fibers and minerals, and modest amounts of proteins, avoiding sugars and fat. Fruit or fruit juice; whole grain cereal with a banana or dried fruit; low fat milk or natural plain yoghurt; whole grain bread. Try to eat breakfast at least an hour before the start of your tour and at least two hours before really hard mountain climbing sections.

☐ *Lunch:*
On the road, aim for a relatively light lunch after a big breakfast, again containing more starch than proteins, avoiding fats and sugars. Eat salad with bread or other starch foods, combined with small quantities of meat, fish, egg or cheese. A sandwich should not be lots of meat or cheese with a little bread, but rather lots of bread with little meat or cheese and very little in the way of butter, margarine or mayonnaise. Drink plain water, tea or low fat milk, and have a desert of plain yoghurt and fresh fruit.

☐ *Supper:*
When bicycle touring, this should be the heaviest meal of the day and the one time to include more protein foods, though it will still be preferable to go easy on tender (read: high-fat) meats. In addition to meat or other protein foods, eat generous quantities of starch foods and fresh or cooked vegetables and fruit. Drink water, tea,

natural fruit juice or low fat milk. Hold off on salad dressings, gravies and sauces. Try to have dinner relatively early in the evening. Get some light exercise, even if it is only a 20 minute walk, after dinner to help digestion.

☐ *Snacks:*
If the urge strikes during the day, the active cyclist can indulge in snacks between meals. In fact, it will be even wiser to eat six small meals than three big ones during a cycling day. When eating between meals, avoid junk food, though. Instead of sugared and fatty stuff, choose any of the relatively light foods that give you something to munch on and which contain starch, fibers, minerals and vitamins. You can eat fruit, crackers, raw or cooked vegetables and plain yoghurt; drink water, tea, low fat milk or unsweetened natural fruit juice.

On the road, it will be smart to have some snacks for nibbling readily accessible. For long rides in relatively deserted terrain, you may also have to carry supplies for at least one meal, sometimes more. Try to adjust your eating pattern to the above recommendations, so the items for lunch are easy to carry, and the meal quickly prepared on the road during a picnic break. The larger meal at night and the preparations for some of the next day's meals are taken care of at the location of your overnight stay. In the Bibliography, you will find references to some books with recipes for dishes that can be easily prepared on a little camp stove with a minimum of simple ingredients.

18
Bicycle Camping

Although you are free to stay in any type of accommodation you choose, most touring cyclists finish up camping at least some of the time on longer tours. Done properly, that can be a very enjoyable experience. Without the right equipment, inadequately prepared or with the wrong attitude and expectations, on the other hand, bike camping can be quite frustrating. In the present chapter you will find the advice needed to make your bicycle camping experience a pleasant one.

In most cases, you probably want the emphasis of your trip to be on the cycling aspect. That is perfectly legitimate, providing you pay just enough attention to the camping aspect so it does not result in excessive work or frustration. That would spoil the fun of cycling as well. In short, taking the various considerations necessary to make you as competent a camper as you are as a cyclist, will be handsomely rewarded. You'll have a more enjoyable touring experience.

Mountain bikers camping in the Colorado mountains. (Photograph David Epperson / Bicycle Sport)

The correct selection of your camping equipment is of course of utmost importance. In order to handle the selection process most competently, I suggest you read through Chapter 7 once more. In addition, it may be a good idea to get several catalogs of camping and backpacking equipment suppliers. You may also consider the possibility of making some of your own gear. If you are not already an experienced lightweight camper and an accomplished seamster, you should only venture out in that particular field with the aid of very thoroughly tested patterns. You may be as impressed as I was with the sew-it-yourself kits developed by the Frostline company.

After solving the equipment selection problem, that of packing it all in the various bags and attaching these to the bike will be the most important. Refer to the relevant advice in Chapter 5 for the selection of bicycle bags and Chapter 13 for the choice of items to take and the way to pack them. If you stay the night in tent and sleeping bag, you will have so much more to carry on the bike that all these recommendations become even more critical than they are for other bicycle tours.

Camp Sites

Assuming you have managed to work out all the equipment and packing questions satisfactorily, you will now be faced with the practice of camping. Even if you have often spent the night outside before, it will not be quite the same as when you are backpacking or travelling by car. Unlike the backpacker, you will probably travel quite significant distances between overnight stops, and your camp sites generally have to be those along the road. Many of those, you'll soon learn to your considerable disappointment, are less idyllic than you may have imagined.

In the first place, these sites may be quite far apart, since motorists – for whom these sites are primarily intended – don't mind travelling a hundred miles out of their way. As a cyclist, you probably object to 'wasting' even ten miles. In addition, most of these camp sites are overrun by people in cars. There'll be lots of trailers (caravans to the English) and mobile homes, not to mention the televisions, refrigerators and other achievements of modern civilization that go wherever mechanized people penetrate. But there are other drawbacks. In the USA, I have more than once found camp sites paved wall to wall with asphalt, where pitching a tent was plainly impossible.

Even so, all in all, there are enough adequate camp sites, though it will be smart to plan your trip carefully to make sure the ones you intend to use are equipped for your kind of use. The positive side of the motorist domination is that there will almost always be a little corner for a cyclist and his tent somewhere, even on a site that is otherwise full. And, as a cyclist, you can more easily pitch your tent outside the official camp sites, much like the backpacker. Certainly in the US, where private property is a fetish, I must recommend not doing that on clearly privately owned land without specific permission from the owner. In areas where people live near the land they work, it should often be possible to round up the owner, who will rarely object when asked for permission.

Personally, I have had some of my most memorable experiences camping with permission on private land. Many land owners were delighted to have a visitor, and quite a few were extremely helpful and hospitable. This does seem to work out best in foreign countries, since most people feel a particular obligation to show themselves from their most favorable side when they are given an opportunity to help strangers. I have been invited in for meals and baths, spent long nights in animated discussion and made good friends in such cases. Certainly if there are only one or two in your group, this can be a wonderful way to camp.

Many of the roadside camp sites have the advantage of very sophisticated facilities, though they are often rather expensive. The opportunity to take a shower, do your laundry or buy many of your essential supplies will be particularly welcome to the cyclist. To make maximum use of these advantages, get an up-to-date guide that shows the facilities available at all the camp sites in the relevant area.

The biggest problem is that you may have an awfully long way to go if the anticipated facilities are for some reason not available, for instance to obtain the food you thought could be purchased locally. However, you can probably find a

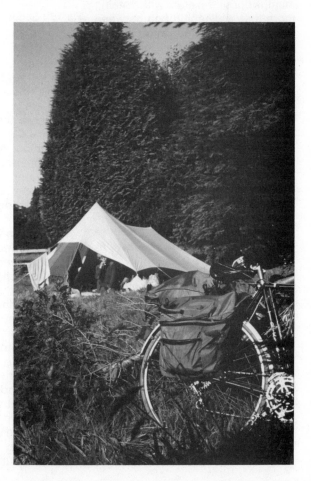

Bicycle camping in England. Especially in a rainy climate, a tent with a full size fly sheet and a large covered entrance will be very convenient.

motorist at the site who will either give you a ride to the nearest store or bring you something back. In countries like the US and Canada, this nearest store may at times be beyond cycling reach, certainly after you've already spent a long day in the saddle. If you can't get a ride or if even the remote shop is closed, motor campers often have so much in the way of supplies (and compassion) that you can scrounge enough for one or two meals without difficulty or embarrassment.

Pitching the Tent

The ultimate way of camping, to my mind, is under the stars with nothing more than a sleeping bag between you and the heavens. Unfortunately, a tent can rarely be considered dispensable. Although it may at times be quite possible to camp without putting up a tent, I suggest you carry one on all camping trips, especially if rain, insects or the need for a modicum of privacy may become a problem. When bike touring, one or the other of these criteria seems to apply most of the time. In this section I will discuss the considerations needed to put up the tent wisely.

The tent should properly be considered a shelter that can be used to protect you from rain, wind, cold, insects and improper curiosity. Clearly, it must be pitched with the relevant objectives in mind. In addition, you will want to be assured of a reasonable night's sleep, so it will be necessary to put the tent in such a way that a level surface allows that. Here are the considerations necessary when surveying the overall site as to just where you choose to pitch the tent:

☐ The spot for the tent must be level, free from protruding rocks,

Fig. 18.1 Suggested arrangement of tent and site

and large enough to accommodate the tent, allowing all guy lines to be extended.

☐ If there is any chance of rain, find an area that is elevated slightly above the rest of the terrain; at a minimum, avoid a location that is just below a likely downward path for water.

☐ If strong winds are likely, make sure the tent opening faces either a dense and high windbreak or the downwind side.

☐ Keep adequate distance from your present or future neighbors, public facilities, car parking areas, roads and pathways.

☐ Find a place so generally sheltered that you have at least a modicum of privacy.

☐ Before pitching the tent, remove all sticks, stones and other protrusions that might damage the ground sheet and fill up any holes that would make it uncomfortable to sit or sleep.

☐ Make sure you can keep your bike locked up close to the tent and within your view.

Inside and Around the Tent

The way you arrange your household in and around the tent can be of great significance for the comfort and convenience of your camping experience. Having everything needed regularly within easy reach, while keeping things you don't need where they are out of your way, must be learned. Experience eventually solves that problem, but a little thought and practice beforehand may be very helpful. Don't hesitate to try it all out in your own back yard or in any public place, before you actually go out on your first serious camping trip. Even then, I would suggest you start off with a weekend trip to get additional practical experience. Either way, thinking it all out beforehand, as well as during the time you are out there, will make the whole experience more enjoyable and efficient.

Fig. 18.1 shows a suggested layout for the tent and your equipment. As you can see, the tent's central area should be its entrance. When sitting in the entrance, and protected within the tent, though maintaining access to the things arranged to either side of you, everything may be taken care of conveniently. The things that must be kept dry at all cost, such as clothing and sleeping bag, are kept inside the tent, near the back. Cooking equipment, including camp stove, pots, utensils, food and water container, are arranged to one side, just outside the entrance, under the shelter of the tent's forward extended fly sheet.

Items to which you need quick access, such as matches and utensils, are near the side of the tent. The stuff you don't need to get at very often can be kept just outside the tent under the extended sides and in the back under the fly sheet. Near the entrance of the tent, the ground is covered with a small extra ground sheet. Shoes and rain gear, if appropriate, are also near the entrance. Items of value are kept in a bag in a fixed place, that should not be too obvious to others. This allows you to take them with you whenever you leave the tent, certainly when you do not have a companion with you who can guard tent and gear while you are gone.

My observation is that most less experienced campers are either sitting inside their tent with the opening closed, or standing outside it. The experienced camper, on the other hand, has found the method explained above much more effective. This way you are acting at the interface between your tent and the outside world. Getting up to fetch water, or to take care of any other chore, is no problem. Even if it is windy or rainy, this arrangement, together with the smart selection of the location and orientation of the tent, sees to it that you are adequately sheltered. You can cook or do other household chores from your station at the front, without getting smoke, flames or fumes inside.

If it does get too cold, you can still close the tent opening and move the entire operation in by about two feet. That way you'll bring the dangerous cooking operation into the tent as well, so you must take a little more care to avoid fires, breathing in fumes or spilling the contents of your pot. The entire cooking procedure is a tricky thing, but I'm afraid doing it really effectively with the limited facilities takes more than anybody can adequately describe in a book.

You'll learn as you go along, especially if you give the whole operation some thought and if you plan ahead.

Working in the right sequence, it is possible to cook an entire meal on only one flame, using only two or three saucepans and a frying pan. You can keep items just cooked warm on top of the pot with the next dish you prepare. Alternately, you can wrap certain items up in a towel and a sleeping bag to keep them warm (that's the ultimate way to cook rice, to give just one example).

Excellent freeze-dried dishes are available in great variety in most parts of the world these days. Although specialized backpacking stores may have the most complete (and the most expensive) selection, you may find enough variety in ordinary supermarkets at home or along the way. But you need not limit your cooking to the reconstitution of freeze-dried mixtures. Preparing meals from scratch is not impossible on a camp stove either. This makes even more sense if you are a larger group. If you are travelling in a group of three or more, you can carry two separate cookers and enough pots to prepare a full meal using fresh foodstuffs. Just select the ingredients with the required preparation time in mind, and shy away from dishes that need too many different ingredients or spices. Those few spices you do need should be selected before you leave, and they can be carried in small waterproof containers, such as empty film canisters.

Sleeping in the Tent

At night, also arrange everything with some thought. To make sure your pad will be comfortable, you can try out the ground before you even pitch the tent. Sometimes pitching the tent a few inches one way or the other can make all the difference in comfort. Keep the sleeping bag packed away until you are ready to go to bed, though the mattress pad may be used during the day to sit in the tent more comfortably, especially if it is cold.

Arrange all the items you will not be needing during the night or when getting up in the morning along the back and the sides of the tent. Articles you may need during the night or when first getting up, such as matches, candle or flash light, shoes, jacket or rain wear and the next day's clothing, should be easily accessible near the entrance, as appropriate to their function. In addition to your sleeping bag and pad, you probably want to have something that can serve as a pillow – if nothing else, fold some clothing together and wrap it in a towel under your head.

In very cold weather, you may find even your sleeping bag is not enough to keep you warm. You can easily extend your bag's comfort range by wearing socks, a sweater and a woollen cap, in addition to your usual night wear. I like to use a sheet sleeping bag liner inside my down bag, to keep the latter clean under normal circumstances. Putting this sheet bag around the outside of the down bag will keep you quite a bit warmer in the cold, thin though it is. In particularly hot weather, you may want to make do with sleeping on top of the opened sleeping bag, sleeping uncovered or with only the sheet bag. Sleeping directly under the stars without a tent, keeping the tent open, or closing only a mosquito netting flap, will also keep you a lot cooler during a hot night.

Breaking Up Camp

Next day, if you intend to continue on the bike right away, you may either pack up before breakfast, or you can first treat yourself to a comfortable breakfast in camp. It all depends on the time you get up and the number of hours you want to spend on the bike. If you have a long trip ahead of you, it will make a lot of sense to hold off with breakfast, breaking up camp right away instead. If you stay in camp until after breakfast, first hang your sleeping bag out to air or dry, assuming it is not raining. Keep the tent pitched until all is taken care of, packing the tent last of all, especially if the weather is cold or wet. Make sure you forget nothing and that everything is properly packed on the bike.

If you are in a hurry to get back on the bike, you may have to pack up in a bit of a rush, so you may not have time to air your sleeping bag or to eat breakfast. Take the time for a proper breakfast after one or two hours, especially if you anticipate some hard cycling that day. While stopped for breakfast by the roadside, air the sleeping bag, the tent and any laundry or other clothing, if it was not completely dried when you packed up.

This late breakfast after one or two hours of cycling can be taken in the form of a roadside picnic. Buy your supplies fresh along the way, and stop in a scenic location. It is perhaps one of the most delightful experiences, to be having breakfast under the sky at a time long before most others are travelling. You will feel even better when you realize

View from the tent. Though your bikes may not be the most scenic object in view, it will be a good idea to keep an eye on them, especially on public camp grounds. And don't forget to bring everything out of the bags into the tent. I have had bags and gear stolen off the bikes myself. (Photograph Darryl Skrabak)

Small saddle pouch by Eclipse. Unlike the large British bags, this otherwise well designed and constructed model, is not big enough to carry more than a few essentials.

that you have already covered twenty, thirty or even more miles of cycling, bringing you that much closer to the day's destination. On a really long trip, you can even have supper on the way, continuing the bike trip afterwards, to put up camp quite late. This is particularly suitable in Northern regions in the Northern hemisphere – or far South in the Southern hemisphere. In spring and summer, days are very long in those regions.

If, on the other hand, you want to make the most of your camping experience, and want to keep the day's cycling distance down to something manageable without interruptions, you may decide to cy-cle only half days, either mornings or afternoons. In the former case, have an early breakfast at the camp site and get going early. Travel up to a late lunch, which you have at the next camp site. This way you will have the entire afternoon to spend in camp, which will be very desirable if you are camped in a location where some activity – whether sightseeing, a museum visit or an afternoon at a swimming pool – is possible conveniently close to the camp site. Conversely, you can stay put until after lunch; in that case, cycle only afternoon and evening, getting to the next campsite in time for supper.

19
Bike Touring Abroad

Bicycle touring, most of those who have tried it agree, is a fine way to travel in foreign countries. The formalities and the material risks associated with travelling abroad by car are eliminated. At the same time, you retain the freedom to travel at will at your own pace and to your own schedule, where you want and when you want. It is usually both more convenient and cheaper than conventional ways of travelling. The latter applies especially if bike touring is combined with camping or staying in youth hostels. This chapter is devoted entirely to the specific problems associated with travelling abroad by bike.

As an additional bonus, you may consider combining your tour abroad with some bicycle-related activities. Perhaps you'll have an opportunity to watch a major stage race, such as the Tour de France, while touring on the European continent. A visit to a major manufacturer's plant may well be an eye-opener to the interested bicyclist. On a more practical level, you may be able to purchase some of the

Photo stop along the romantic route. Spectacular scenery showing man's hand as well as God's in Southern Germany more exotic bicycles, bike components, bike components or bicycling clothes that are not readily available at home. Or how about a visit to the Science Museum in London or another one of several European museums with extensive bicycle collections?

Clearly, riding a bike in a foreign country is not very much more difficult than it is in your own. Though the roads may be better paved here than they are there, the traffic less murderous in one society than it is in the next, the weather more congenial to cycling here than it is there, the differences are gradual, rather than absolute. In fact, you are likely to encounter at least as many positive and negative extremes in your own country as you will abroad.

Preparation

Of course, it will pay off to prepare well for your tour, because purposeful preparation and planning is critical to the success of your bike tour abroad. But so they are when travelling abroad with any other means of transportation. Adjusting to foreign motoring habits or parking restrictions, getting used to railway time tables or staying sane aboard a guided touring coach are at least as tricky, and they require the same kind of thorough preparation if you want to do it successfully.

Much of the work that goes into preparing your tour abroad can be done the same way it should be done for any other kind of travel, providing you keep your particular mode of transportation in the back of your mind. In fact, my experience is that some of the guides and route descriptions purportedly written specifically for and by cyclists are about the most useless of all the books I've read. You will always be dealing with material prepared by people who have very limited general background information and often suffer from significant prejudices about the things bicycle tourists can handle or should be interested in. Only *you* know what you want out of a bike tour. You can only arrive at a satisfactory program if you are given a chance to base your decisions – to take one route or another, visit one place or the other, go at one season or another – on comprehensive and unbiased information.

Most of the items that matter to other tourists abroad are just as important to the cyclist. You will need some kind of identification, and perhaps other travelling documents. Depending on your destination, that may include anything from a simple ID or Driver's License to a passport, a visa or special exemptions. For the countries immediately bordering the US, a Driver's License is usually all you need, except if you are a resident Alien, as I am. In that case you will need more – if only to get back into the US. Passports and visas are required for some other countries, and in some cases you will need vaccinations. If you are in doubt about these matters, enquire about such things at the host country's consulate or travel bureau.

Of course, you will also need foreign money, although it will usually be much easier to exchange dollars into local currency once you are abroad than it is to get money changed anywhere in the US. This is something to keep in mind if you are living in another country and visiting the States. Almost all the information about preparing for your tour, ranging from these formalities and money matters to specific suggestions about the things to do at your destination, can be learned from the kind of general guide book other tourists would use.

Tourist Information

Excellent tourist guides of this type are available for most countries and for many general or specific regions. Of these, the Michelin guides, which are available in English for many countries, are perhaps the ultimate. In a very systematic way and with astonishing economy of space and language, these guides present the essential information about a region and each of the individual points of interest.

Even if no Michelin guide is available for the country or the area you plan to visit, I suggest you take a close look at one of these for another country or region. Compare the guides that exist for your destination with the way the Michelin guide is arranged. If the other one appears to be similarly encyclopedic, it may well suit your purpose admirably. If, on the other hand, it is less systematic, wordier or with too

Shared land use: off-road bike touring in the Canadian Rockies. (Photograph courtesy Backroads)

much emphasis on pretty pictures, it may perhaps be useful only to get background information before setting out.

In that case you'll probably have to choose another book to help you along with more practical matters along the way. A second series of useful books are those based on the scheme of the original *Europe on $5 a Day* (yes, really: that was in the late 'sixties) by Arthur Frommer. These guides are especially suitable if you are on a budget, don't want to go camping, and are more interested in the towns than the country. A few less well known, though excellent guides for the major continents are included in the Bibliography.

An additional good, if subjective, source of information will be the host country's national tourist board in your home country. Many countries maintain tourist offices in major cities abroad, others have at least one office in the USA and other major countries, with whom you can deal by mail or telephone. They will send you free maps, schedules of

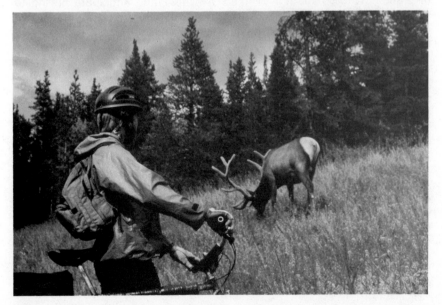

events and hotel or camp site direc- tories. Of course, these tourist boards are set up primarily to deal with conventional tourists who travel by car or plane – people who like to visit beaches or overrun tourist traps and stay in expensive hotels. Just the same, upon request, most of these offices will provide the specific type of information that interests you. That is under the proviso that you give them enough time: start your preparation at least three months before leaving.

Let me give you an example of the type of bicycle-specific information that may be obtained from a tourist board. In many countries you may at some time or another wish to travel some distances by public transpor- tation. For that purpose, it will be a good idea to ask in writing for the schedules of major carriers and an English-language copy of their policy on transporting passenger- accompanied bicycles. In most cases, you will receive adequate information to plan your tour, so you'll know where you can take the bike and how to go about it. Even if some local station officials, drivers or conductors balk or don't know the policy, assuming they just can't take a bike, the polite and respectful confrontation with a copy of the letter you received from their na- tional tourist office usually has the desired effect.

Another example of such very important kind of general informa- tion pertains to cultural or commer- cial customs and opening hours. Anybody who has ever tried to get a drink or food at an English pub, or who has attempted to do grocery shopping evenings, weekends or certain weekday afternoons in countries like England, Holland or Germany, or to go to a museum on Mondays, can confirm the useful-

ness of exact information about these matters. Don't think foreign visitors to America have fewer diffi- culties: just try changing money or even doing any dealings with an American bank, if you are used to European banking convenience.

In addition to the conventional guide books and tourist board infor- mation, which both almost invariably show the sunny side of a country, you would do well to charge yourself up with some socially, culturally and environmentally relevant informa- tion. Read, cut out and collect all the articles that appear about your destination in the newspapers and other periodicals, so you are up to date on relevant current issues. Inform yourself regarding the geographic details on the country in a school atlas, almanac or encyclo- pedia. This will make you an informed visitor – one who under- stands and appreciates what he sees and experiences.

Maps are another essential ingredient of the preparation pro- cess. Enquire locally what maps are available, and anticipate having to buy the more detailed ones at your destination. In most big cities there are book stores that specialize in maps and other travel literature, so try to find such a store in or near your home town. The minimum you will need is an overall map, showing the entire country or region you intend to visit in relief, to use as a prelim- inary planning tool. In addition, get a road map, showing the area in one piece and, if possible, some more detailed maps, on which you can plan out the actual route and itiner- ary more accurately with the help of your tourist guide book and other literature.

Finally, another source of pre-trip information should not be over- looked: talk to those who have visited the country of your destination, preferably people who have travelled by bike themselves. If you are not talking to a cyclist, make sure you don't get carried away with reports of ventures that will be much harder or impossible on the bike. On the other hand, you are not married to your bike, so you could well consider the possibility of leaving it in safe keeping, while you go off on a shorter trip by bus, train, ship, plane or on foot. Good places to leave bikes reasonably safely in most countries are the railway stations.

Getting There With Your Bike
Unless you live close to the border and want to visit the neighboring country, you will have to consider the transportation problem. Getting yourself to your destination is easy enough: the same way any other tourist would go about it. But you'll want to get your bike out there too.

Bicycle ferry service across the Vecht, one of the many smaller rivers in the Rhine delta in Holland.

From the US, different airlines have different policies. Many either leave it to their airport personnel or the latter take it upon themselves to make or bend the rules. This practice may work in your favor or against you, as I have experienced myself at different times.

There are elegant and strong packing cases on the market these days, but what do you do with an expensive 4 x 3 x 2 foot plastic case, while you are cycling around the countryside? So if you can't package it that way, the safest way to put the bike on a plane is undisguised. Turn the handlebars in line with the bike and reverse the pedals (pointing in), perhaps with something wrapped around the frame tubes to protect the paintwork. That way everybody can see it's a bike, and not some anonymous cardboard box that can be thrown about and may end up at the bottom of a pile, covered by much heavier articles.

The problem is that most airlines don't accept bikes that way. They insist you put it in a box, and if you're lucky there is at least one airline desk that sells such things. Depending on the size of the box, you may have to partially dismantle the bike. And at the other end you'll be stuck with a box you can't carry around with you. If you're lucky the airline may offer to keep that box for your return trip. If you're not lucky, or if you return from another airport, the same hassle starts all over again on the return journey.

Enquire at the airline office at least four weeks before departure date. If you do that in writing, you can also expect a written answer. Use that to back up your claim at the airport if it should be more favorable than what you are told at the check-in counter. Even so, a little polite charm may get your bike on, though it may backfire in some cases, in which case only money will solve your problem – or you may have to go on another carrier, losing some time.

You may be charged a hefty sum, especially if the total weight of bike and luggage exceeds the personal weight limit. To avoid or minimize that, make sure you pack for absolute minimum weight, keeping the weight of the items you hand in at the counter to no more than 20 kg (44 lbs). Put all heavy items in a bag that can be carried on. Usually you can get away with carrying a small backpack and a hand-carried bag on board as cabin luggage.

If it all sounds like too much of a challenge, you may consider renting a bicycle at the other end. Whether you can rent an acceptable machine will depend on the country of your destination and on your taste in bicycles. In France and England reasonable bikes are readily availa-

ble for rent, while you may as well forget it in most other countries, unless you have been able to secure the use of a suitable machine by mail in advance. On the other hand, don't insist too much on the kind of equipment you are used to: the bikes available for rent at your destination may be quite suitable for the terrain encountered, even if you think they are heavy clunkers – it's probably what the locals use, and they get by somehow.

Foreign Road Maps

Maps for trips in foreign countries present essentially the same problems as maps for your own country. Consequently, you are referred once more to my comments in Chapter 14 about route planning and those in Chapter 18 about orientation. Once you have learned to handle a domestic map effectively, you will have no problems gleaning the essential information from a foreign map. The legend of many foreign maps is actually printed in English, as well as in the native tongue. If not, the country's tourist board or your domestic touring or automobile association may be able to provide a list of translations of such terms. Similarly, you can generally obtain a guide to the meanings of road signs – both directional and regulatory ones.

The criteria for a good cycling road map are the same abroad as they are at home: a detailed scale of about 1 : 200,000, not too much distortion in the road widths and other topographic details, and the need for reliable information pertaining to elevations. Finally, it should be as up to date as possible, to avoid frequent surprises with freeways and other man-made barriers that are not shown on the maps. In almost all Western countries, you will be able to find several adequate series of maps once you get there. In Eastern Europe and some other more totalitarian societies, suitable maps are hard to get locally. Thy may even be illegal to import, since the use of a map there seems to be associated solely with the trade of espionage.

You may want to do some off-road cycling when you are in the country of your destination. To find your way off-road, you will need maps to scale 1 : 50,000. Generally, it will be impossible to obtain such detailed maps, except locally. Don't cover all

the terrain with maps of that scale: a friend of mine carried three pounds of mapping material just to follow the Rhine from its source downriver for about 300 miles. Instead, decide ahead of time where will be a good area to cycle off-road, and buy topographic maps only to cover that specific region.

In most cases, you will have to wait until you are in the country of your destination before buying the detailed maps. Once you get there, that should be your first priority of things to take care of. Even there it may take a search for a special book

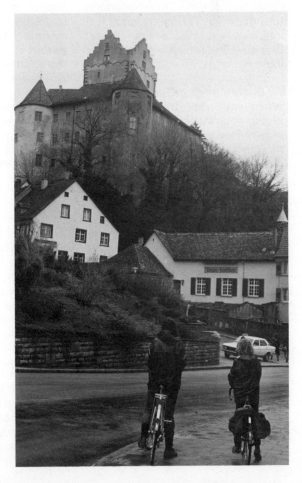

Meersburg Castle near Lake Constance on the German/Austrian border. In Germany youth hostels are often located in such buildings, and most lie similarly high on a hill.

store to get hold of the right maps. At the first shop you find, don't just ask for the particular maps: if they don't have them, buy something else and ask for the address of a shop that would have the kind of maps you are looking for.

Done even slightly diplomatically, you will find out the source for good maps quite soon. Once you have discovered such a store, buy all the maps you think you may need, erring rather on the high side than risking the chance of your trip taking you to uncharted regions. Perhaps that does not sound very adventurous, but most experienced travellers agree that a trip without reference to a good map brings a much less intensive experience than a well prepared and properly documented journey.

Understanding One Another
When you have to ask the way during your trip, always consult the map at the same time. You will find that, though the locals perhaps do not understand your pronunciation of a place name, they will recognize it when you are pointing to it on the map. Similarly, it will be much easier to follow their instructions while making reference to the map. Even if you soon forget the verbal instructions, you will find it quite easy to reconstruct the route with the aid of the map.

In most foreign countries you will have to overcome the language barrier. Even between English speaking countries there are problems, since different words may be used for the same things, while the same word may mean different things either side of the Atlantic. That the Englishman calls an intersection a junction, and means the sidewalk when he says pavement, are just a few examples.

Much more unexpected sources of confusion sometimes completely obliterate sensible communication. Thus, the American asking for a rest room in England or Australia should have a strong bladder, while the Englishman looking for the same institution is probably unaware how much embarrassment he causes the American when asking in his national vernacular. Seems trivial, and it is, except that people have got hopelessly lost on account of such differences in language.

Whether you are travelling in another English speaking country or in a place where a truly foreign tongue is spoken, it must not be impossible to prepare for sensible communication and understanding. Before you leave on your tour, take the trouble to get familiar with the differences you can expect to encounter.

Of course, there are also weights and measures to consider, where the difference between metric, American and imperial systems can be quite bewildering. Don't think it's impossible: converting pounds to kilograms and kilometers into miles or vice versa is just as easy as it will be to convert meters into feet when it comes to expressing elevations. Table 4 in the Appendix will prove quite helpful in this respect.

Not only different variants of English, but even foreign languages can easily be learned well enough to allow the very basic level of communication required to avoid getting lost. Simple expressions like left and right, straight ahead and about turn will be quickly learned in any language. Similarly, you can learn to pronounce the names of most towns and major landmarks with some semblance of the authentic. It's a matter of preparation, and it adds to the interest of the tour when you at least manage to come across as somebody who tries, rather than as the proverbial ugly American. Be receptive to your hosts and their language, and you and your country will be treated with equal respect.

When to Go

One of the charms of foreign or otherwise remote regions is the fact that the weather can be quite different at certain times of the year. Thus, you will find that when it is high season and too hot to do anything enjoyable in your part of the world, it may be quite delightful and not half as overrun with people somewhere else. Conversely, you may be able to benefit from the relative unpopularity of early or late season travel to get to an area where the weather is just perfect for cycling at that particular time, a subject that was covered in Chapter 12.

This is again the kind of information to be found out when doing your preliminary planning. In general, I suggest you shy away from the summer months in flat and lower lying regions, as well as from popular summer seaside destinations. The weather prevalent there at such times may be acceptable to those who prefer to stay in a hotel swimming pool most of the day, but it won't make for enjoyable cycling.

On the other hand, really high mountainous areas can be incredibly cold, especially in the late and early season, and high summer may be the only even remotely comfortable period there. Of course, these considerations also apply when travelling in your own country, certainly if it is a land as big as Canada or the USA. However, the views of foreign countries in our minds are colored by their generalized representation. Consequently, it may be as hard to imagine a heat wave in Canada or Iceland as it is to believe that there is perennial snow on Indian and central African mountains, or for that matter that the French Alps can get quite chilly, while sun-tanned beauties bathe topless at the beaches only two hundred miles away.

It will also be smart to try and avoid major public holidays, such as Easter, in most catholic countries, especially in religious or cult centers. Of course, that advice does not apply if your particular interest is precisely in witnessing such a celebration. The problem is usually that accommodation and travel are greatly hindered during such events. If you're not coming for the show, especially if you are not prepared, it can be quite frustrating to be stranded somewhere on account of a head hunting heyday or an Easter procession.

Where to Travel

Whether at home or abroad, major roads are generally the most convenient routes to follow. Of course, it will be wise to steer clear of heavily travelled arterials and real freeways (certainly where it is illegal to use them with a bike) and to avoid roads that form direct connections between neighboring major centers or a metropolis with its satellites and suburbs.

Some people like to avoid all major roads, fearing motor traffic more than getting lost or stuck in the dirt. In some countries, it is quite possible to avoid really major roads, and still travel on well paved roads with good facilities. France is a good example. In that country most major roads are quite closely paralleled by nearly equally direct minor roads. These may be just as well paved but carry much less motor traffic. Besides, they lead through many more interesting places and are generally more scenically attractive.

In some other European countries you will find specific bicycle paths. In some countries, such as Holland and Denmark, these paths are generally of adequate quality, certainly if you don't use very delicate equipment. In other countries, like Germany, these facilities are created solely to expel bicyclists from the much safer and better surfaced roads. In general, even the best bicycle paths are more dangerous and less convenient to cyclists than just about any road. For that reason, I suggest you try to steer clear of them as much as you can. Wherever a parallel connection exists without separate bike path, use it in preference if you want to enjoy your trip, while maximizing your chances of living to tell others about it.

Mountain bike or all-terrain cycling is quite a new development in the US, although it has long been practiced in many other countries by folks who never knew they were doing it. In several countries, there is an entire network of paths and trails that are off-limits to motorists. A mountain bike allows you to combine transportation rides on regular roads with sections that go cross-country to explore the more remote terrain. In general, you will do better not to try and ride off-road for an entire tour. Instead, combine regular travel on the road with excursions and short sections cross-country. See Chapter 22 and the remarks on maps above, to make sure you are adequately prepared.

Where to Stay

In numerous foreign countries the accommodation available is generally quite a bit more primitive or harder to find than it is at home.

When doing your general preparation for the tour, also establish what type of accommodation to expect where. Their availability, their accessibility and the services provided may well influence your choice of accommodation. Thus, in a country where hotels are few and far between and where cyclists are frowned upon, you may decide to camp out, since in many cases camp sites are actually more numerous and adequately equipped.

If you want to go camping, also use the host country's tourist offices. Most of these have specific materials available for people who go camping. Certainly the list of official camp sites and the country's police policy regarding camping on private or public land will be of great importance to you, if that is the way you intend to spend the nights. If not available from the tourist office, your own country's automobile association or certain book stores that cater to travellers will be able to supply you with a camp site guide, or you may have to wait until you arrive at your destination.

Don't expect foreign camp sites to be similar to the way they are in your own country. Read up on the facilities offered and any regulations that may apply. To give just a few European examples, French and Danish camp sites are each in their own way superb for cyclists, while Dutch camp sites generally have so little available space and so many restrictions, that I prefer to steer clear of them. In other countries, for example in Eastern Europe, there are only very few and extremely large camp sites, set up for people who spend three or four weeks in the same spot.

In most European countries, but more and more also on the American continent, there is a type of accommodation known as youth hostels. These offer separate dormitory sleeping facilities for men and women, though differing quite a bit from one country to the next as regards the services and supplies available. Enquire at your local or national youth hostel association about the facilities in the country of your destination, if you are interested. I have my own prejudices as to which of these I like and which not. Try them out and decide for yourself whether you prefer the regimented type with clean trim and noisy school kids or the slightly run-down variety with interesting people to meet. In the USA, their existence seems to be a guarded secret, hardly known to those for whom they are intended. Here they are frequented mainly by European visitors and America's vagrant unemployed.

Each country has its own peculiarities with respect to overnight accommodations. Thus, the British and Irish Bed & Breakfast houses and the German, Swiss and Austrian private Pensions are excellent tips – they are found everywhere, except in the big towns. In addition, many of the national cycling organizations, such as the British CTC and the American bike touring associations have listings of cheap or free overnight facilities. Some of these are as

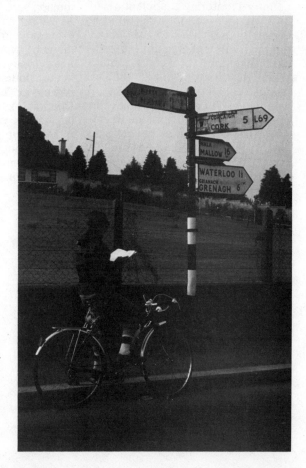

Finding the way in Ireland. As also used in many parts of England, Holland and Denmark, these directional signs are just right for cyclists. Located at the actual intersection, they show the destinations within the immediate area and don't keep you in the dark about the distances.

good as staying in a commercial facility, while all will help you keep within a more modest budget, even if you don't want to spend every night in such simple quarters.

Staying Healthy Abroad

The chances of getting sick or hurt while travelling abroad are – if anything – higher than they are at home. Yet most people are both hopelessly unprepared for this, and do little to prevent it. By way of preparation, make sure you know what kinds of medical services are available in the host country and check into the best form of insurance. The better conventional tourist guides or your own country's motoring association can give you information about what is available and how to go about getting treatment. See any independent insurance broker to obtain travel insurance coverage that includes accident and health risks, as well as liability and theft. Take the appropriate health insurance ID and any other documents that tell you what to do when you go on your trip.

If you do get sick, you will perhaps be better off if you can locate a physician who is used to dealing with English-speaking patients. In the address list in the Appendix you will find the address of the International Association for Medical Assistance to Travellers, who can supply you with a directory of English-speaking doctors in the country you will be visiting. All member physicians agree on a modest standard fee per consultation and accept certain forms of insurance.

To prevent health problems from developing or getting serious, follow all the precautions commonly suggested. Make sure you have an adequate supply of any prescription medicines you regularly need, kept in a water proof container. Take care to feed yourself well, especially making sure that your diet is at least as varied as it would be at home. Protect yourself and your companions by avoiding excessively strenuous trips without adequate rest. Make yourself familiar with the basics of first aid, checking with Chapter 11 for particularly relevant issues for bicyclists. Finally, minimize accident risks by studying the traffic peculiarities in the host country and being particularly careful while cycling or walking in city traffic.

20
Touring with Children

Bicycle touring with children is not impossible, even though it presents some additional problems that are not encountered when cycling with adults alone. If you are willing to take the special needs and wishes of your offspring into consideration, all of you will find it to be an enjoyable and educational experience, whatever the children's age. My parents have taken me touring and camping from the time I was a toddler, and I only

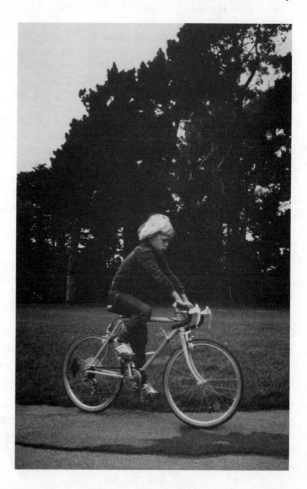

Children's bikes of adequate quality are hard enough to find. Even this French machine with 20 inch wheels, shown here in its original state, had to be modified considerably before it was suitable for serious touring. Matching aluminum rims, luggage racks and fenders were all extremely hard to find in the US.

regret not having been able to share real bike touring with my own children quite as much as they did. Even so, I and my family have gathered enough of the direct experience needed to help you in this chapter. You will learn how to make the most of your touring with children.

I feel a full awareness of the children's bicycling needs and abilities on the part of the parents is a basic criterion for successful family touring. However, if you are not an experienced cyclist yourself yet, there is no need to shy away from sharing your own learning experience with the entire family. In that case, just avoid the really ambitious tours. It will be smarter to first get used to competent cycling together and individually, before setting out on a major tour. Together, go through the basic advice contained in the first two parts of the book, and practice what you learn, going on modest family trips first.

The Child's Age and Ability

The most important thing to consider when planning a family bicycle tour is the child's interest and ability. Though younger children are not always very demanding, your first task as a parent is your responsibility to the child. The touring schedule should primarily be determined by what corresponds to the child's needs, not by what you would do if you were travelling alone. On the other hand, there is no need to subordinate your own wants completely. There will be instances when the child has to wait his turn, just as there are many times when you have to accommodate to the child's special needs or wishes.

Of course, each child is an individual – though they all go through similar development stages. At a very early age they are quite satisfied sleeping and idling. After some time they want to be occupied, meanwhile learning to keep themselves busy, which occurs in the next stage. Then comes the stage of interaction, when they need the presence and response of others. Finally, they have developed into youngsters, who distinguish themselves mainly from adults in the particular nature of their interest: whereas the parents may want to converse about one thing, their offspring may be more interested in another; while the parents want to visit a museum, they'd rather spend their time at play.

The age at which a child is in any particular stage is not quite as fixed as to allow categorizing. It is more important for the parents to be aware of the particular stage the child is in and what interests him most at this time. Your children will not be replicas of mine, just as my daughter was no carbon copy of her elder brother, and neither of them are similar to me or my sister at corresponding ages. If you occupy yourself with your children enough at other times as well, you should be able to evaluate their development and interests. This in itself should make it relatively easy to consider these factors when planning your family bicycle tours.

Unless your child happens to be one of those rare creatures who themselves want to ride a bike for its own sake, make sure the tour also serves other purposes. If your children are interested in horseback riding, try to combine the tour with one or more visits to rental stables. If the children are fascinated by sea and bathing, plan your tour to include some opportunities to go to the beach. If your children don't feel happy without other companions, suggest taking one or more of their friends along. In the latter case, start off with some practice rides together, to get the friends used to responsible bicycling practices.

Allow the child to participate in the preparations for the tour right from the start. Consult him when doing initial planning and when selecting particular destinations within the tour's itinerary. Convince the child you take him seriously, by actually including as many of his suggestions as possible and heeding his warnings. Even during the tour, the child can be given the feeling of being a full fledged participant. Invite and respect feedback and suggestions. Don't be too rigid in your planning, since it is only too easy to overestimate the abilities of a child, which would not only spoil this one tour, but may also nip a developing cycling career in the bud.

Teach the child the basic skills of effective bicycling, as well as some appreciation for the various aspects of touring. Children can develop an understanding for where they are and how much work it will be to get to the next place. A child old enough to learn reading and writing is also adequately developed to understand the principles of mapping, including the distances to be covered and the symbols used to represent various landmarks on the map.

Especially when the child rides a bike himself, you may be astonished at the insatiable appetite he or she develops. I found my nine-year old daughter eating like a grown man, devouring food she would have declined back home. That makes the family experience all the more pleasant, and increases the children's willingness to participate in the jobs of shopping and cooking. When camping, delegate certain responsibilities to the child – provid-

ing they are not only the kind of chores the child detests. Try to include jobs that can be seen as a kind of reward for his performance during the day. By involving the child in this manner, you will find the tour can be a delightful communal experience.

After completion of the tour, or shortly before the goal is reached, is a good time to reward your children with a durable memento of the tour in the form of a desirable or practical present. Things like a bicycle speedometer, a Swiss army knife, a pair of binoculars or a simple camera make excellent presents. You may look for things that increase the child's interest in bike touring, as well as providing something enjoyable in and by themselves. It all depends on the child's interest – another child may

Effective head protection is as important for children as it is for adults. Bike helmets are now available in all sizes. (Photograph courtesy Backroads)

be more interested in a doll or a book.

Ways to Carry Children

Depending on the children's age and development, there are a number of different potential methods of taking them along when cycling. Not all of these methods are equally recommended or suitable for serious bike touring, but here they are summarized:

- [ ] in a papoose type backpack (also referred to as Gerry Pack) on the back of one of the parents;
- [ ] on a child's seat mounted in the front of the bike;
- [ ] on a child's seat mounted in the back of the bike;
- [ ] in a trailer or a side car, pulled by one of the parents;
- [ ] on the back seat of a tandem;
- [ ] on a bike of his own.

During the first six months or so, when the child can not keep its back upright, the only even remotely satisfactory solution would be to carry the child in a sidecar or trailer, equipped more like a baby carriage or perambulator. Hardly the thing for long tours, but it has been done successfully.

Carrying the child papoose-style on the back of one of the parents only lends itself to very limited use, for transporting small children up to the age of perhaps 18 months. It is potentially unsafe, uncomfortable to the parent and not much better for the child over a longer distance. Though possible for short trips – we often carried one of our children this way if we had to take two on one bike – I'd consider it totally unacceptable for touring over longer distances.

A front-mounted seat can be suitable for younger children. Whether it is safe to do so depends on a number of factors. The child's seat must be installed firmly to a fixed part of the bicycle, not to the steering system. The feet must be well protected from accidentally getting caught between the spokes of the front wheel. The frame must be so long and the handlebars so high, that the parent's sight of the road and control over the bike are not imperilled. Provided that all these criteria are met, this position allows good interaction between child and rider. It also gives the child a chance to see more than it can in the back. Children over the age of about four are generally too big for this method of carrying.

Children's seats installed in the back of the bike are by far the most common. The same criteria regarding sizing, foot protection and mutual interference as in the front apply *mutatis mutandis* in the back. Since some of these seats are intended, or will be used, for quite sizable kids up to the age of perhaps six, you will have to make doubly sure the construction is really adequately sturdy to take the weight and to offer sufficient support and protection to the child.

When choosing a child's seat, and before you buy it, try it out. Install it on the bike, and put the child in it. Now take the bike by the handlebars and sway it in a lateral motion. If the whole affair starts oscillating precipitously, the seat's carrying frame and attachment are not adequately rigid. When a child is carried in the back, assuming you have found a suitable seat, you will have to transfer some of the luggage otherwise carried there to the front with the aid of a sturdy low-rider front luggage rack and sizable front panniers.

Trailers and side cars are now available in quite a number of different versions, although not many are really adequately equipped to carry children. The trailer should be equipped with smoothly running wheels, incorporating high pressure tires and ball bearings. It must be big and sturdy enough, so the child's movements would not tend to upset its balance or negatively affect the bike's handling and steering characteristics. Finally, it must be equipped with an adequately safe seat, complete with harness and weather protection. Give the younger child some toys that are tied on to the trailer, so they can't be lost on the way.

Children's Bikes and Tandems

Children over the age of seven or eight are usually strong and coordinated enough to participate in bike tours on their own bike. That only applies under close parental supervision, since children up to age ten are neither sufficiently coordinated, nor mentally advanced enough to understand some of the basic phenomena necessary to ride safely in traffic. At this stage, they can not decide by themselves what is the right action in a critical situation on the road. Before going on a tour, take the child out cycling together on several trips, and get him used to the skill and routine of predictable cycling. Make him understand and execute your advice and commands while riding. Develop a communal riding style and, conversely, learn to observe the child to estimate what its needs are.

A child's bike should be selected just as carefully as an adult's machine and ought to be of comparable quality. That will make it about as expensive too, since the price of most components is not a function of their size, but rather of the care that went into making them. Do not purchase a bike that is clearly too big for the child, assuming he will eventually grow into it. He probably will eventually, but before he reach-

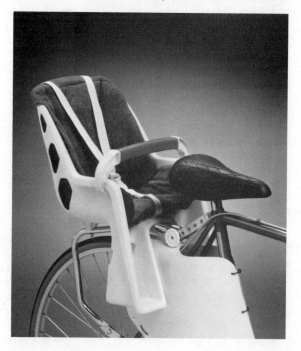

Excellent seat for small children by Troxel. The integral foot rests and the wheel covers protect the child against the most frequent cause of injury: getting the feet caught in the spokes. The handle and the harness give sufficient hold.

es that stage, he may have learned to hate cycling on that unsafe and uncomfortable machine that is too big.

Unfortunately, there are only few stores – and even fewer manufacturers – that offer an adequate selection of high quality children's bikes, while suitable components and accessories may be even harder to locate. You will probably find the few stores that do stock such items by simply asking other cycling parents who appear to have found good equipment for their offspring. If you should ever get abroad, you will find France and Italy to be wonderful places to purchase high quality components for children's bikes. So you may want to take the opportunity to investigate purchasing certain parts or even complete bikes while you are there. Similarly, tandem parts, including conversion kits to make the tandem suitable for a child stoker (that's cycling jargon for the rear rider), are more readily available in England and France than they are anywhere on the American continent.

This chapter is not the appropriate forum to show how you teach a child bicycle riding skills. However, it will be imperative that the child must be adequately prepared and has developed all the basic skills necessary. Once he has learned these basics, the only proper way to prepare him for serious touring is to take him along on as many supervised rides as possible. Instruct junior in the kind of lessons contained in the chapters of Part II of this book. Even on the tour, remain aware of the child's probable need for instruction – just avoid bombarding him with unwanted warnings and superfluous advice.

Depending on the child's development, you can load his bike up with

Fig. 20.1 Children's crank adaptor for tandem

some luggage. Making even the smallest member of the party carry at least something, will boost his confidence as a full fledged participant. Younger children's bikes should of course be loaded lightly: give them items that are relatively bulky for their weight. I've always made my children carry their own sleeping bag and clothing, right from the first trip. Later we added some of the other items that have to be carried. By the time my son was 14, he was indeed carrying as heavy a load as that of an adult.

Perhaps the best way to introduce a child to bicycle touring is on a tandem as the stoker. If the child is still quite small, you will need either a specially built tandem with a very small rear frame, or an adaptor kit to raise the rear cranks to a level that suits the child's leg length. Although the latter gadget, illustrated in Fig. 20.1, seems more like a do-it-yourself solution, it is in some ways the preferable way: the child sits so high that he sees more than the parent's back, and it is easier to adapt when junior grows bigger. If money is no object, you can get an experienced tandem frame builder to construct a special tandem that is designed right from the start for a short but growing stoker. At a later age, a standard tandem with a suitably small rear frame may be used.

Even tandem riding has to be learned and practiced beforehand – both for the person in front and the one in the rear. However, it can be mastered quickly if you put your mind to it. The tandem has less luggage carrying capacity than two individual bicycles. That needn't be a serious drawback, since you would probably not load the child's bike up with very much luggage anyway. For additional advice, you are referred to Chapter 21, which is devoted specifically to tandem touring. There you will find general comments regarding this type of bicycle and the special problems associated with its use.

Overnight Stays with Children

The first few trips with children should probably be short ones. Very soon, it will be possible to make tours that include overnight stops. I have found that children prefer to stay at camp sites and youth hostels. Neither camping in isolation in the wilds, nor staying in the boring solitude of a motel, nor the organized splendor of most hotels, seems to satisfy their need for relaxation and playful activity. The only drawback of camping is the fact that quite a bit of luggage has to be carried.

At camp sites, they usually find other children with whom to spend their time and whom they can impress with their bicycle touring achievements. Generally, they seem to enjoy getting involved in the improvised household chores associated with camping. Youth hostels are appreciated for similar reasons, especially in those countries where it is customary for the visitors to prepare their own meals. Many hostels offer family rooms, in addition to the characteristic sex-segregated dormitory accommodation. The advantage of youth hostels over camping is the reduction in the volume of luggage that must be carried: neither tent, nor cooking equipment, nor down sleeping bag will be required.

Certainly when camping, it will be a good idea to occasionally stay two nights at the same site. This should be made dependent on the degree to which the children feel at home at one camp site or the other. When you have reached a site where the children find plenty of playmates or absorbing occupations, the suggestion to stay on an additional night will probably be welcomed enthusiastically. An occasional rest day like this is probably just as enjoyable and relaxing to parents as it is to the children. You may take the opportunity to visit some local places of interest on unloaded bikes, either with or without the children, or you may just loaf about if that's your preference at the time.

Hotel and motel stays require even less in the way of essential equipment. On the other hand, perhaps the main reason for kids to object to that kind of accommodation is the fact that they feel out of place in their cycling garb. In fact, children are generally even more concerned about their parents' appearance than they are about their own clothing. So you would do well to make sure you carry enough civil looking clothing for children and adults alike to come across to the other guests and personnel as quite respectable visitors, who may have arrived in a car like everybody else. That may well be the way you feel yourself, once the bikes have found a safe place.

Contrary to popular fears, cyclists are not treated like paupers or poor relatives at most hotels. That applies to most places, both abroad and at home, including really fancy hotels. You may find that many people have an innate sympathy for those who do something different and more interesting than what they encounter every day. In fact, staff or owners often go out of their way to make sure their young cycling guests lack nothing. In most cases they will also help you find a safe place to put your bikes.

21
Tandem Touring

In recent years the tandem has become increasingly popular for bike touring. It has several important advantages that make it ideally suitable for touring purposes. You can cycle together without losing one another. You will always be close enough for communication. It allows riders of unequal abilities to go at the same pace. Besides, since the wind resistance of a tandem is much less than the total for two single

bikes, driven by the same two human motors, tandem riders usually move faster and smoother.

In the preceding chapter I had already emphasized the value of the tandem for family cycling. You are referred to the information contained there for specific comments about the adaptation of a tandem to carry children. In the present chapter many of the general issues relevant to tandem touring and the technical peculiarities of the machine will be covered in some depth.

Delightful though it is, tandem touring has disadvantages too. In the first place, you can carry less

Well constructed touring tandem from the German frame builder Mittendorf. With its double central diagonal bracing tubes, this frame design – also used by some American and British frame builders – probably results in the most rigid tandem possible.

luggage on one tandem than you can on two single bikes. That makes the tandem somewhat less suitable for camping, although the smart selection of lightweight equipment, together with good luggage racks and bags, or the use of a luggage trailer, can overcome most of the tandem's inherent weaknesses in this respect.

Tandem riding is a very unique experience, and the problems associated with it are equally singular. Other and more experienced tandem riders are your best source of relevant information and advice. In Great Britain there is an active organization of tandem riders, the Tandem Club, whose address can be found in the Appendix. This association forms what is probably the world's greatest storehouse of technical and practical expertise in the field, and their Handbook is far and away the most comprehensive printed source of Tandem facts. A membership in the Tandem Club is highly recommended to present and prospective tandem riders alike, wherever they live.

Transporting a Tandem

Like any other bike, the tandem is most practical when you ride it: transporting it any other way can be a bit of a headache. These things are mighty big. Whereas a normal bicycle is about 1.70 m (5 ft 8) long, the typical tandem measures a full 2.40 m (8 ft). And when you remove the wheels, the difference seems even more striking, since the tandem frame turns out to be nearly twice as long as that of a normal bike. That's not a problem in everyday use, but it becomes apparent when the thing has to be put in storage or transported.

Except in a full-size station wagon, you will usually find no room for the tandem in a car, and it will be equally hard to transport one on a trunk-mounted rack. In America, the Amtrac railway system does not accept tandems on account of their length. An unreasonable ruling, because Amtrac's luggage cars are big and empty enough to handle a whole flock of tandems. Bus drivers probably don't welcome tandem patrons either. Most airlines balk when you arrive at the check-in counter with a tandem. If they accept it at all, they may charge a hefty excess luggage surcharge, even if the overall weight of your luggage – including the bike – stays within the total allowance for the number in your group.

You may have to be particularly inventive and imaginative to solve some of the transportation problems you'll encounter with a tandem. When carrying it by car, only a specially adapted roof rack will do the trick. In the case of public transportation, enquire well ahead of time how it can be done. And if all else fails, decide not to transport the bike, except the way it was meant to travel in the first place: on its wheels, with you and your companion in the saddles. That limits your range of operation a bit, but it may save you a lot of headaches.

A tandem couple of my acquaintance had travelled much of the Middle East. Finally, they discovered that getting the bike back to Greece from the African continent would be nearly impossible, at least within their budget in terms of time and money. So they did something original: with a hacksaw, they severed the rear triangle, shortening the frame just enough to allow transportation as regular airline luggage. Upon their arrival in Greece, they went in search of a competent bicycle mechanic, who joined the two parts up again with the aid of accurately fitted reinforcing inserts and brass brazing technique. I'm not suggesting you do that each time the tandem has to be shipped, merely that you often have to be imaginative when it comes to overcoming tandem difficulties.

It is not impossible to rent a tandem, and could certainly be recommended − if only tandem riders weren't so fussy. And with good reason, because a tandem is a lot more than a bike with two saddles. It has to really stand up to its task, and there are but few bicycle shops that are familiar with the problems associated with tandem set-up, riding and maintenance. Consequently, most of the tandems offered for rental are not adequate for serious touring over longer distances. In France and England you will probably be able to find respectable tandems, as you may in those places in the US where a local bike shop has attained some standing as a tandem specialist. But, by and large, however inconvenient it is to transport a tandem, it will be the lesser of two evils.

Mechanical Problems

At least equally serious as the transportation problem is another one: the frequency of mechanical breakdowns with a tandem, and the associated difficulties in getting repairs executed satisfactorily. In subsequent sections of this chapter you will be introduced to some of the equipment selection considerations relevant to the purchase or modification of the machine, to minimize the likelihood of such mishaps. Before you take up tandem riding, though, it will be fair to warn you of the kind of hardships you may be saddled with.

The touring tandem is always a heavily loaded machine. Carrying twice the weight, accelerating twice the mass, with twice the propulsive output, often at a significantly higher speed, it is subjected to hard punishment. In addition, all these higher demands are placed on a structure that is considerably longer between supports (the wheel axes). To the mechanically or structurally enlightened, that translates into potential trouble. Consequently, tandem design is a serious matter. Only the products of specialized tandem frame builders and manufacturers should be considered.

Important tandem details. The adjustable eccentric bottom bracket and an oval connecting bottom tube between the two bottom brackets. Shown here on a Jack Taylor tandem, the former allows adjusting the connecting chain tension, while the latter gives adequate frame rigidity. (Photograph Michiel Sablerolle)

Fig. 21.1 Tandem frame loading

Not only the frame, also the various other components get a lot of abuse. Wheels, brakes and drive-trains are heavily loaded and often fail. That is the time the unprepared tandem rider gets the next shock, because most of these tandem components are non-standard. Consequently, the repair or replacement of even a relatively minor component may be quite expensive and time consuming.

To prevent such difficulties, which of course are most likely to happen when you are touring far away from home with limited time available, always choose the sturdiest, rather than the lightest or most fashionable equipment, for use on a touring tandem. As an additional safeguard, ride and treat your machine carefully. When in doubt about the quality of the road, go slow or even get off the bike. Get up from the saddle when riding over bumps, if they are unavoidable. Walk up the very steepest hills and slow down enough to eliminate the need for excessive braking when going downhill.

Tandem Frames

The frame of a tandem bicycle is a very heavily loaded structure. Fig. 21.1 illustrates the major points where forces are applied to it. The various forces working on the frame result in the tendency to twist around an axis that runs from the rear wheel axle to the head tube, also represented in the illustration. To satisfy the structural and mechanical criteria for adequate strength and reliable tracking, steering and braking, the torque-induced movements around this axis must be kept to a minimum.

The structural design of the tandem frame determines whether or not adequate rigidity around the torque axis is achieved. Frame builders and tandem manufacturers have come up with several designs to try and achieve the desired effect without making the bike quite so heavy and stiff as to be uncomfortable. Structurally ideal would be a very large diameter tube that runs the length of the chain-dotted line in Fig. 21.1, split only in the rear portion to accommodate the rear wheel.

This design is indeed used by some manufacturers. Unfortunately, it involves a number of practical problems, brought about by such factors as material and parts availability, poor shock absorption due to excessive vertical rigidity, and the visual impact on the observer. Consequently, various other, more or less adequate designs have been used. Several satisfactory designs for touring tandems are illustrated in Fig. 21.2. All these have sufficient rigidity, which distin-

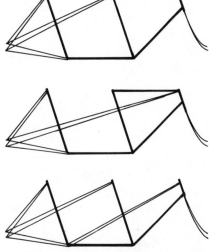

Fig. 21.2 Touring tandem frame designs

Fig. 21.3 Inadequate tandem frame types

horizontal top tube. 'Women's' designs, on which the rear top tube is either lacking or lowered to run parallel to the down tube, are no-no's for touring tandems. Furthermore, diagonal bracing in the form of twin lateral tubes, as shown in the RH detail of Fig. 21.3 contributes little, if anything, to the desired rigidity, which is so critically important for the stability and integrity of a touring tandem.

As for the size of the frame, these machines are usually available in a stepped design, on which the forward seat tube is about five cm (two inches) longer than the one in the rear. That suggests a convention guishes them from the three examples of common, though inadequate, designs represented in Fig. 21.3.

As you can tell from the positive and negative examples of these two illustrations, the most critical thing to avoid is an open frame design, even if only in the rear. Both parts of the frame should have a continuous which is indeed very hard to break: the big man as captain in the front, with his small companion, usually female, as the stoker in the back. I don't agree that it must necessarily be this way, and feel that many women would feel better about tandem riding if they could take the reigns in their own hands. Conversely, I'm not macho enough to consider the place in the back with disdain for a male rider.

If you agree, you may have to order a custom-built tandem, with equally long seat tubes front and rear. In fact, even a reverse design, one that's bigger in the rear than it is in the front, should be possible. If you choose the front of a conventional design small enough to accommodate the smaller partner, you may still be able to swap places by using a special (strong and long) seat post in the rear. In recent years such items have become readily available for mountain bike use.

Fig. 21.4 Tandem drivetrain configurations

Tandem Drivetrains

The most popular set-up for touring tandems includes fifteen-speed gearing. The problem with this configuration is that it locks you into special tandem components for most of the drivetrain parts. I feel that for most applications a ten-speed design may be quite satisfactory. This allows the use of a standard triple chainwheel crankset in the rear and a single chainring model in the front.

Actually, in less undulating terrain five- and ten-speed systems would usually be quite adequate. These are less complicated to operate and maintain. In that case, choose big steps between the individual sprockets, to obtain reasonably wide range gearing. For any given type of terrain, tandem riders generally need somewhat more widely spaced gears than those listed for solo riders in Table 9.I in Chapter 9. Invariably, wide range derailleurs should be selected for touring tandems.

Fig. 21.4 illustrates a number of different drivetrain configurations. Those that keep the two chains on the same side allow the use of con-

Fig. 21.5 Parallel and off-set tandem cranks

ventional components, as long as you are satisfied with a five- or ten-speed system. Special tandem drivetrain components are expensive and hard to find, especially if you get into trouble on your tour far from home. If one accepts the need for special tandem components, then most experienced touring riders seem to agree that the rather odd looking arrangement with the very long chain, driving the rear wheel from the front crankset, is the most convenient to use.

The connecting chain between the front and rear cranksets must be kept reasonably taut. This may be either achieved with a spring-loaded chain tensioning device, or by adjustment of the position of one of the crank spindles. For the latter purpose, most quality tandems are equipped with an oversize forward bottom bracket shell and an eccentrically located set of bearings. By selecting a different eccentric orientation of the bearings, the spindle can be moved further to the front or the back, thus loosening or tensioning the connecting chain. Ideally, the system with a long driving chain should have this adjustable bottom bracket in the rear, while tensioning and loosening are achieved by adjusting it in the opposite directions, respectively.

Many touring tandem riders like to modify the synchronization between the two sets of cranks so that the cranks are not parallel, as shown in Fig. 21.5. This way, the propulsive power output is more constant, since the one rider's minimum and maximum power points in the dead center and forward crank positions, respectively, never coincide with the corresponding orientations for the other rider's cranks.

This off-set can be achieved by undoing the connecting chain and putting it back when the cranks are held in the desired relative orientation. Alternately, a 90 degree difference may be achieved by undoing the cranks on one crankset, reinstalling them in the off-set position. It's a matter of preference, but it is certainly worth trying to see whether you and your tandem partner benefit from this configuration.

Tandem Wheels

The most trouble-prone parts of a tandem seem to be the wheels. Reasonable enough, if you realize that they have to carry twice the weight as compared to what similar wheels used on single bikes have to stand up to. It should be obvious that tandem wheels must be selected on the sturdy side, rather than on the light side. If you've ever heard the tales of broken spokes and bent rims told by most tandem riders, you'll feel no desire to take any chances yourself.

The advent of the mountain bike is perhaps the best thing that has happened to tandem wheel design in recent years. Now once more regularly available are sturdy hubs with solid axles, held by means of axle nuts with integral washers. Such hubs should be suitable for relatively thick spokes, preferably at least 13 gauge or 2.2 mm diameter. Also available are strong aluminum rims (though, like the hubs, they are not generally designed for 40 or more spokes) and strong fat tires, that nevertheless take a high air pressure. All these are essential factors in the construction of a satisfactory tandem wheel.

Of course, the tandem frame geometry must be designed generously enough to accept these rather hefty mountain bike wheels, with their slightly smaller diameter and much greater tire cross section. However, the narrowest mountain bike tires of size 26 x 1.5 in, also known by their ETRTO designation 559 x 38 mm should be about the right size to fit many properly designed touring tandem frames. As long as the brake pivots for cantilever or cam-operated brakes are mounted in the appropriate relative position, as explained in the final section of this chapter, such wheels are eminently suitable for tandem touring use.

Tandem Brakes

The much bigger mass put on the road by a loaded tandem can become correspondingly much harder to slow down than that of even a heavily loaded single bike. Add to that the higher speed at which tandems roll downhill, and you should be able to appreciate how difficult it can be to provide adequate tandem brakes. For touring machines, the industry standard has become cantilever brakes on both wheels and an additional drum brake, which is usually mounted on the rear wheel.

Due to the tandem's great length on the one hand, and the strength of a properly constructed tandem fork on the other, it does not much matter whether this additional brake is installed in the front or the rear wheel. Either brake solution, however, frequently seems to be associated with the incidence of spoke breakage. Make sure the thickness of the hub flanges matches the bend at the spoke heads, or install thin washers in between flange and spoke head, to make up any difference that may be present. Keep those spokes tight by frequently adjusting the nipples, and you'll avoid the most common problems of this kind.

The use of cantilever brakes (or some of the modern frame-mounted cam-operated models) brings with it the question of the location for the pivot bosses. These are usually set for a specific rim size. Though the difference between the formerly most common sizes 630 mm (for 27 inch wheels) and 622 mm (for 700 mm wheels) is so small that adjustment of the brake shoe location generally provides adequate compensation, mountain bike wheels, with their much smaller and at the same time wider rims, require different boss locations. Make up your mind about the wheel size and brake model to be used before ordering the frame, so these bosses can be located appropriately. If you are buying a standard factory-made tandem or frame, you may have to get the bike shop to arrange for their relocation by a competent frame builder.

22
Mountain Bike Touring

The greatest cycling revolution of the 'eighties has doubtlessly been the sudden emergence of mountain bikes or ATB's, as intended for off-road cycling. Off course, this modern fat-tired bicycle lends itself to much more than cross-country cycling alone. It has indeed become the favored machine of many experienced and novice bicyclists alike. Despite its presumed slightly lower efficiency when it comes to cycling on the open road, its advantages are not lost on many touring cyclists. It is an excellent choice for heavily loaded bicycle touring, especially when less than perfectly paved roads are encountered, as will often be the case abroad.

The mountain bike and its application have so many fascinating aspects that distinguish it from regular bicycles and their use, that I should recommend the interested reader to purchase a copy of a special book devoted to the subject. In this vain, you may find my *Mountain Bike Book*, also published by Bicycle Books, of considerable benefit. However, to go touring, there is no need to know quite that much about the mountain bike. The present chapter will probably suffice to get the most out of your mountain bike for touring purposes.

Off-Road and
Rough Road Cycling

When people talk about *off-road*, *cross-country* or *all terrain* cycling, they don't usually really mean what they say. In fact, the majority of cycling done with most mountain bikes is probably on the same kind of roads as you would use with a regular bike. And even if you leave the regular smoothly paved road, that doesn't necessarily mean you're in the jungle, the mountains or the desert. In practice, off-road cycling generally means nothing more than

(Photograph David Epperson / Bicycle Sport)

Fig. 22.1 Mountain bike

riding on any non-asphalted surfaces, be they fire roads or forest paths.

Without knowing it, I have been doing this kind of cycling since I was a kid. In Holland and England, as well as many other countries, cyclists are less obsessed with asphalt than Americans used to be before the advent of the ATB. We rode our ordinary bikes, which admittedly were not equipped with narrow lightweight tubular tires, on dusty paths and gravel trails, cobblestone streets and muddy tracks quite frequently, without thinking anything of it.

We didn't make quite the spectacularly fast progress that can be attained on smoothly paved main roads, but this kind of cycling always had a charm all its own. What a difference it makes, not to hear the constant rumble of motor traffic. How delightful to meet nothing but walkers, cattle and a few other cyclists for miles on end. No anxious looking back, ready to dive into the ditch, should an overtaking motorist threaten your right to the road. No

inhibitions about suddenly turning off without concern about following traffic. Everybody probably needs to experience this from time to time, if only to realize what he has to endure the rest of his cycling life.

Even when I settled in California, back in the late 'sixties, I sometimes left the beaten track and found short cuts and paths that few other cyclists seemed to have discovered, or didn't care to use if they had. Some local cyclists shared my appreciation of the unpaved outback, but not until the mountain bike boom of the mid 'eighties, did it even begin to get crowded on any trail. Even today, only a very few of the many paths seem to have been discovered by the mountain bike masses. And that is in Marin County, the nation's number one off-road cycling area. There must be lots of trails left for uncrowded off-road cycling all over the country.

Much of the country, as well as millions of square miles elsewhere, is criss-crossed with trails that are virtually undiscovered by bicyclists, though they offer the potential for great off-road cycling. It can be done with any good touring bike, providing it is not equipped with the skinniest tires. It's even more accessible with a real mountain bike. In the section that follows we shall have a closer look at this fat-tired machine. Before we do, let me once more give you the advice not to skimp on the price when buying one of these: the more expensive models definitely pay off the price difference in greater riding pleasure and reduced trouble.

The Mountain Bike

Essentially, the mountain bike or ATB (all terrain bike) is nothing but a derailleur bicycle with fat tires and flat handlebars. In practice, these machines are generally characterized by a few additional features, though most of these may be lacking on one machine or the other, without disqualifying it as a true mountain bike. Fig. 22.1 shows the various parts that may be considered characteristic for these machines.

In addition to the things you can recognize immediately, there are some more subtle features, which will be covered here. In the first place the frame. On a good mountain bike, it is not identical to that of a regular bike. To increase stability, to accommodate the fat tires, and to allow using it on very uneven terrain, it should be dimensioned differently: longer, with shallower angles and bigger clearances. In addition, it should be constructed with tubes and other components of slightly larger diameters and wall thicknesses than what is typical for regular bikes of comparable quality.

The mountain bike rider will probably also choose his bike slightly smaller than a regular bicycle. This is also in part predicated on the frame's different geometry. Since the bottom bracket is higher, to clear obstacles, and since the rider may want to sit low enough to put a foot on the ground, the seat tube should perhaps be up to two inches shorter than that of a touring bike for the same rider, as listed in Table 1 in the Appendix.

Of course, the frame must also be equipped with the pivot bosses that allow it to take cantilever or other frame-mounted brakes, but these are nowadays common on touring bikes as well. Their size will be different, though: mountain bikes are generally equipped with larger versions of the same types of brakes. The pivot bosses must be positioned to accommodate these larger brake arms and to accept the different rim sizes used for the mountain bike's differently dimensioned wheels.

These wheels usually do not have quick-release hubs, although that is getting fashionable for the front, in order to facilitate transporting the bike. The rims are of a dimension to fit the special fat, knobby tires designed for them. Nowadays, the industry standard is rims with a rim shoulder diameter of 559 mm and a width of 22–25 mm. These rims are designed for tires of 26 inch nominal size in the American designating system. The international size will be e.g. 54-559. That means the tire has a cross section of 54 mm (2.125 inch) and fits a rim with a shoulder diameter of 559 mm. That will be one of the fattest models; today's trend is towards narrower tires, and I feel these really fat tires may be on their way out for non-competitive off-road cycling.

Just the same, for people who really do cycle more off-road than they do on the road, especially if they travel on loose dirt or sharp rocks a lot, these thickest tires are the ultimate. Most people seem to prefer thicknesses of around 38–47 mm nowadays, and this is certainly a fine compromise for mixed use. The secret to low rolling resistance, as well as rim and tire endurance, is tire pressure. Skinnier tires are more easily constructed so that they endure the higher pressure. In addition, they will weigh a little less, although I have also seen some really fat tires that were beautifully light and flexible, while accepting a pressure of 5 bar (72 psi) without problems.

The gearing set-up for a mountain bike should be similar to that of a good touring machine: fifteen speed derailleur systems with widely spread gears. In general, these gears will be selected by the manufacturer about 5–10 inches lower (0.4 to 0.8 m less development) than they would be for a regular touring bike. This is necessary to account for the greater incidence of really hard cycling, either uphill or on ground that provides a higher rolling resistance.

The handlebars are flat and wide, although narrower ones are getting increasingly popular. Some riders actually have started using dropped handlebars that are only slightly modified. To adapt racing handlebars for off-road cycling, bend them out slightly, as shown in Fig. 22.2. The very wide, flat handlebars can be cut down to a more civil dimension with the aid of a hacksaw. Unless your name is King Kong, 55 cm (22 inches) is probably as wide as can be comfortably handled. The narrower bars make it much easier to ride sharp curves, since you don't have to twist your upper body as far. These mountain bike handlebars are not wrapped with handlebar tape; instead, they are equipped with

Fig. 22.2 Widened drop handlebars

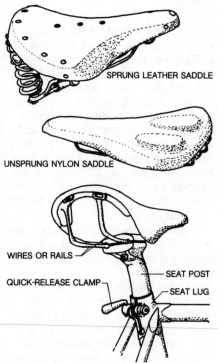

Fig. 22.3 Mountain bike saddle

Fig. 22.4 Filler piece for double wire saddle

closed cell foam grips. These grips dampen road shocks quite a bit, while still allowing excellent control over the steering and handling operations.

The mountain bike should have an easily adjustable saddle. A quick-release binder bolt allows height adjustment in combination with a very long and (hopefully) strong seat post. In addition, there may be a device that allows quick forward adjustment of the saddle. If a spring support, such as the Hite Rite, is installed between seat post and binder bolt, the height adjustment can actually be carried out while riding. It also prevents the theft of the too easily portable saddle and seat post combination.

Since more of your weight rests on the saddle than would be the case on a regular derailleur bike, on account of the high handlebars, the saddle should be particularly comfortable and a little wider than usual. To my mind, the ideal mountain bike saddle is the Brooks 66 Champion. Unfortunately, this model does not by itself fit a regular adjustable alloy seat post, due to its double wire construction. However, it can be used on one of these with a filler piece, such as the one marketed by Joe Breeze. This accessory is available at many bike stores that deal in quality mountain bikes. Fig. 22.3 shows the regular mountain bike saddle with its quick-release, while Fig. 22.4 shows a home-made filler piece to adapt a regular seat post to a double wire saddle model.

The same kind of accessories as for regular touring machines are now available in special versions for mountain bike use as well. These should indeed be specially designed for mountain bike or off-road models, since the equipment suitable for normal touring bikes does not fit in most cases. Special luggage racks for the front and the rear, matching bags and packs, map holders, fenders, warning devices and lighting equipment will be just as useful on a mountain bike used for touring as they are on a regular touring bike. Refer to the appropriate chapters of Part I, and keep the different dimensions in mind when selecting such accessories for a mountain bike.

Off-Road Cycling Skills

To really appreciate the difference between a mountain bike and a regular touring bicycle in a positive sense, you have to use it off-road, even though these machines do quite well on surfaced roads as well. Before you take your mountain bike on an extensive bicycle tour, get familiar with the art of off-road cycling closer to home and without luggage. For this kind of work you need not find a spot of real wilderness, since suitable terrain to practice the kind of maneuvers required can be found almost everywhere.

Practice riding on soft ground and rough terrain. Get a feel for the gearing ratios and the pedalling rates best suited for certain conditions. Learn to climb in the saddle and out of the saddle, to mount and dismount quickly, without stopping or falling. Get used to the feel of braking under off-road conditions, going steeply downhill or riding on ground that is either soft or so uneven that the bike bounces wildly about.

All these things can be learned with a little conscious practice, since they don't really differ completely from the techniques described in the various chapters of Part II. It's not an absolute difference, but one of degree. If you practice enough, you can teach yourself these skills, as indeed most of today's successful off-road racers have done. Once you can ride confidently off-road, try doing the same with a loaded bicycle, certainly if that is what you will be doing on tour. If you want to delve further into these matters, you are referred to my *Mountain Bike Book* for more detailed instructions and advice.

Cross-Country Touring

There are three perfectly respectable ways to use your mountain bike for touring:

☐ instead of a regular touring bike on normal roads;
☐ on normal roads with occasional off-road excursions;
☐ for real continuous off-road touring.

No doubt the latter is the ultimate, but I suggest you start off by selecting one of the two less stringent alternatives. This way you learn to appreciate the advantages and disadvantages of this kind of equipment under different circumstances. That will help you select the riding style and equipment optimally to match terrain conditions encountered during subsequent tours.

If your choice is to tour on regular roads and to see your mountain bike rather as a more rugged type of regular touring machine, you are in a position to travel on rougher roads and to take steeper terrain than you would otherwise have been able to handle. There are parts of the world where this is obviously beneficial. My first trip to Baja California was in a car, but it immediately became clear that bicycle touring in that environment would require something like a mountain bike – which unfortunately did not exist yet at the

time. The same can be said for much of Latin America and in fact for all countries outside the industrialized Western world.

To find your way on this kind of tour, you will need the same type of maps as you would choose when riding a regular bike. After all, the roads are not of a different category but of a different quality within the given category. Even so, you should probably count on making less rapid progress, while you may need more orientation and map-reading stops in this kind of terrain. For that reason, I still suggest you use topographical maps in addition to regular road maps, whenever you can get hold of the former in the less well mapped parts of the world where this is of particular relevance.

If you want to use your mountain bike to combine a longer tour on regular roads with excursions into the outback, I suggest you concentrate these trips to only one or two areas within your overall tour. National or state park lands, wilderness areas and the like, all lend themselves to this kind of use. One way is to plan your tour to include one or more stops, perhaps at a camp site in or near such an area. Make your excursions from there, returning to the base camp after the day's ride. In many popular mountain biking areas, this kind of thing is also possible using a mountain bike that is rented on the spot for the day or for a longer period.

A more demanding, but also more flexible, method is the one I would recommend you use. Plan your tour through such an area with good paths for off-road cycling and several camp sites or other facilities. Travel to that destination on regular roads, covering considerable distances each day, until you get to a base camp. Next day, load the bike up with your camping gear again, to venture out on the trails to another camp site at a day's distance in off-road cycling terms. That distance is probably less than half what you may be used to doing on the road, though still quite a bit more than backpackers can cover. You'll be camping out in the wilds, meeting at best some backpackers and at worst a bear. Take all the precautionary and other measures with respect to food and safety you would take as a backpacker.

For this kind of touring, you can get by using perhaps only one or two detailed topographical maps for the off-road area you cover, in addition to road maps to cover the entire tour. Except for having to dismount each time you consult the map, orientation is no more problematic on the bike than it is when hiking, and it is no more difficult doing it this way than when making day trips. The added advantage is that, should you get lost, at least you have the equipment and the time to stay out

Organized mountain bike touring in Northern California. (Photograph James Cassimus / Bicycle Sport)

another day before you have to get concerned about finding your way back to the civilized world.

Once you have tried this technique, you may be ready to move up to the ultimate in off-road bike touring. That would be an entire vacation, travelling essentially only off-road. To reach the start of the mountain bike tour, you can travel by car or bike to a base camp. From there, take the bike and your camping equipment for a tour through woods and mountains, deserts and plains – a tour that may be purposely designed so as to avoid the roads as much as possible. In some areas, you need not even bring your own mountain bike for a trip like this, since you may be able to rent a perfectly good mountain bike and have it equipped with the appropriate luggage racks before you leave for the back country.

You will have to take a lot of food, and you should plan quite accurately how, when and where you can get to a town or a store to replenish your supplies. I have never ventured into the wilds this much myself, but those who have done so agree that it is a most impressive experience. You may be most surprised to note what distances you can cover on a tour like this. Travelling back along the road, you may be following your earlier cycling route for hundreds of miles from some distance away.

This will probably do much for your appreciation of the wonderful means of individual transportation the bicycle is. A machine that allows you to go where no other vehicle can, and to cover unbelievable

A beautifully built Mountain Goat off-road tandem by Jeff Lindsay. Though off-road tandem riding is rather tricky, a machine like this is excellent for tandem touring on any kind of roads and can be equipped with luggage racks.

distances in a limited time. With a mountain bike, this can be done miles away from the rush of everyday traffic that otherwise seems so pervasive and omnipresent in our society.

23
Keeping a Record of Your Tour

It is quite possible to ride a bike for years, without ever feeling the need to preserve any of your experiences – whether for posterity or for your personal pleasure. If so, don't feel obliged to bother. However, if you are like most people I know, you will consider many of your bicycle tours so enjoyable or eventful, that they warrant keeping some kind of mementos. From a more pragmatic standpoint, whether the whole trip was that enjoyable or not, each of your touring experiences can be used to advantage as a learning factor for the future. For all of these reasons, it is a good idea to keep a reasonably accurate and systematic record of your bicycle tours.

The simplest and most useful form of record keeping is the pocket diary. If you don't keep writing the most important facts down from day to day, you won't have travelled very far before you have forgotten how many days you've been gone, how far you've travelled, what day it is and what point you had intended to reach tomorrow. Though the modern digital wrist watch with display of weekday and date can help you keep on track as far as the date is concerned, keeping a minimal daily record in your diary seems essential for a successful trip. There are, however, more comprehensive, systematic and rewarding ways of recording your touring experiences, which will be covered below.

The Photo Log

One obvious way of tying your records together is by means of a photo log, collecting the photographs you take while touring systematically. In its simplest form, the photo log is no more than a conventional photo album. Most people take photographs here or there along the route. These can be organized in the photo album in such a way as to remain in their context as records of a specific trip to a defined goal at a known point in time. If you take slides, which almost invariably offer a higher quality picture than what is customary for color prints taken from negatives, you can of course do the same with your slide collection, keeping the pictures from one trip together with the notes that pertain to them. You can also have both, since good enlargement prints can be made as well of slides that are correctly exposed.

For the photo album, arrange your photographs in the sequence of the tour on one or more two-page spreads. Add references to the locations, the dates and the names of the participants. Perhaps you include a piece cut out or photocopied from a map in which the route is drawn in, referencing the places where you took the individual pictures, as well as start and finish and the locations of your overnight stops. Any additional pictorial mementos, ranging from picture post cards to hand drawn sketches, from ferry tickets to dried plant or flower leaves, can also be added.

To do this really effectively, it will prove very helpful to maintain a systematic record during the tour. Keep a little note pad and pen with your camera, so you can record when and where each photo was taken, what the subject was and whether it contains any additional details that you might overlook or forget when you put the photos in the album, once you get home. Doing this conscientiously helps you get the most out of your photo records, and it avoids a lot of frustration later on. You may refer to Chapter 13 for some remarks about the selection of a camera and the best way to carry photo equipment on the bike.

Getting Published

Some of your photographs and writings may well be suitable for publication in one of the increasing number of bicycle, camping or adventure magazines. If that doesn't boost your ego, at least it can provide some additional income. For that purpose, your photographs had better be good: only perfectly exposed and brilliantly sharp color slides will be approved to maintain today's standard of publishing in this field. Instead of color slides, perfectly sharp large glossy black and white enlargements (at least 5 x 7 inches) may be accepted, but color prints just won't pull.

If you are more artistic and skilled than most of us, really good drawings or water colors may also be highly suitable, and are gladly accepted by most editors. Whatever the chosen form of illustrations for this purpose, they are of no use unless they bear directly on the text of the article. The latter should be relatively short and to the point, avoiding any unnecessary detail and background information. Include a clear description of the location and distance of your tour, as well as a map showing the route. Take a critical look at some of the other materials published, to give you an idea what editors and publishers are looking for.

The Touring Log

The concept of the note book, mentioned above for recording information about the photographs you take, can be expanded to provide an even more useful set of records. Take a 4½ x 6 inch note book (or the international size A-6), and keep all your records pertaining to your touring experiences in there. I already suggested such a note book in Chapters 13 and 14, where I proposed using it to write down your various remarks about the items to take and the route to follow. Combine it with the kind of information used to back up your photographs, and you'll have a pretty compact and complete record of your tour.

Use a new booklet for each season or for each longer tour. Start off by collecting the preliminary systematic and random notes taken while preparing for the trip. As you go along, add the day-to-day remarks, specifically remembering to record the date, day of week, starting and termination point and a few details about the route as it was planned. During the day, add the details about the places where you stopped, as well as the subjects and locations you photographed. At the end of each day, update all this with remarks about the actual trip.

All this may seem trivial, and it is to those who operate systematically by nature. But for us, basically disorganized and impulsive folks – I guess we are about 99 percent of the populace – this must be organized consciously to be done right at all. What we also have to learn is to write so legibly that it can be deciphered upon our return. It is also useful to keep the book in such a place and in such a state that the information can be located and the book can be found when it is need-ed. Take the trouble to go through all these notes almost immediately upon your return, when the experiences are still fresh in your mind, to get the maximum benefit from them.

The Mapping Log

In addition to the note book, maps are your most valuable and concise recording tool. Some people cringe at the thought, but maps are more useful if you add your own remarks to them. Recording the locations of your stops makes it easier to find your way on the map as you are travelling. It helps even more in reconstructing your overall tour at the record keeping stage. Certainly the beginning and end points of each day's ride with the relevant

Mountain bike touring in the Colorado mountains. (Photograph courtesy David Epperson / Bicycle Sport Magazine)

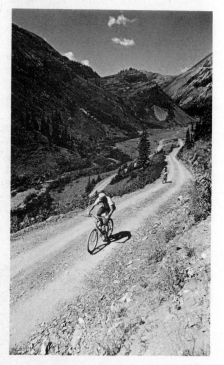

date are worth recording on the map, using an indelible pen.

Then there are those who take a big marking pen and draw in the proposed route long before they set out. I've ruined perfectly good maps myself that way. However, I have never managed to adhere to those routes as I went along, nor has anyone else I know. In practice, you will soon find out, as I did, that the actually travelled route only rarely coincides with the one you had initially planned to take. The actual route you follow evolves as you go along, and the very purpose of a map is to find your way in the field, much more than planning it out at home.

The time to draw in the route you followed is *after* the day's ride. Only then can you be sure which way you went, while it is still fresh enough in your memory to remember the exact routing. In addition, this is the time to make some comments about the trip, perhaps drawing in some records of your own. The sites from which you took photographs are just as useful to indicate as the precise locations of worthwhile places to stop, scenic sections and really bad parts of the road, to give some examples.

These remarks will not only help you reconstruct the tour when collecting records afterwards, they also serve several other important purposes. You can learn from earlier experiences in bike touring, as in other pursuits, by referring to your records, whether consciously or not. Having recorded on the map where it was good or bad may help you seek out or avoid either the same sites or those that are characterized by the same features in other locations. Finally, you will be able to use these records to help others who are planning to travel in an area where you have been. If you can show on a map where you went and how it was, your friends are much better prepared when they leave on their trip.

All this record keeping, whether documenting photos, routes or anything else, is of course strictly up to you. Many cyclists don't want to be bothered, since they enjoy the experience of riding more than that of digesting their experiences. Others have such organized minds that they can do without, although these are more typically exactly the ones who keep meticulous paper records as well. And finally, my way is not the only right way to do it. This description may help if you don't know at all how to go about it, but it is entirely up to you to find a method of recording your touring experiences, using the tools and the form you enjoy most. You may choose not to keep any records at all, except in your mind. However, I know lots of people who were sorry they did not take systematic notes afterwards, while I have never met anybody who regretted keeping such a record of his touring experiences.

Appendix

Table 1. Frame sizing table

| leg length | | max. seat tube height (A) | | | |
| cm | in | touring bike | | mountain bike | |
		cm	in	cm	in
72	29	50	19	46	17.5
73		51	19.5	47	18
74		52	20	48	18.5
75		52	20	48	18.5
76	30	53	20.5	49	19
77		54	21	50	19.5
78		55	21	51	19.5
79	31	56	21.5	52	20
80		57	22	53	20.5
81	32	58	22.5	54	21
82		59	23	55	21.5
83		60	23	56	21.5
84	33	61	23.5	57	22
85		62	24	58	22.5
86	34	63	24.5	59	23
87		64	25	60	23.5
88		65	25	61	23.5
89	35	66	25.5	62	24
90		67	26	63	24
91	36	68	26.5	64	24
92		69	27	65	24

Remarks:
1. This table applies to bicycles with 26 in, 27 in, 650 mm and 700 mm wheels.
2. Inside leg measurement is taken per Fig. A.
3. Maximum recommended seat height as defined in Fig. B, dimension X. If measured per dimension Y, a nominal frame size must be selected that is 1.5 cm or 0.5 inch smaller.
4. See Chapters 2, 8 and 22 for additional explanations.

Fig. A. Inseam leg length determination   Fig. B. Frame size determination

Table 2. Gear table in inches

number of teeth chainwheel

number of teeth sprocket

	24	26	28	30	32	34	36	38	40	42	44	45	46	47	48	49	50	52	53	54	55	56
12	54·1	58·5	63	67·5	72	76·5	81·1	85·5	90	94·5	99	101·2	103·5	105·7	108	110·2	112·3	117	119·3	121·5	123·7	126
13	49·8	54	58·1	62·3	66·4	70·6	74·7	78·9	83·1	87·2	91·4	93·4	95·5	97·6	99·7	101·8	103·9	108	110	112·1	114·2	116·3
14	46·2	50·1	54	57·8	61·7	65·5	69·5	73·3	77·1	81	84·9	86·7	88·7	90·6	92·6	94·5	96·4	100·3	102·2	104·1	106	108
15	43·2	46·8	50·4	54	57·6	61·1	64·8	68·4	72	75·6	79·2	80·9	82·8	84·6	86·4	88·2	90	93·6	95·4	97·2	99	100·8
16	40·5	43·7	47·2	50·6	54	57·2	60·9	64·1	67·5	70·9	74·3	76	77·6	79·3	81	82·7	84·4	87·8	89·4	91·1	92·8	94·5
17	38·1	41·2	44·4	47·6	50·8	54	57·2	60·3	63·5	66·7	69·9	71·5	73·1	74·6	76·2	77·8	79·4	82·6	84·1	85·7	87·3	88·9
18	36	39	42	45	48	51	54	57	60	63	66	67·5	69	70·5	72	73·5	75	78	79·5	81	82·5	84
19	34·1	36·8	39·7	42·6	45·5	48·2	51·1	54	56·8	59·7	62·5	64	65·3	66·6	68	69·4	71·1	73·9	75·3	76·7	78·1	79·5
20	32·4	35·1	37·8	40·5	43·2	45·9	48·7	51·3	54	56·7	59·4	60·8	62·1	63·4	64·8	66·2	67·5	70·2	71·5	72·9	74·5	75·6
21	30·8	33·4	36	38·6	41·1	43·7	46·4	48·9	51·4	54	56·6	57·9	59·1	60·4	61·7	63	64·3	66·9	68·1	69·4	70·7	72
22	29·4	31·9	34·3	36·8	39·2	41·6	44·2	46·6	49·1	51·5	54	55·2	56·5	57·6	58·9	60·1	61·4	63·8	65	66·2	67·5	68·7
23	28·1	30·5	32·8	35·2	37·5	39·9	42·4	44·6	47	49·3	51·6	52·8	54	55·2	56·3	57·5	58·7	61	62·2	63·6	64·5	65·7
24	27	29·2	31·5	33·7	36	38·2	40·5	42·8	45	47·3	49·5	50·7	51·8	52·9	54	55·1	56·3	58·5	59·6	60·7	61·8	63
25	25·9	28	30·2	32·4	34·6	36·7	38·9	41	43·2	45·4	47·5	48·6	49·7	50·8	51·8	52·9	54	56·2	57·2	58·3	59·4	60·4
26	24·9	27	29	31·2	33·2	35·3	37·4	39·5	41·5	43·6	45·7	46·7	47·8	48·8	49·9	50·9	51·9	54	55	56	57·1	58·1
28	23·1	25	27	28·9	30·8	32·8	34·8	36·6	38·6	40·5	42·4	43·7	44·4	45·3	46·3	47·2	48·2	50	51·1	52	53	54
30	21·6	23·2	25·1	27	28·6	30·6	32·4	34·2	36	37·5	39·6	40·5	41·4	42·1	43·2	44	45	46·8	47·5	48·6	49·4	50·2

Remarks:

1. The gear numbers (in inches) shown here are valid for 27 inch and 700 mm wheels, though 650 mm and 26 in wheels are so close that the same values may be used as a rough guide.

2. See Chapter 9 for derivation and explanations.

3. See Table 3 for the conversion of gear number in inches to development in meters.

Table 3. Conversion between gear number in inches and development in meters

Gear number (inches)

30	40	50	60	70	80	90	100	110	120	in
2,0	3,0	4,0	5,0	6,0	7,0	8,0	10,0	11,0		m

Development (meters)

Remarks:
1. See Chapter 9 for derivation and explanations.
2. See Table 2 for gear numbers in inches.

LOW GEAR
SHORT DEVELOPMENT

◄

HIGH GEAR – LONG DEVELOPMENT

◄

Table 4. Conversion factors

multiply	by	to obtain
Distance and length		
km	0.62	mile
m	3.28	ft
cm	0.39	in
mm	0.039	in
Speed		
km/h	0.622	mph
Mass and weight		
kg	2.20	lb
N (Newton)	2.23	lbf
g	0.035	oz
Volume		
l	0.26	gal (US)
l	0.22	gal (imp)
l	1.89	pint (US)
l	1.76	pint (imp.)
gallon/pint (imp.)	1.15	gallon/pint (US)
gallon/pint (US)	0.87	gallon/pint (imp.)

Temperature
degrees C = 0.56 x (degrees F − 32)
degrees F = (1.8 x degrees C) + 32

Pressure and stress		
bar	14.3	psi
psi	0.07	bar
Work and energy		
kgm	7.25	ft lb
kcal	4.20	kJ
kJ	0.24	kcal
Power		
hW	1.34	hp
hp	0.74	kW

Table 5. Suggested packing list

Note:
This compilation is only intended as a starting point to help the reader make up his own packing list. Select only the appropriate items from the various groups applicable to your situation, delete or add items and avoid duplication.

Removable bike accessories
pump
lock
water bottle
map holder
lights
warning device
rear view mirror
saddle cover
bike cover
straps / belts / bungees

Tools, etc.
tool pouch
screw driver
patch kit
3 tire irons
Allen keys
wrenches (spanners)
adjustable wrench
pliers
spoke wrench
crank tool
chain tool
freewheel tool
spray lubricant

hand cleaning paste
cleaning cloths
repair instructions

Spare parts
brake cable
gear cable
electric wire
spokes
light bulbs
batteries
inner tube
chain links
brake blocks
special spares

Bike clothing
shorts
jersey / shirt
socks
underwear
shoes
gloves
helmet
visor

Take along these tools: screwdriver, tire irons, patch kit, Allen wrench, adjustable wrench and needle nose pliers. On a longer trip you'll need more tools. And never go without a pump.

Cold weather wear
long pants
sweater
thick socks
lined gloves / mittens
jacket
scarf
helmet liner
long underwear
pedal covers

Rain gear
jacket / cape
helmet cover / Sou'wester
spats / leggings
shoe covers / pedal covers
overshoes / plastic liners

Off-bike clothing
shoes
socks
shirt
slacks / skirt / dress
jacket
swim wear
track suit
pajamas

First aid
first aid pouch
band aids
aspirin
tweezers
scissors
prescription medicines
insect repellent
insect bite ointment
disinfectant
water purification tablets

Toilet gear
small and large towels
toilet bag / pouch
soap
wash cloth
tooth brush
dental floss
tooth picks
tooth paste
cotton swabs

shaving equipment
mirror
comb / hair brush
nail scissors
nail file
comb/brush
shampoo
sun screen/lotion
tissues/toilet paper

Documents etc.
document pouch/wallet
cash
ID/driver's license
credit cards
foreign currency
address/phone no. list
transportation tickets
insurance documents

Orientation aids
maps
spare map pouch
map cover
curvimeter
compass
binoculars
note book
pen/pencil

Various
pocket knife
can opener
scissors
sewing kit
cold water detergent
chamois cream
laundry line
clothes pegs
clip board / plain board
protector for stationary etc.
stationary
envelopes
stamps
note book
pen /pencil
flash light (torch)
camera
camera accessories
films

spare glasses
sun glasses
literature
pocket radio
wrist watch
tissues
toilet paper
plastic bags
carrier bag
small backpack

For roadside eating
pouch for utensils
knife, fork, spoon
flat tray / bread board
cup
bowl / plate
can opener
dish towel
plastic sheet

For foreign touring
passport
visa
vaccination record
foreign curency
traveller's checks
special insurance
guide book
phrase book
dictionary
special address list
special medicines

For camping
ground sheet
sleeping bag
sleeping pad/ air mattress
cushion
sleeping bag liner
tent with accessories
spade
electric light / candle
wind shields
stove
fuel
cooking pots
can opener
matches / lighter
salt / spices
staples (sugar, flour etc.)
dehydrated / canned food
storage bags or containers
plastic screw-top bottles
water container
wash basin
dish washing liquid
dish brush
scouring pad
dish towel
(also see *Roadside eating*)

Addresses

Alliance Internationale du Tourisme (AIT)
Department de Cyclisme
Quai Gustave Ador 2
1207 Geneva
Switzerland

American Youth Hostels, Inc.
1332 - I Street
Suite 800
Washington, DC 20005
USA

Association of Cycle and Light-weight Campers
11 Grosvenor Place
London SW1W OEY
Great Britain

Australian Cycling Council
153 The Kingsway
Cronulla
Sydney 2230
Australia

Bicycle Federation
1055 Thomas Jepherson Street
Washington, DC 20007
USA

Bicycle Federation of Australia
399 Pitt Street
Sydney 2000
Australia

Bicycle USA
League of American Wheelmen
P. O. Box 988
Baltimore, MD 21203
USA

Bikecentennial
Box 8308
Missoula, MT 59807
USA

British Cycling Federation
70 Brompton Road
London SW3 1EN
Great Britain
Touring Bureau
3 Moor Lane
Lancaster
Great Britain

Camping Club of Great Britain and Ireland, Ltd.
11 Lower Grosvenor Place
London SW1
Great Britain

Canadian Cycling Association
Touring Department
333 River Road
Vanier, Ontario KIL 8B9
Canada

Canadian Youth Hostel Association
268 First Avenue
Ottawa, Ontario
Canada

Countryside Commission
John Dower House
Crescent Place
Cheltenham GL50 3RA
Great Britain

Cyclists' Touring Club
69 Meadrow
Godalming, Surrey GU7 3HS
Great Britain

Effective Cycling League
726 Madrone
Sunnyvale, CA 94086
USA

International Association for Medical Aid to Travellers
736 Center Street
Lewiston, NY 14092
USA

National Parks Foundation
PO Box 57473
Washington, DC 20037
USA

Sierra Club
530 Bush Street
San Francisco, CA 94108
USA

Rough Stuff Fellowship
c/o F.E. Groatcher
65 Stoneleigh Avenue
Worcester Park, Surrey KT4 8XY
Great Britain

Tandem Club
c/o Peter Hallowell
25 Hendred Way
Abingdon, Oxfordshire OX14 2AN
Great Britain

The Youth Hostel Association
Trevelyan House
8 St. Stephen's Hill
St. Albans, Herts AL1 2DY
Great Britain
Travel and Services Department
29 John Adam Street
London, WC2
Great Britain

Bibliography

Advanced First Aid. New York: Doubleday / The American National Red Cross, 1973.

American Youth Hostels Handbook. Delaplane, VT: American Youth Hostel Association, (annual).

Ayres, M., *Cycles and Cycling.* London: Butterworth, 1981.

Ballantine, R., *Richard's Bicycle Book.* New York: Ballantine, London: Pan, 1978.

Bicycle Touring Atlas. New York: American Youth Hostel Association, 1969.

Biestman, M., *Travel for Two:* Sausalito, CA: Pergot Press, 1986.

Bridge, R., *Freewheeling: The Bicycle Camping Book.* Harrisonburg, PA: Stackpole Books, 1974.

–, *Bike Touring.* San Francisco: Sierra Club Books, 1979.

Brooks, J. and Candy, J. (ed.), *The South America Handbook.* Bath (GB): Mendip Press, Chicago: Rand McNally, 1980.

Bunelle, H. and Sarvis, S., *Cooking for Camp and Trail.* San Francisco: Sierra Club Books, 1984.

Campground and Trailer Park Guide. Chicago: Rand McNally, (annual).

Carlson, R. (ed), *National Directory of Budget Motels.* New York: Pilot Books, (annual).

Climates of the States. Port Washington, NY: United States National Oceanic and Atmospheric Administration, 1974.

Coles, C. W., and Glenn, H. T., *Glenn's Complete Bicycle Manual.* New York: Crown Publishers, 1973.

The Complete Guide to America's National Parks. Washington, DC: The National Park Foundation, 1984.

Crane, N. (ed.), *International Cycling Guide.* London: The Tantivy Press, New York: Zootrope, (bi-annual).

The CTC Handbook. Godalming, Surrey (GB): Cyclist's Touring Club, (annual).

Cuthberson, T., *Anybody's Bike Book.* Berkeley, CA: Ten-Speed Press, 1984.

–, *Bike Tripping.* Berkeley, CA: Ten-Speed Press, 1984.

Cyclists Reference Dictionary. London: F. C. Avis.

Davis, A. (ed.), *The On Your Own Guide to Asia.* Rutland, VT: Charles E. Tuttle, 1979.

DeLong, F., *DeLong's Guide to Bicycles and Bicycling.* Radnor, PA.: Chilton Books, 1978.

Eastman, P.F., *Advanced First Aid for All Outdoors.* Centerville, MD: Cornell Maritime Press, 1976.

Editors of Bicycling Magazine, *Best Bicycle Tours.* Emmaus, PA: Rodale Press, 1981.

Faria, I.E., *Cycling Physiology for the Serious Cyclist.* Springfield, MS: Thomas, 1978.

Fletcher, C., *The New Complete Walker.* New York: Knopf, 1974.

Food and Nutrition Board, *Recommended Dietary Allowances*. Washington, DC: National Academy of Sciences, 1974.

Forester, J., *Effective Cycling*. Cambridge, MS: MIT-Press, 1984.

Gatty, H., *Finding Your Way on Land and Sea*. Brattleboro, VT: Stephen Green Press, 1983

Gausden, C. and Crane, N., *The CTC Route Guide to Cycling in Britain and Ireland*. Oxford: Oxford Illustrated Press, Harmondsworth: Penguin Books, 1980

Greenhood, D, *Mapping*. Chicago: University of Chicago Press, 1964.

Hawkins, K. and G., *Bicycle Touring in Europe*. New York: Pantheon Books, 1980.

Hefferson, L., *Cycle Food*. Berkeley, CA: Ten Speed Press, 1976.

Howard, J., *The Cyclist's Companion*. Brattleboro, VT: Stephen Green Press, 1984.

Inside the Cyclist. Brattleboro, VT: Velo-news, 1984.

International Bicycle Touring. Mountain View, CA: World Publications, 1976

Kals, W. S., *Land Navigation Handbook*. San Francisco: Sierra Club Books, 1971

Kellstrom, G., *Map and Compass*. New York: Charles Scribner's Sons, 1973.

Knotty, P., *Cycle Touring in Europe*. London: Constable, 1976.

Murphey, D., *Full Tilt: Ireland to India with a Bicycle*. London: J. Murray, 1978.

National Atlas of the United States. Washington, DC: US Department of the Interior, Geological Survey.

Palister, N. (ed.), *NOLS Cookery*. Emporia, KS: Emporia State Press, 1974.

Rostaing, B. and Walton, B., *Bill Walton's Total Book of Bicycling*. Bantam Books, Toronto, New York, 1985.

Sloane, E., *Eugene A. Sloane's Complete Guide to All-Terrain Bicycles*. New York: Simon & Schuster 1985.

–, *The New Complete Book of Bicycling*. New York: Simon & Schuster, 1981.

Thomas, D., *Roughing it Easy*. Provo, UT: Brigham Young University Press, 1974.

Van der Plas, R., *The Bicycle Repair Book*. San Francisco: Bicycle Books, 1985.

–, *The Mountain Bike Book*. San Francisco: Bicycle Books, 1984.

–, *The Penguin Bicycle Handbook*. Harmondsworth (GB): Penguin Books, 1983.

–, *Roadside Bicycle Repairs*. San Francisco: Bicycle Books, 1987.

Watts, A., *Instant Weather Forecasting*. New York: Dodd Mead & Co, 1968.

Whiter, R., *The Bicycle Manual on Maintenance and Repairs*. Chicago, IL: Contemporary Books, 1972.

Whitt, F. R. and Wilson, D. G., *Bicycling Science*. Cambridge, MS: MIT-Press, 1982.

Wilhelm, T. and G., *The Bicycle Touring Book*. Emmaus, PA: Rodale Press, 1980.

Youth Hosteller's Guide To Europe. London: Youth Hostel Association, Riverside, NJ: Collier Books, 1977.

Index

Other books published by Bicycle Books, Inc.

The Mountain Bike Book
Choosing, riding and maintaining
the off-road bicycle
by Rob Van der Plas
ISBN 0-933201-10-9
6 x 9 inches, soft cover, 144 pages,
with 200 photos and line drawings.
US price $ 7.95

The first and still the most authoritative
book ever published about the modern
ATB or mountain bike. Shows how to
select, equip, ride and maintain this
wonderful machine. Lavishly illustrated
and clearly written, this is the most
useful 'accessory' for any mountain bike
rider.

The Bicycle Repair Book
The complete manual of bicycle
care
by Rob Van der Plas
ISBN 0-933201-11-7
6 x 9 inches, soft cover, 144 pages,
with 300 illustrations.
US price $ 7.95

The most thorough and systematic bicycle repair manual on the market today. It
covers all repair and maintenance jobs
required on any kind of bicycle.
Complete with step-by-step instructions, clear illustrations and an extensive
troubleshooting guide.

The Bicycle Racing Guide
Technique and training for bicycle
racers and triathletes
by Rob Van der Plas
ISBN 0-933201-13-3
6 x 9 inches, soft cover, 256 pages,
with 250 photographs and line
drawings.
US price $ 9.95

The most concise and useful book for
those who want to increase their cycling
speed. Includes an introduction to the
sport, as well as complete instructions
for scientific training methods and practical advice for racing and training situations.

Roadside Bicycle Repairs
The simple guide to fixing your bike
by Rob Van der Plas
ISBN 0-933201-16-8
4⅜ x 6 inches, soft cover, approx.
100 pages, with 120 illustrations.
US price $ 3.95

The book for those who want to fix their
bike when they need to – nothing more,
nothing less. Systematically arranged
and clearly illustrated, this easy-to-
follow guide to essential bicycle repairs
can be taken along on any trip, since it is
small enough to fit anywhere.

Available July 87

Major Taylor
The extraordinary career of an early
American champion bicycle racer
by Andrew Ritchie
ISBN 0-933201-14-1
6⅜ x 9⅛ inches, hard cover, approx.
200 pages, with over 100 photographs.
US price $ 18.95

Beautifully illustrated and vividly told,
this is the authentic story of the dramatic life of one of the earliest great black
American athletes. Bicycle racer 'Major'
Taylor vanquished his American, European and Australian competitors at
home and abroad some eighty years
before Greg LeMond won the Tour de
France.

Available February 88

All books published by Bicycle Books, Inc. may be obtained through the book or bike trade. If not available locally, use the coupon bellow to order directly from the publisher:
Bicycle Books, Inc.
1282a – 7th Avenue
San Francisco, CA 94122
Tel. (415) 665 8214

☐ Check here if payment enclosed

Please send the following book(s):

The Bicycle Repair Book	_____ copies x $ 7.95 =	$ _____
The Mountain Bike Book	_____ copies x $ 7.95 =	$ _____
The Bicycle Racing Guide	_____ copies x $ 9.95 =	$ _____
The Bicycle Touring Manual	_____ copies x $ 9.95 =	$ _____
Roadside Bicycle Repairs	_____ copies x $ 3.95 =	$ _____
Major Taylor	_____ copies x $ 18.95 =	$ _____
Sub total		$ _____
California residents add tax		$ _____
If not paid with order, add $ 1.00 P&H per book		$ _____
Total amount		$ _____

Name: _____

Address: _____

City, state, zip: _____

Telephone: (_____) _____

Signature: _____ Date: _____

Bicycle Books, Inc. will pay postage and handling if payment in full (check or money order) is enclosed with order form. California residents add 6 % tax. If payment does not accompany order, books will be sent COD and customer will be charged for postage and handling at $ 1.00 per copy. Allow three weeks for delivery. Make check or money order payable to Bicycle Books, Inc. and mail to Bicycle Books, Inc., 1282a – 7th Ave., San Francisco, CA 94122.

